**FUNDACION BBV**

# The Human Genome Project: Legal Aspects

## Volume III

Fundación BBV

*The decision of the Fundación BBV to publish this document does not imply any responsibility regarding neither the content nor the inclusion of complementary materials and information provided by the authors, those being the sole responsible for the content of this book.*

Translated by Larry Lilue

*The Human Genome Project: Legal Aspects*
© Fundación BBV Documenta
Edited by Fundación BBV
Plaza de San Nicolás, 4
48005 Bilbao
Registered number: M-2407-1996
I.S.B.N.: 84-88562-31-4 (Complete work)
I.S.B.N.: 84-88562-60-8 (Volume III)

Cover Ilustration:
© Yves Tanguy. VEGAP. Madrid 1994

Printed by Sociedad Anónima de Fotocomposición
Talisio, 9 - 28027 Madrid

# The Human Genome Project: Legal Aspects

# TABLE OF CONTENTS

*Papers*

# HUMAN GENOME AND INSURANCE LAW

# PRESENTATIONS

# GENETIC INFORMATION AND ACCESS TO HEALTH INSURANCE

# Thomas H. Murray*

Director, Center For Biomedical Ethics, Case Western Reserve, Cleveland, Ohio. United States of America.

The Human Genome Project is expected to increase dramatically our ability to predict the likelihood of disease in an individual. Though it is important to reject the myth of genetic determinism –the simple-minded belief that such complex outcomes as heart disease, cancer or autoimmune diseases are caused exclusively by particular genes– it is equally important to acknowledge that in at least some individuals, genes may play a role in making one more or less susceptible to such diseases among others. The ever-growing prospect of genetic prediction, spurred by the Human Genome Project, has implications for such social practices as insurance, in which predicting the risk of disease or death plays a crucial role. Concerned that enhanced genetic prediction might have unfortunate social consequences unless the impact of such predictions were anticipated, and changes made to accommodate them, the US Human Genome Project's Working Group on Ethical, Legal and Social Issues established in May 1991 a Task Force on Genetic Information and Insurance. The author of this article was appointed its Chair, and an eminent scientist and member of the ELSI Working Group, Jonathan Beckwith, was named Co-Chair.

---

\* Moderator.

The Task Force membership was chosen to represent a mixture of those with substantial interests in genetics and insurance along with experts in important aspects of the problem. Representing those at risk of genetic discrimination were individuals from The Alliance for Genetic Support Groups and the Federation for Children with Special Needs, and the Tourette Syndrome Association. Representing insurers were individuals from the Blue Cross Blue Shield Association, the largest group of not-for-profit health insurers representing 71 member plans, the Health Insurance Association of America, representing approximately 300 commercial health insurance companies, and the American Council of Life Insurance. Also among the Task Force members were scholars in the fields of law, public policy, medical genetics, and bioethics.

The Task Force was given an eight-point charge:

1. Gather information on insurance issues from the insurance industry, insurance regulators, consumers, professional groups, ELSI grantees and other researchers.

2. Facilitate collaboration among ELSI grantees conducting insurance-related research and serve as a clearinghouse for the products of their research.

3. Identify important new areas for ELSI research related to insurance issues.

4. Develop clear descriptions of current health care financing, life and disability insurance practices relevant to assessing the impact of genetic information on public access to insurance.

5. Develop clear descriptions of emerging advances in genetics and their relevance to insurance practices.

6. Identify and define the primary policy issues raised by genetic information for access to health care financing and life and disability insurance.

7. Develop policy options for addressing the major issues.

8. Report its findings to the NIH-DOE ELSI Program and the ELSI Working Group in a document accessible to policy makers, insurance companies, self-insured corporations, insurance applicants, and other interested parties in May, 1993 [1].

---

[1] Task Force on Genetic Information and Insurance, Genetic Information and Health Insurance. May, 1993. Bethesda, MD: National Center for Human Genome Research.

The Task Force met seven times over its 2-year life. The first year was devoted primarily to mutual education and to learning the concerns, and even the special terminology, of each of the participants. Insurance industry representatives began to hear the concerns expressed by representatives of those at risk of genetic disease, just as other participants were made to hear about insurance industry concerns. The Task Force brought in consultants to analyze the scientific, medical and technological advances that would shape the questions we had been charged to address. Insurers brought in experts who explained how and why risk underwriting is done.

By the end of the first year, the Task Force had reached several tentative conclusions. Most importantly, we became convinced that the problem posed by increased genetic prediction in insurance was a genuine and important one. When we began, the danger seemed plausible but uncertain. The information we gathered in that first year persuaded us that genetic prediction of disease was in one sense already with us, and in another sense, likely to grow massively within the foreseeable future.

A conceptual distinction was also crucial in that first year. Insurance representatives insisted upon distinguishing fair from unfair genetic discrimination. Their view was something like this: insurers have a right, possibly even an obligation, to avoid what the industry terms «adverse selection» —selling a policy to someone likely to experience claims in excess of premiums. For example, health insurers do not wish to sell policies, at least at standard rates, to persons infected with HIV. Such persons can be expected to make extensive claims for reimbursement of treatment expenses. Insurers describe denying a policy to such persons, or other practices such as charging very high premiums, or selling policies that exclude coverage for HIV treatment as «fair» discrimination. «Fair» discrimination for genetic disease might include similar policies for persons with symptomatic sickle-cell disease or G6PD or other genetic diseases resulting in substantially increased health care costs. «Unfair» discrimination, in contrast, would discriminate against people with genetic conditions that do not result in increased health care costs. One case in the US involves a family with children who have fragile-X syndrome, a dominant inherited disease that can result in retardation. The available evidence, however, indicates that children with fragile-X do not have significantly higher health care costs.

All members of the Task Force agreed that «unfair» discrimination as insurers described it was undesirable and should be eliminated. But it soon became clear to the Task Force that what insurers regarded as «fair» discrimination also had the unfortunate result that many people who needed health care experienced great difficulty in getting it financed. The concept of «fair» genetic discrimination implied that it was acceptable to deny health insurance to people with symptomatic genetic disease, as well as to people at substantially increased risk of symptomatic disease. Continuing «business-as-usual» became increasingly difficult to justify if it resulted in a lack of access to needed health care.

A second clarification was equally important. The Task Force was established because of concern over future increases in genetic testing. Insurers claimed, with good reason, that they were not systematically employing genetic tests. They argued that at this time genetic tests were too expensive, that they were useful only for detecting people with relatively rare genetic diseases and that their usefulness in actuarial prediction was not established. In short, genetic tests were not yet cost-effective. The evidence presented to us by scientists, clinical geneticists and commercial test developers indicated that genetic tests were likely to become cost-effective in the not too distant future. But a closer examination of the concept of genetic tests showed other characteristics that were significant. The core notion of a genetic test was a direct DNA test– that is, a test that showed whether an individual had a particular DNA sequence for an allele associated with some characteristic of interest, such as risk of disease. But one could also test for a genetic risk by looking for the absence or presence of a particular gene product, or a metabolite of that product. Indeed, the possibilities of testing for genetic risk were limited only by the ingenuity of test developers.

It became clear that a narrow definition of genetic testing was inappropriate. It also became clear that plenty of genetic information about individuals was already available, especially in the form of the standard health history. Knowing what one's parents died of is potentially useful genetic information in predicting one's risk of disease. These considerations compelled the Task Force to turn away from a narrow consideration of direct DNA tests to the broader concept of «genetic information» which includes such tests, but also encompasses a wide range of other kinds of information relevant to genetic characteristics.

By the end of the first year the Task Force was also narrowing its charge. In the context of a US health care system in which at any given time 31 to 37 million Americans have no health insurance, and over the course of a typical year some 63 million Americans will go without insurance for a portion of the year, health insurance was by far the most critical problem. Also, Task Force members came to agree that the ethical issues were clearer in health insurance than in other forms of insurance, and that the phenomenon of adverse selection which insurers emphasized was less significant in health insurance than in life or disability income insurance. Genetic data in life and disability income insurance were clearly important issues, but the Task Force chose to devote its time and energies primarily to health care coverage. This decision was ratified in the second year.

Early in the second year, as we faced the prospect of making specific recommendations for policy, differences among Task Force members sharpened. Nonetheless, we were able to devise a set of recommendations calling for radical changes in US health care policy. It is important to indicate that in the end not all Task Force members were able to agree with the final set of recommendations. The ACLI chose to formally oppose the Task Force's recommendations. The HIAA, though praising the report in general terms, took an official stance of neutrality with respect to the report. All other Task Force members, including the Blue Cross Blue Shield Association and representatives of those at risk of genetic disease, endorse the report.

The Executive Summary of the report, which includes seven specific recommendations, is incorporated as part of this article. As the precise wording of the recommendations was painstakingly negotiated, I am reluctant to paraphrase them. It is better to let them speak for themselves. I will, however, comment on what I believe are two crucial conclusions that shaped the report.

First, we became convinced that a policy that would prohibit consideration of genetic risks by health insurers but that would permit consideration of other predictors of disease was conceptually untenable, ethically indefensible and practically infeasible.

Second, we came to believe that the only defensible and practical policy solution was to reform radically the US health care system so that all members of the community would have full access to the health care they genuinely needed. The logic that lead to this conclusion followed roughly these lines:

1. It is unfair to deny health care to people whose need for it is the product of some genetic condition.

2. For the purpose of determining who should have access to health care, there is no practically sustainable distinction between genetic and non-genetic diseases.

3. As a practical matter, a fair health care system would not deny health care to those individuals most likely to need it. Hence, risk underwriting by health insurers would have to be eliminated for those services that respond effectively and not wastefully to genuine health needs.

The report also includes a warning. It is a virtual certainty that whatever changes are made to the US health care system, there will continue to be a distinction between a package of basic services which will presumably be available to all, and a system of voluntary supplementary services, which may continue to permit risk underwriting. The Task Force report has this to say about such a two-pronged health care system:

The Task Force has no objection in principle to such a mixed system, as long as the program of basic health care services provides adequately for the genuine medical needs of people. If needed and appropriate genetic services and health care for genetic diseases are not included in the program of basic health services, then the concerns about unfairness and genetic discrimination that motivated the work of the Task Force will simply migrate to the supplementary programs.

It cannot be emphasized too firmly that the program of basic health services must respond adequately to the health care needs of the American people, or the ethically troubling features of our current system will reappear in the market for supplementary coverage [2].

Much work remains to be done on genetics and insurance. The Task Force set aside life and disability income insurance so that it could address what it believed was the most pressing problem –health care coverage. But genetic prediction in life and disability income insurance is an important issue and deserves continued attention. In the short term, the Task Force will work to see that its recommendations are incorporated into the proposed reform of the US health care system.

## Summary

*Report of the Task Force on Genetic Information and Insurance*
*NIH/DOE Working Group on Ethical, Legal and Social Implications*
*of Human Genome Research*

One of the ironies in the current health care coverage crisis is that developing more accurate biomedical information could make things worse rather than better.

In the current American health care system, information about an individual's risk of disease plays a crucial role for many people in determining access to health care coverage. This link between

---

[2] *Ibid.,* pg. 10.

the likelihood of needing health care and the ability to obtain coverage for that care has the unfortunate result that those most in need may have the greatest difficulty finding affordable health care coverage. New advances in human genetics are transforming medicine by making available increasing amounts of such information about risk.

Biomedical science and the delivery of health care are being reshaped by advances in our understanding of human genetics. New insights into health and disease, new diagnostic and prognostic tests and the possibility of new therapies reflect significant investments by the public and by private business and are no longer limited to the uncommon disorders traditionally labeled as «genetic diseases». Among the first products of genetic research is information useful in predicting the likelihood that an individual will develop particular diseases, opening the door both to preventive strategies that we would welcome, such as changes in diet and exercise patterns, and to the unwelcome possibility of genetic discrimination.

Injecting information about genetic risks into the current health care system could result in ever more refined risk rating by insurers and ever greater difficulty in finding affordable health care coverage for large numbers of people. At a minimum, people could be discouraged from obtaining genetic information that might be useful in disease prevention and early treatment or for case planning and management because that same information could jeopardize their access to health care coverage in general, or to treatment for a condition excluded from coverage because it was «preexisting». Under other circumstances people might be compelled to provide genetic information as a condition of obtaining affordable health care coverage Genetic risk information carries an additional, wider burden because information about an individual's genetic health risks may also be information about the risks of children, parents, brothers, sisters, and other relatives.

One suggested approach –providing special protection for genetic information– is unlikely to succeed. This special protection has been suggested because of the relevance of genetic information to family members and its implications for reproductive choices, potential discrimination and stigmatization. Genetic privacy ought to be vigorously protected; however, other varieties of health related information are equally sensitive. Furthermore, as a practical matter genetic information is not segregated from other health related information in, for example, medical records.

Special protection for genetic information is also difficult to enforce because of the «genetic revolution» in medicine. Diseases increasingly are coming to be seen as having both genetic and non-genetic components, making it ever more difficult to classify health related information as wholly genetic or non-genetic. The standard personal medical history, for example, is a rich source of genetic information. Policies intended to protect genetic privacy will need to address the privacy of health related information in general. If we want strict standards to safeguard genetic information, then those same standards will have to extend to all health related information. The Task Force considered these factors carefully.

In anticipation of fundamental reform in the financing and delivery of health care in the US, the Task Force on Genetic Information and Insurance offers the following recommendations. The recommendations concern health care coverage and should not be applied uncritically to other forms of insurance, such as life or disability income insurance.

1. Information about past, present or future health status, including genetic information, should not be used to deny health care coverage or services to anyone.

2. The US health care system should ensure universal access to and participation by all in a program of basic health services * that encompasses a continuum of services appropriate for the healthy to the seriously ill.

3. The program of basic health services should treat genetic services comparably to non-genetic services, and should encompass appropriate genetic counseling, testing and treatment within a program of primary, preventive and specialty health care services for individuals and families with genetic disorders and those at risk of genetic disease.

4. The cost of health care coverage borne by individuals and families for the program of basic health services should not be affected by information, including genetic information, about an individual's past, present or future health status.

5. Participation in and access to the program of basic health services should not depend on employment.

---

* We use the phrase «program of basic health services» to describe the array of services that would be available to all after implementation of major health policy reforms, such as those being considered by the President's Health Policy Task Force. We explicitly reject all connotations of «basic» as minimal, stingy or limited to such services as immunization and well child care. A program of «basic» health services could encompass a broad range of care for those most in need.

6.  Participation in and access to the program of basic health services should not be conditioned on disclosure by individuals and families of information, including genetic information, about past, present or future health status.

7.  Until participation in a program of basic health services is universal, alternative means of reducing the risk of genetic discrimination should be developed. As one step, health insurers should consider a moratorium on the use of genetic tests in underwriting. In addition, insurers could undertake vigorous educational efforts within the industry to improve the understanding of genetic information.

# INSURANCE AND GENETICS: A PURPOSIVE ANALYSIS

*Alexander Morgan Capron* *

Professor of Law and Medicine, University of South California, Los Angeles. United States of America

The task of addressing the complex subject I have been assigned —insurance and genetics— in the time allotted is made somewhat easier by the topic itself. Why? Because many of the germane issues are being addressed in other sessions: to see what I mean, we need only consider why the topic of insurance has achieved such prominence in the ethical, social and legal examination of the human genome mapping project, when compared with earlier debates about bioethics issues. In those debates, insurance was never a major issue —not in the discussion of death and dying (although it is certainly relevant, especially in the context of euthanasia), not in the behavioral and neurosciences, not in human experimentation, and not in other areas of genetics, such as genetic engineering. Regarding all these other topics, insurance issues received at best glancing treatment while other issues predominated.

Why, then, is insurance a major topic in examinations of the social and legal implications of human genome mapping? Because it is the field in which the fruits of genome mapping appear likely to have most direct (and perhaps negative) effects on the lives of

---

* Keynote Speaker.

most people. For the average person, the other issues raised by genome mapping appear irrelevant or at best esoteric. Few of us see ourselves directly implicated in the criminal justice system —so that the issues of criminal responsibility and of genetic fingerprinting do not hit close to home. Likewise, genetic patents remain matters solely of intellectual interest. Finally, genetic experimentation remains of concern to the relatively few who have rare genetic diseases that might be manipulated at a molecular level

But insurance —and the related area of employment— are arenas in which people are already seeing the effects of increased genetic diagnostic capabilities from the genome mapping project. As documented by people like Dr Paul Billings and as widely reported in the press, ordinary people find themselves suffering consequences, which gene mappers themselves recognized to be a risk as long as a decade ago and ethicists worried about 20 years ago.

Thus, if the major impact of genome mapping for most people will be an increase in the ability of biomedical science to screen for genes of interest, the major areas of concern about this increased ability are insurance and employment, which are seen as the setting in which screening is most likely to raise concerns about freedom, responsibility, and confidentiality —all of which are topics separately addressed at this meeting.

I hope I will not be misunderstood: I am not saying that the other issues raised by genome mapping are unimportant. Indeed, I regard some of the issues around experimentation and patenting to be extraordinarily complex and profound. Nor am I suggesting that an issue's importance is properly gauged by the amount of anxiety it provokes in the average person. I believe, for example, that a great deal of the anxiety that was felt by the general public —or at least articulated by public representatives— about genetic engineering rested on a misperception of that field of science and of the moral or conceptual issues it implicated.

Nonetheless, in looking at the program for this meeting, I think it is notable that the related areas of insurance and employment, which largely involve matters of *private* conduct, receive such attention, whereas the sorts of concerns that one might expect to see about governmental conduct, having to do with eugenics, are further in the background. Why? Because I believe it is assumed, rightly or wrongly, that the tragic experiences of this century with eugenics have put us on guard to avoid the major misuse of the fruits of gene mapping by governments, while at the same time we find ourselves with much less confidence that the enormous powers wielded by private companies —as insurers and employers— will be used in a beneficent fashion if those companies find ways to use genomic knowledge to further their own interests.

To summarize, then:

1. Insurance is a topic in this area of bioethics because it is perceived to be an arena where the findings of genome mapping will have their major impact on the lives of most people.

2. Much of the interest in insurance is not due solely to the actuarial or related insurance issues (to which I will now turn) but arises because insurance is the arena in which other issues arise most immediately, around, for example, personal freedom and the confidentiality of especially sensitive personal and familial data.

In my remaining time, I would like to sketch out what I see as the major insurance issues and to describe the legal response in the United States thus far, knowing that subsequent speakers will fill in the many important facets of the topics that I only have time to sketch quickly. Specifically, I will address four points:

1. Predictive medicine.

2. Discrimination and the tension it creates in insurance.

3. The varied purposes of insurance.

4. The role of underwriting in health and life insurance.

## Predictive medicine

«Predictive medicine» is a term used to describe the ability of physicians to foretell with specificity the diseases that patients will suffer in future years. Beyond allowing the monitoring and even treatment of people who are still asymptomatic, predictive medicine will enable physicians to become better counselors for their patients, whose attention they can direct to those aspects of their lives —such as what they eat and how they live— that involve particular risks to their well-being. Such advice, tailored to the susceptibilities of each patient, is the *good* side of predictive genetics.

But these abilities to forecast people's lives also raise important issues. First, they mean a change in the thinking of physicians, both in replacing the idea of simple «genetic disease» with an understanding of diseases with multiple causes (one or more of which are inborn), as well as in preparing physicians (and other personnel) to be informed and helpful counselors and decision-enhancers (a task for which present health care personnel are, sadly, inadequate).

## Discrimination and the tension it creates in insurance

Second are the issues that arise from what we might term the negative side of predictive medicine: the use of the information by others for their own ends. This raises the issue of *discrimination,* a topic of great interest to the law in a democratic society. A fundamental principle in such societies is the equal worth of every member and thus a major object of legal regulation has been to ensure that organs of the state —and in recent years, a growing array of private parties in more and more settings— are prevented from discriminating, in the sense of treating one individual differently than another for illegitimate reasons.

The classic definition of unlawful discrimination —which rests on very deep moral principles— is that it is wrong to classify a person based upon his or her membership (or perceived membership) in a group or category (being a woman, being a person of color, being a Jew, being a foreigner, etc.) rather than on his or her individual attributes.

The law's concern with discrimination extends to the field of insurance. In the United States, most regulation of insurance occurs at the state rather than the federal level. And the two issues with which insurance commissioners have been primarily concerned are, first, the solvency and financial management of insurance companies, and, second, that their rating charts and underwriting practices not be based upon unlawful discrimination.

Therefore, it is easy to see why I suggested that a major tension arises around the issue of discrimination when we look to a future in which genome mapping will have made it possible to make many predictions about a person's future health based on his or her genes. Clearly, any use of genetic information to classify people —a process called underwriting— can be seen as a form of unfair discrimination, at least by those people who are either forced to pay higher premiums for coverage or who are denied insurance altogether. Yet rather than being the sort of discrimination that is usually forbidden, it is actually the type of differentiation that is at the heart of most private insurance.

Thus, the use of genetic predictions raises two related issues that are often confused:

1.   Is any degree of differentiation fair?

2. Is particular differentiation fair? That is, does the particular differentiation fulfill the criteria that underlay an affirmative answer to the first question?

Why do I say these questions are often confused? Because much of the public discussion in the United States has proceeded in the following way: Instances are cited (and condemned) in which people have lost insurance because of genetic factors. As part of this condemnation, it is pointed out that the tests involved are not accurate yet, or that their predictive value is much less than necessary for the conclusions being drawn from them. It is also noted that many other genetic conditions —perhaps much worse— are as yet not identified (an arbitrary and unfair consequence of how scientific progress has occurred). Furthermore, the severe adverse consequences for people in losing health insurance are asserted. From this it is concluded that it is wrong to use genetic information in insurance.

## The purposes of insurance

But these instances, although perhaps probative on the second question —«is this particular differentiation fair?»— really don't answer the first question, whether any degree of differentiation in insurance is ethically acceptable and hence should be legal. To answer that question —and hence to develop criteria for when, if ever, genetics has a role in insurance— we must ask and answer several more basic questions.

First, what is the purpose of insurance?

Second, when is underwriting compatible with that purpose (or purposes)?

I suggest that we answer the first question in two parts.

1. What are the general purposes of all insurance?

2. What are the specific purposes of particular types of insurance?

Insurance has several major purposes. It is intended to spread risks and thereby to minimize their adverse impact on individuals and their total costs for society. These purposes are served differently by different types of insurance.

Sometimes the objective to spread risk broadly predominates. To do so most efficiently, we use what is often termed «social insurance» —that is, a program that encompasses everyone and typically that is paid for by broadly based means (typically, taxes) unconnected with individual risk. Over the past century, the major industrial democracies have created many insurance schemes along this model– to provide health care coverage and old age pensions, for example. These programs involve benefits that are seen as essential (namely, health care and income maintenance), that are almost universally relevant (that is, nearly everyone gets sick at some point and most retirees need some pension to support them in old age), and where, therefore, social insurance not only minimizes administrative costs but also serves the valuable function of building social solidarity by manifesting the sense of community and commonality that is an important characteristic of viable societies.

Let me contrast this type of social insurance program with another type of insurance that most societies seem to leave to private entities –namely, liability insurance. Here we recognize that risks are highly variable, based on the characteristics of the insured and the activities in which the insured engages. Hence, the goal of risk spreading is tempered by the goal of cost minimization: if we spread the costs of accidents from running a fleet of trucks onto all commercial activities, for example, then relatively safe activities (like flower arranging) will subsidize trucking, and we will have too much trucking and too little flower arranging. Furthermore, by allowing insurers to engage in risk classification –by charging truck owners different premiums than flower arrangers– we actually help insureds to recognize (and internalize) their costs of doing business, which should encourage them to minimize those costs –and we buttress that encouragement with the assistance that insurance underwriters can provide in singling out certain ways of conducting the business more safely (for example, through testing the knowledge and skills of the people they hire to drive their trucks).

To summarize this point, then: Having identified three general purposes of insurance –loss spreading, avoidance of severe impact on individuals and minimization of total costs– we have seen that different forms of insurance –such as general social insurance and highly differentiated private insurance– can each serve those purposes depending upon particular characteristics.

## The role of underwriting in health and life insurance

Let us look, then, at the characteristics of the two types of insurance –health and life– that are most often discussed in the context of genetic screening. To focus and speed up this analysis, let's at the same time ask whether underwriting for genetic risks is compatible with the purposes of these two lines of insurance. To come quickly to the point –why is it widely believed that genetic differentiation is inappropriate for health insurance but more widely acceptable for life insurance?

What are the characteristics of health insurance? First, the events it insures against are at once *universal* (everyone gets sick) yet quite *variable* (the costs of care can range from small to catastrophically large); second, the lack of insurance can (and does) result in a lack of care, which in turn can have a *decisive and even devastating adverse effect* on a person's life prospects; third, the *risks are subject to the control of the individual only to a minor degree* (hence, the problem of «moral hazard» is less pronounced than in other types of insurance); fourth, activity —health care— is one of great *symbolic importance* (human caring in the face of illness, suffering and death); and fifth, the activity (health services) is directly connected to the *production of the information that would be used for differentiating* among individuals (thus, ironically, the provision of health care could be adversely affected if the information it generated for preventive reasons were used as a ground to disqualify the person from obtaining the insurance necessary to obtain health care).

For these reasons, it is not surprising that direct underwriting plays a small role in health insurance —which is either encompassed (in most nations) under a form of social insurance or (in the United States) provided through a mixed program of governmental and group insurance. Private health insurers in the United States realize that any use of genetic factors or other individualized risks to rate applicants for health insurance only fuels the movement toward a universal, single-payer system of health insurance.

This is not to say that underwriting does not occur. Indeed, it does —in fact, most potential insureds who have average or below-average risks are covered by group insurance leaving to individual policies those members of the population who are higher than average risks, which has the effect of driving up premiums and thereby further encouraging adverse selection (that is, the higher the premium, the more likely that those who choose to buy the insurance will be those who know or believe themselves to be at high risk of getting sick).

Compare health insurance with life insurance. Again, the event insured against —death— is *universal* but the potential exposure of the company is fixed by the amount of the policy, not variable as with health care costs; second, the lack of insurance will have an adverse impact but usually *not a devastating* one (assuming that a minimum level of income maintenance is provided through social insurance programs); third, the *risks are subject to substantial control by the insured* (and hence moral hazard is more of a problem);

fourth, life insurance has *little symbolic* significance; and fifth, the activity –which relates to estate planning– is *not directly connected with the source of the information* (i.e. information about genetic or other risks that is generated through health care).

Thus, given the purposes of this type of insurance, it is much less likely that society would find unacceptable were some segments of the population charged higher premiums or even denied life insurance because insurers find their risks to be too great.

Furthermore, because much more life insurance is sold individually rather than to groups and because many people chose not to insure and hence the pool of insureds is very subject to adverse selection (that is, the people who are most at risk buying the largest amount of insurance they can), insurers have a great interest in being as well informed about their applicants' risks as they can, especially when they believe the applicants may be aware of their own risks.

Thus, it is unlikely that insurance companies will launch programs of generalized genetic screening any time in the near future –because the cost of generating information through such screening is likely to far exceed the contribution of the information to intelligent underwriting decisions. But at the same time, insurers *are* interested in uncovering any genetic risk data that applicants themselves already know. To have a solvent insurance pool, one must be able to predict the risks of those covered and to change appropriate premiums in light of those risks.

## American legislation

Not surprisingly, the laws enacted by several American states over the past few years aimed at genetic testing by insurers have not precluded life insurance companies from using such tests. For example, in 1989, Arizona became the first state to enact protection based on «genetic conditions» generally, but it merely brought such conditions within the prohibition of unfair discrimination, while permitting insurers to consider genetic risks that substantially affect actuarial predictions.

In April 1992, Florida took the stronger step of requiring informed consent for DNA analyses, except in criminal investigations. Results may not be disclosed without the consent of the person tested, but insurers are apparently free to use them to determine eligibility and rates, provided that the tester reveals this to the person tested. Should insurance be denied, the test «must be repeated to verify the accuracy» of the results. But this provides only limited control over insurers, since «accuracy» here refers to the reliability of the test; insurers are not to required to provide data establishing a connection between a genetic condition and long-term consequences for the insured.

Probably the strongest statute is the one that became effective on 1 July 1992 in Wisconsin. It provides a preview of what are certain to be an increasing number of efforts to limit «genetic testing», defined in the Wisconsin act as a test using deoxyribonucleic acid extracted from an individual's cells to determine the presence of a genetic disease or disorder or the individual's predisposition for a particular genetic disease or disorder. Under the statute, insurers (as well as employers that self-insure) are not only prohibited from requiring genetic tests but also from requesting information about previous tests. Furthermore, coverage may not be conditioned upon having a genetic test nor may rates be determined upon test results. *None of these restrictions apply, however, to life insurers,* which are mandated only to behave reasonably when setting rates based on genetic data.

What is so fascinating about the Wisconsin statute is how, once again, it shows what I call the genicity of certain issues. In this arena, the fears aroused by novel molecular tests cause them to be singled out even though in the not too distant future, the new knowledge of genetics is likely to result in the development of more screening tests for gene products (such as enzymes and metabolites) rather than requiring DNA analysis to reach a «genetic diagnosis». Furthermore, we have long tolerated insurers' use of medical histories, simple clinical tests (like blood pressure, blood tests, and EKGs) and family histories as part of underwriting. Yet these measures are mostly aimed at making predictions about health and life expectancy that would be made more accurately by using so-called «genetic testing». That is to say, the reason for asking about one's medical history or finding out whether one's parents and siblings have suffered health problems is to see whether the applicant's inherited predisposition to a medical problem is greater than average. To preclude genetic tests —which could pinpoint whether a familial disorder has actually been inherited, for example— is rather like the policy being developed on gays in the military. That policy is called «Don't Ask, Don't Tell». Placing a limit only on direct DNA testing could be called a policy of «Don't Test, Just Guess». The time will soon come, I believe, when we ask is it better to insist on the use of surrogate markers than the real thing? And hence, if we have a problem it is not with the genetic tests as such but with the use of genetic factors in underwriting.

## Conclusion

In this discussion, I have focused on the legitimate and illegitimate uses of genetics-based «discrimination» in insurance by taking a look at the purposes of particular lines of insurance. I will leave to others the examination of other aspects of the interplay of insurance and genetics and will merely note that questions about the reliability and partiality of early genetic screening tests must be satisfactorily answered to avoid compounding the problem of unlawful discrimination, not say nothing of «blaming the victim». I suggest that the objective of policymakers and insurance alike should be to keep a balance between the purposes of particular insurance and the means used to draw appropriate categories of insureds. Thus, in the early phases of the genome mapping project it might be appropriate to place a moratorium on the use of genetic factors in rating/underwriting until we possess more complete data and better knowledge of its true significance for people's life and health status, along with a more open discussion of the purposes of insurance and the degree they are compatible with underwriting.

# THE GENETIC CODE AND INSURANCE CONTRACTS

## Aurelio Menéndez Menéndez *

Professor of Commercial Law, Universidad Autónoma of
Madrid. Spain.

1.  As has been often stated, by the beginning of the 21st century
    scientists will have investigated the basic secrets of human
    genetics. All over the world, and particularly in countries
    pursuing specific research projects, the search goes on for
    «the most intimate essence of humanity». The 21st century
    «shall be the era of the gene» (T. Wilkie). At present the
    Human Genome Project and advances in the field of mole-
    cular genetics are surging forward. Understood as an orga-
    nism's hereditary substance or the sum of the hereditary
    information existing in a cell, the genome and its analysis
    already offer the possibility of obtaining information on inhe-
    ritance, including information on inherited predispositions to
    certain diseases (E. Deutsch). It is equally true that we have
    only very partial knowledge of how different traits and pro-
    cesses are coded in the genes of a chromosome. It is nonet-
    heless expected that the mapping and sequencing of most of
    the human genome will be completed in the coming years.
    This would give us the key to unlocking the genetic disposi-
    tion of a genome and furthermore allow us to determine the
    order of the different steps in a DNA segment (P. Präve).

---

\* Keynote address.

When taken as a whole, this research, the results thus far attained and those that we can now foresee, warrant the observation that the Human Genome Project and its related programmes will pose –are posing– «society with a number of major ethical problems, as well as the possibility of great benefits» (S. Grisolía). The «discovery» of the human genome, the «genetic profile» or «map» of each of the 50,000 to 100,000 genes found in the genetic endowment of each human cell, could be the levers of an unprecedented revolution in human history. Today we know that these breakthroughs in genetic technology, as part of biotechnology, will radically affect human life for good or for bad, be it for the prevention or cure of genetic disorders, for the determination of human conduct, or for possible genetic manipulations of unforeseeable consequences.

2.  Neither the law nor students of the law can fail to be moved by a challenge of this magnitude. It is true that in all great political revolutions legal systems naturally tend to trail events, often acting as a curb on innovative tendencies and therefore criticized for their conservatism. But something different occurs in the midst of a scientific revolution in which, as is the case with the Human Genome Project, research results already impact health and life sciences and foretell a radical overhaul of the pre-existing value system and, in short, of human and social life over the coming decades. In this case, the need for legislative intervention has begun to be felt during the course of the ongoing advances in genetic investigation. This impact has already been noted «in relation to assisted fertilization, artificial insemination and other such manifestations, though not enough protection has been provided by the barriers established by the legislator», in view of which it has been added that this historical conflict will be accentuated «if from here to 15 years the so-called Human Genome Project, flagship of modern biology which Watson has said represents the "most important instruction book that can be attained by human beings" achieves its goals» (Martín Mateo; with respect to the time frame, such a leading authority as the Nobel Prize winning human genome investigator Dulbecco has recently said that «in 5 or 6 years the complete genetic map of all human chromosomes will be finished»).

In order to perceive the importance of the legal questions raised by these developments we need not enter into the numerous implications of genetic investigation for human freedom, or the sharp debate over the human genome as a «heritage of humanity» (or, stated more clearly, the question of whether or not genetic discoveries are patentable), or the tension between findings in the field of human genetics and respect for human dignity. It is sufficient to allude schematically to some questions arising from genome analysis and the detection of predispositions to certain diseases: genome analysis and consent of the interested person, genome analysis and confidentiality of the results, genome analysis and prenatality, genome analysis and employment contracts, genome analysis and social security, genome analysis and criminal culpability, genome analysis and private insurance, etc. Fundamental parts of the entire legal edifice are affected and must be studied or revised.

The many legal questions now on the agenda have thus far not brought forth legislative reaction in the different countries, even in those where genetic investigation has made the most progress. I do not mean to thereby assert a complete legal vacuum as to the implications of genetic innovations, but rather that there will be an ever more pressing need for positive legal regulation in keeping with the varied important questions posed by the ongoing investigation of the human genome. In our own country there are already some significant provisions having direct or indirect bearing on genetics-related issues. This is the case, as has been stated elsewhere, with paternity disputes (article 39.1 of the Constitution and section 171.1 of the Civil Code) and, more directly, with the December 28th 1988 Act for the regulation of the «donation and use of human embryos and fetuses or their cells, tissues or organs» and November 22nd 1988 Act regulating «assisted reproduction techniques». These laws will have counterparts in criminal law if approval is given to the draft Criminal Code which envisages, in its sections 164 to 167, infractions relating to «the genetic manipulation of human embryos and fetuses and unauthorized artificial insemination» (Romeo-Casabona and Bustos Pueche). But there is still no regulation of major questions of civil, commercial, criminal or labour law (to cite branches of law particularly affected by these questions), and unless such regulation is enacted great interpretive effort will have to be made in order to apply the legal provisions now in place to deal with the ethical and social exigencies arising from genetic investigation. Hence the importance of Spanish jurisprudence focusing attention on genetic issues, for notwithstanding some estimable contributions in that area, such attention has been limited, especially when compared to the treatment dispensed by legal sciences in other countries. And thus the importance of this workshop on «Human Genome Project: Legal Aspects», a follow-up to the two previous workshops held in Valencia in 1988 and 1990 on scientific cooperation and the ethical aspects of the Human Genome Project, both organized by Professor

Santiago Grisolía (Chairman of the UNESCO Committee for the Human Genome Project), sponsored by the Fundación Banco de Bilbao Vizcaya and the Valencian Foundation for Advanced Studies.

3.   The foregoing analysis is intended as an introduction to the subject at hand: the genetic code and the insurance contract. This paper will contemplate the implications of genetic investigation for insurance contracts. I will begin by recalling that within the range of justified human ambitions few legal institutions play so important and far-reaching role as that fulfilled by the insurance contract in shifting and eliminating risks. The historic expansion of this institution has permitted the establishment of a safety net underpinning all human activity. Knowledge of the genetic code will present us, and is presenting us, with some delicate questions relating to the continued expansion of private insurance without detracting from the necessary respect for personal freedom and human dignity. These questions are substantially centred on the potential impact of insurer insistence that the insured submit to genetic testing and disclose the results prior to making the insurance contract.

This simple introduction allows us to frame the question before us. The following analysis will not delve into property damage insurance, where the insured interest consists of concrete things or the overall estate of the insured. What concerns us here is the impact of genetic testing on insurance contracts involving human lives, and this study will therefore focus on personal insurance, that is, on insurance aimed at covering risks to people.

I should furthermore point out that within personal insurance a distinction can be made between insurance in respect of the risk from events that can affect the person's very existence (life insurance), from the possibility of bodily harm (temporary or permanent disability, or death) due to violent external causes (accident insurance), and, from the danger of disease (health insurance). In all these the insurer considers it necessary to know the *state of health* of the insured. The insurer therefore wishes to ascertain that state of health by means of questionnaires, and possibly with medical examinations using the clinical tests deemed appropriate. It is here, as we will see, that the question of the legal regard for genetic analysis takes on special significance. I might add that the question can be posed in similar terms for all these types of insurance, though noting that in accident insurance medical examinations, or more specifically, genetic screening, only make sense with respect to diseases that increase the likelihood of accident, and that in health insurance, more similar to objective indemnity insurances, there are those who justify genome analysis of the insured in order to better avoid risks, with such analysis aiding in selecting the insured and calculating premiums (E. Deutsch). As one final introductory remark in defining the question of the implications of genome analysis for personal insurance I will add that this concern only makes sense in whole life insurance policies. In the case of endowment insurance, declarations as to the health status of the insured are obviously irrelevant to the insurer, and it therefore makes no sense to discuss genetic screening of the insured.

In light of the foregoing points we can conclude that the delicate insurance law problems raised by genome analysis are in connection with the different types of personal insurance, except endowment insurance. The above reservations having thus been made, we can now proceed to contemplate these issues in connection with life insurance.

4.  The considerable progress being made in genetic research, and more specifically the legal implications of genome analysis, do not affect the very existence of life insurance. To be more precise we might say that all this genetic knowledge does not affect risk as the causal assumption of insurance contracts. I will not here enter into the debate over life insurance as assuring an indemnity or as assuring abstract coverage of a need. What matters here is that no matter which conception is invoked, it cannot be forgotten that as a general rule without risk there is no insurance, irrespective of whether that element of risk is understood for all types of insurance as «the possibility of a harmful event» (the unitary conception of the insurance contract) or for life insurance as «the possibility of an economic need» (the dualist conception of the insurance contract). In any event, for risk to exist we must always be able to speak of «possibility». This implies two things: that we are considering a *future* and *uncertain* event. This «uncertainty» need not be absolute *(incertus an, incertus quando)*: in life insurance the uncertainty is only relative, that is, it is known that the insured event (the death of the insured) will take place but not when *(certus an, incertus quando)*. Hence my belief that risk, the basic precondition for an insurance contract, exists regardless of the information provided by genome analysis. Genetic screening may eventually point to many pathological predispositions in the insured that could not be determined until now but will not eliminate uncertainty as to *when* death would take place, such uncertainty being sufficient to warrant speaking of a risk to the insured.

5. For these reasons the question posed pivots on the content of the insured's duty to declare. The purpose of this obligation is for the insurer to acquire the necessary knowledge of the insured's state of health in order to adequately evaluate the risk of death. This duty to declare is usually satisfied by means of a questionnaire accompanying the policyholder-insured's application. I will first make some observations on the following aspects of this duty: the questionnaire and the insured's duty to respond, the duty to declare in relation to the acquired immune deficiency syndrome (AIDS) and the duty to declare of the insured in life insurance contracts.

a) The health questionnaire is increasing complex and detailed. It effectively transforms the policyholder-insured's duty to declare into a *duty to respond,* in the sense that the policyholder-insured must answer the questions truthfully and completely, without omitting, falsifying or concealing any information, always keeping in mind that these declarations in the form of answers to the questionnaire are the basis on which the insurer studies and assesses the risk.

As provided in section 10 of the Spanish Insurance Contracts Act, «It is the duty of the policyholder, before the contract is made, to declare to the insurer, in accordance with the questionnaire submitted by the latter, all circumstances known to him that may affect the valuation of the risk». Our insurance laws clearly circumscribe the policyholder-insured's duty to declare to the duty to respond, and without any reservation whatsoever, to the questionnaire submitted to the potential policyholder-insured by the insurer. Section 10 refers to all circumstances known to the policyholder, but it is clear that those circumstances are restricted to those which are formulated in the questionnaire (Sánchez Calero). The second sentence of paragraph one of the afore-cited section 10 leaves no room for doubt: «He shall be relieved from such duty if the insurer does not submit a questionnaire to him, or where, despite submitting the same, circumstances are involved which may influence the valuation of the risk and are not included therein». Consequently, if the insurer fails to include in the questionnaire some question about one or another relevant circumstance, such omission cannot be used in prejudice of the insured's interests. It is fitting to add that this questionnaire is in practice used in whole life insurance, although on occasions it is not used or is limited in scope according to the amount of the policy to be underwritten.

In life insurance policies for amounts exceeding the automatic subscription limit (in Spain the ceiling usually established is five million pesetas for insureds under 50 years of age, and half that amount for those over 50), the questionnaire is normally accompanied with certain tests and, in particular, by a medical report which may include clinical and radiological tests. The insured must accept this medical examination as part of his precontract duty, such that refusal to undergo medical examination or the attendant tests closes the selection process and releases the insured from any commitment to make the contract and issue the policy.

b) Although I will refer to this later, it seems appropriate to make mention here of the impact of the acquired immune deficiency syndrome (AIDS) on the insured's duty to declare, especially as regards certain population groups. The close relation between the onset of the disease and death generated great alarm among insurers throughout the world, who quickly adopted risk selection measures for new insurance contracts. As regards Spain, changes were introduced in the questionnaire so that the duty to declare include statements as to whether or not the insured belonged to one of the risk groups and whether or not he had undergone AIDS testing. In recent years the blood test for insurance of over a determined amount have included the test for AIDS. Consequently, a strict respect for confidentiality as manifestation of professional secrecy was imposed in connection both with the answers to the questionnaire and with the results of the AIDS or blood tests (Tirado Suárez).

In any event, the opposition of certain pressure groups to such mandatory testing placed the insurance industry of some countries in a dilemma: on the one hand, an important part of the public opinion was opposed to the test, while, on the other hand, insurance companies «were obliged to pursue sound commercial management». The solution to this dilemma in some countries consisted in requiring the test for AIDS in cases where the underwritten amount was important (G.W. de Wit). Something similar occurs in our country, where, as mentioned above, the health questionnaire has been expanded to include questions directly touching on detection of this disease, and where screening for the presence of the retrovirus is required in the precontract stage when the insured capital exceeds a certain amount. As far as I know this practice is being pursued without opposition from the insured, and the insurer's right to oppose the contract and not issue the policy if the insured resists the obligatory AIDS screening or declarations has gone undisputed.

It should be stated here that it would be incorrect to equate the case of AIDS with the situation of genetic information. There are no sufficient grounds for drawing such a strict analogy. As has been rightfully pointed out, AIDS is fundamentally classified as an *avoidable disease*, whereas genetic anomalies are *inevitable* given that they are genetically built into the person (G.W. de Wit).

c)   As a concluding remark on the duty to declare, I will point out that this duty falls on the insured. This observation, though it may appear as trivial to some, is necessary because under Spain's Insurance Contracts Act, both section 89 on life insurance, which insofar as concerns the duty to declare defers to section 10, and the latter section itself, which lays down that duty for all forms of insurance, provides that the person bearing this obligation is the *policyholder*. This criterion is acceptable for insurance on one's own life, where the policyholder and insured are one and the same person, but not when a policyholder takes out insurance on the life of a third party (and the structure of the contract is even more complicated when the beneficiary is different from the policyholder and the insured). In the latter case the «risk carrier» is the insured and, in principle, the duty to declare should fall to him. The Insurance Contracts Act sets down in section 7 that «if the policyholder is different from the insured party the obligations and duties deriving from the contract are for the policyholder» but immediately qualifies this by adding «with the exception of obligations and duties which, by their nature, must be fulfilled by the insured party». The duties which «by their nature» must be fulfilled by the insured no doubt include the duty to declare in personal insurance and, specifically, in life insurance for a third party, where the policyholder and insured are not the same person. And this is the case for individual and for group life insurance, for even in the latter case the duty to declare does not directly fall to the policyholder as representative of the group but to the individual insureds which make up the group, because this duty only makes sense with respect to the state of health of each one of them. Another matter is when, in any of the cases cited above, the policyholder fulfils this duty by forwarding to the insurer the correct and adequate information provided him by the insured.

In this case the policyholder is acting as a representative or proxy for the insured. The latter is the genuine risk carrier and it is therefore to him that the *state of health* must refer.

6.  Having thus delimited the scope of the insured's duty to declare in connection with a life insurance contract, we can now better take up the problems being raised in some countries by the possibility of genetic screening of potential insureds. Undoubtedly, advances in genetic technology can provide insurers during the preparation of the life insurance contract with exceptionally relevant information as to the insured's predispositions to certain diseases. Such information is of singular importance for evaluating or better analysing the risk as well as for classifying it and calculating the premiums. The current system of making life insurance contracts (in which, as we have seen, the insured's duty to declare takes place within the scope of the autonomy of will, by means of his answering the relevant questionnaire and, where such is the case, undergoing a medical examination) could conceivably allow agreement between the insurer and insured whereby the duty to declare is extended to encompass a medical examination which includes genetic testing to ascertain the insured's predispositions to determined diseases. The testing could be easily performed, given that a drop of blood is sufficient for establishing the hereditary traits, and could therefore be widely applied. Such screening would be of obvious interest to the insurer and could be highly beneficial in the risk selection process.

The same does not occur, however, with the insured. Opposite the insured's legitimate interest in excluding or limiting certain risks stands the equally legitimate interest of the potential insured in exposing the most intimate sphere of his personality only to the extent that can be reasonably expected. This is the case with his genetic characteristics, the disclosure of which could be disadvantageous for the insured, not so much in terms of unfavourable insurance terms as in the possibility of having to give extremely sensitive personal information to strangers (G. Wiese).

7.  The question then is to know which of the two interests should prevail when deciding the possibility of requiring a potential insured to undergo genetic screening as a precondition for entering into a life insurance contract. This debate has been under way for some time among jurists and legal professionals in some countries, with a slight trend toward resolving this conflict of interests in the insured's favour.

The arguments which can be employed by insurers for obligatory genetic testing prior to making an insurance contract turn on the need to not underwrite certain risks or simply to reduce them and demand, in certain cases, higher premiums. All the more in life insurance cases in which the potential insured provides information on a disease in his family during the medical examination and only genome analysis can verify whether or not the insured actually has a genetic predisposition to the disease in question. Along these lines —it is contended— the insurer could invoke the autonomy of will (as the governing principle in this issues, also valid for requiring that the potential insured undergo genetic screening for predispositions to determined diseases). Furthermore, an insured's refusal to undergo genetic screening (with the insurer's consequent refusal to underwrite the policy) does not put him in an «intolerable situation of need»; there are people, after all, who do not have life insurance (even some who are not covered by social security either) and nonetheless do not feel a grave need to seek such coverage.

Conversely, in favour of the potential insured it is said that obligatory genetic testing as a prerequisite for life insurance could produce great distress. The insured would directly or indirectly learn of his possible diseases, either because his policy was rejected or the insurer offered coverage but with a higher premium. And it must not be forgotten that the insured will have to face the knowledge of diseases which may or may not manifest themselves later, or which may be incurable. All this could generate a situation of physical coercion or mental anguish that would seriously condition his life thereafter. There is talk of «transparent citizens», fear of «eugenic discrimination» and the complete genetic profile is likened to the «integral image of one's personality» which violates data protection laws (E. Deutsch). Moreover, it is argued that there is danger of abuse by insurers, who with the data gleaned from the genetic tests would be in a position to elaborate the most intimate profile of the insured.

This has led to proposals for amending the rules of medical confidentiality for doctors employed by insurance companies so that the doctor would only be exempt from his duty of professional secrecy, and therefore entitled to disclose genetic screening results to the insurers, after the results have been conveyed to the insured. Thus if the insured had already consented to undergoing genetic tests, new consent would be needed before the results could be reported to the insurer.

There are voices which insistently point to the danger that breaches of professional secrecy or confidentiality, through negligence or abuse, could lead to highly personal and sensitive information ending up in the hands of third parties (as regards the automated processing of data, see Spain's October 19th 1992 Organic Act on the automated handling of personal data, particularly sections 4, 5, 6, 7, 10, 40 and 44). This danger is particularly pronounced in those countries where, whether by agreement or by custom, the forwarding of data to reinsurers, other insurers and professional associations makes it impossible or very unlikely that knowledge of certain personal information be limited to the insurer and insured (see section 10 of the aforementioned Act on automated handling of personal data and its cautious attitude toward the «duty of secrecy»). It is also pointed out that insurers currently analyse and classify risks without genome analysis and that mandatory genetic screening is therefore not necessary for private insurance schemes to be able to function. Finally, it is added that a genetic predisposition does not necessarily lead to the onset of a given disease, nor influence in the life risk, and that death could even be caused by factors completely unrelated to the disease arising from the genetic predisposition.

Not all these arguments in favour of rejecting insurer demands for genetic analysis as an insurance contract precondition carry the same weight. The one which enjoys the most consideration concerns the insured's individual rights. It is held, and reasonably so in my opinion, that this interest should prevail over the interest of the insurer and, even over the interest of the community of insureds. Although each and every insured has a legitimate interest in keeping insurance premiums as low as possible (something which can only be achieved by allowing insurers greater risk selection), this material interest is overridden by the personal interest of those same insureds in not having to reveal their genetic profile.

This school of legal thought tends to ground the primacy of the insured's position on the constitutional provisions regarding due respect for human dignity and the free development of the individual's personality. Those norms are cited in support of the recognition of a *right of informational self-determination* that guarantees the potential insured's right to decide whether or not to undergo genetic screening and the possible use of the resulting genetic data (this right of self-determination has been recently referred to by Pérez Luño and, in relation to Companies Registry disclosure, by Paz-Ares). According to this right of self-determination it is the insured who shall decide whether or not to know his genetic condition. It is therefore said that this principle of informational self-determination also generates the so-called «right to not know», that is, the right of every person «to not have to know more about himself than what he himself wishes to know»; put in other terms, the insured's right to assure that only he will decide whether he is to know or not know that he is a carrier of a hereditary disorder.

Conversely, if the insured was obliged at the request of the insurer to undergo genetic testing as a prerequisite for qualifying for life insurance, entire population groups (what has been called «the genetic class society» or the «new class of uninsurables») could be excluded from life insurance by means of data banks containing genetic risk information (J. Simon). Such exclusion would be to the detriment of society as a whole and, as has been pointed out, to the state. Taxpayers would have to provide protection for those persons and there would be an inevitable shifting of the risks not covered by private insurance to the government support systems. Here, too, we may recall the current trend away from the «social state» toward the incipient «risk anticipation state», that is, to public coverage of the «future guarantee», understood as the extension of state responsibilities to the risks generated by new technologies (nuclear, informational, genetic engineering, new chemical substances) (López Piña). In line with this tendency, the state would not be able to ignore the vulnerable situation of these population groups excluded from private insurance coverage on the basis of risks detected by mandatory genetic testing.

The criterion favourable to the right of self-determination, or the «right not to know», seems unlikely to triumph in countries, such as Spain, lacking the necessary legal regulation of these matters. Current practice –the obligatory questionnaire embodying the insured's duty to declare, the lack of resistance to medical examination and AIDS testing for insurance exceeding determined amounts– does not hold out much promise of a position favourable to requiring the insurer to make a life insurance contract even where the insured declines to undergo genetic testing. The above-cited sections 10 and 89 of the Spanish Insurance Contracts Act are quite clear as to the potential insured's duty to declare to the insurer «all circumstances known to him that may affect the valuation of the risk». This carries the logical implication that if the insured does not adequately reply to all the questions on the questionnaire regarding his genetic inheritance or which require genetic screening, the insurer has the right to reject the contract or issue the policy.

However, a progressive interpretation, drawing on articles 10.1 and 18.1 of the Spanish Constitution, could contribute to recognizing the «right not to know» as a limit or exception to the «duty to declare of the insured» set down in section 10 and 89 of the insurance contracts act. Both article 10.1 of the Constitution, which protects «human dignity, man's inviolable and inherent rights, the free development of his personality, and article 18.1, whereby «the right to honour, to personal and familial privacy and to personal reputation is guaranteed» (for more on this last precept and corporal privacy, see Martínez de Pisón, pg 112 and ff) provide more than sufficient grounds for the recognition of an informational right to self-determination that would justify obliging the insurer to make the insurance contract even where the insured exercises his rights not to submit to genetic tests. But I consider it beyond doubt that once the means are available for analysing all genetic information in the nucleus of a human cell, there will be a need for legal regulations that dispel all doubts and specifically prohibit insurers from requiring genetic screening as a precondition for making life insurance contracts.

8.  Of course, the issues raised in connection with the insured's obligation to undergo genetic screening at the request of the insurer wane when the insurer and insured are in agreement as to such testing prior to making the contract. In other words, if the insured does not have any objection to submitting to a genetic analysis which will later be examined by the insurer, this problem loses interest (for more on the need for the «express consent of the concerned party» in order for information concerning a person's «health and personal life» to be «collected, processed and passed on» to others see sections 6 and 7.3 of the aforementioned Organic legislative act of October 29th 1992). But the implications of genetic investigation for life insurance do not end here. In addition to the question of genetic testing as a precontract requirement, there is the issue of the potential insured's obligation, once he knows the results of the genetic analysis, to disclose all relevant genetic predispositions in fulfilment of his legal duty to declare.

Before taking up this question it would not be out of place to review the serious consequences incurred by the insured under Spanish law when he does not comply with the duty to declare. The general provision set down in paragraph 2 of section 10 of the Insurance Contracts Act establishes the insurer's right to cancel the contract «by means of a declaration to the policyholder made within the term of 1 month, reckoned from the time the reservation or inaccuracy on the part of the policyholder is made known». This means that both in the case of failure of the policyholder or insured to disclose everything known to him in connection with the circumstances referred to in the questionnaire «which may influence the valuation of the risk» (reservation), as well as where the declaration does not conform to reality (inaccuracy), the insurer is entitled to cancel the contract no later than one month after discovering the reservation or inaccuracy.

The same section 10 also provides that «unless there exists any fraud or serious fault» on the part of the insurer, the latter shall be entitled to «the premiums for the period in course at the time when the insurer makes this declaration» (the declaration of discovery of the reservation or inaccuracy of information by the policyholder or insured). In addition, in case of a claim before the insurer has made the above-mentioned declaration the third paragraph of this section provides that «his payment shall be reduced in proportion to the difference between the agreed premium and the premium that would have been applicable had the true nature of the risk been known», and that in all cases the insurer will be released from any payment «if there existed any fraud or serious fault on the part of the policyholder» (or insured). This regulation is somewhat different for life insurance. In keeping with a widespread life insurance practice, section 89 of the Act provides that for this type of insurance «the insurer may not challenge the contract after the expiry of the term of 1 year, reckoned from the date when the contract was made, unless the parties have established a shorter term in the contract and, in any case, unless the policyholder [or insured] acted fraudulently». As can be seen, a 1 year limit is established on the insurer's right to challenge a contract on the basis of an inaccurate or incomplete (reticent) declaration by the insured, unless —and this is the difference with the general regulations for all insurance— the contract includes clauses providing that it cannot be challenged or cancelled beyond a shorter period of time, whereupon the insurer waives the right to cancel a contract made on an inaccurate or incomplete declaration by the insured. I do not think this should be considered as an innovation with respect to other types of insurance, as such clauses could no doubt be included in other insurance contracts. They are to the insured's advantage and as such qualify for the exemption established in section 2 to the mandatory nature of the provisions of the Act. The said section 2 provides that:

«In the absence of an Act applicable to them, the various types of insurance contract shall be governed by this Act, the provisions of which are of a mandatory nature unless otherwise provided therein. Nevertheless, the clauses of the contract which are most beneficial for the insured party shall be considered as valid».

This is a synthesis of the law's provisions for incomplete or inaccurate declarations by the insured, applicable whenever the insured does not fully or accurately disclose what is known to him in relation with the points of the questionnaire that «may affect the valuation of the risk». These provisions would also be applicable, in principle, to the insured's genetic predisposition to one or another disease, provided such circumstances are of relevance, that is, such as «may affect the valuation of the risk». But if we are to be consistent with the position maintained here with respect to the possibility of obliging the potential insured to undergo genetic testing, it must be recognized that if the insured's obligation is construed to include genetic predisposition we would be accepting an obligation to disclose information about the very core of one's personality. This observation does not hold when the insured does not possess information as to his genetic predisposition, because section 10 of the Act refers to the «circumstances known to him», and irrespective of all the foregoing points on whether or not genetic analysis can be required, there is nothing, under Spanish law at least, that obliges the insured to procure such knowledge.

Somewhat more complicated is the case where the insured is aware of his genetic predispositions, particularly if the insurer specifically includes questions along such lines in the insurance precontract questionnaire. Such situations are covered by section 10: «circumstances known to him [the insured] that may affect the valuation of the risk». But the same principles should apply with respect to arguments in favour of denying the insurer's right to reject a contract if the insured declines to undergo genetic testing. Here, too, the right to informational self-determination can be invoked when dealing with information regarding the essence of the individual's personality. Here, too, the interest of the constitutionally protected right to dignity and to privacy (articles 10.1 and 18.1) should prevail over the interest of the insurer or the community of insureds in curbing costs. But as stated earlier in relation to genetic screening, eradicating any doubts as to the constitutional support for a solution favourable to the insured will require amending section 10 of the Insurance Contracts Act to adequately safeguard the interests of the insured.

It would not be correct, however, to equate the question of genetic screening as a necessary precondition for making the contract and the precontract duty to declare a genetic predisposition known to the insured. Whereas it is possible in the former to invoke the «right not to know», in the latter the insured is already aware of his genetic predispositions. The insured's right to informational self-determination can be defended in both, but while the first is premised on the insured's ignorance of his genetic constitution, in the second the insured knows his genetic makeup. While true that this cannot justify violation of the right to privacy, and this right explains certain currents of legal thought inclined to prohibit the questionnaire from requesting the insured's genetic information, but it does not seem right to make such a conclusion absolutely applicable to all cases.

In my opinion, the search for a more equitable solution justifies limiting the right of the insured. I therefore agree with those who consider that the above conclusion does not release the insured from his obligation to disclose his current *state of health,* and that, consequently, if the insured is sick or knows of the imminent onset of a disease, he is obliged to so state in the questionnaire, irrespective of whether or not the disease is genetically conditioned. In such case, it is a matter of disclosing the current state of health or its imminent worsening, and not a determined genetic condition. That genetic condition, by itself, does not allow prognosis of an eventual onset of the disease and, consequently, is covered by no disclosure obligation whatsoever (G. Wiese). We might say that the boundary of the insured's obligation to declare should be situated between disclosure of a genetic condition and disclosure of a genetically conditioned disease (albeit one that is only about to set in). With respect to the latter case, the application of section 10 of the Spanish Insurance Act would not have to be restricted in any way. Also supporting this position is the basic law on which the insurance contract is based: the insurance policy applicant's duty to declare in *good faith* (Falcao Oliveira) imposed thereupon by the duty to declare when making the contract everything he knows or should know as to whether he is afflicted or will soon be afflicted by some disease. The protection of the individual's right to privacy cannot justify bad faith on the part of the insured. What is more, *good faith* as the basic principle of insurance contracts should in any event impose that if in the above-contemplated conflict of interests no harm is suffered at any time by the insured's interest in the respect for his rights as a person, then the reason for the informational self-determination would be weakened, and the insurer could invoke, on the basis of the principle of good faith, the need for a complete and accurate response to the questionnaire as a guarantee of a fair risk valuation process.

# References

**J. E. Bishop and M. Waldholz:** *Genoma,* Barcelona 1992, pgs. 15 to 29.

**J. E. Bustos Pueche:** «El Derecho español ante las nuevas técnicas genéticas» [«Spanish law and the new genetic techniques»], *La Ley,* July 28th 1992, pgs. 1 and ff.

**M. Clarke and D. Morgan:** *Genome Analysis-Legal Rules-Practical Application,* Workshop on «Genome Analysis», Coimbra, June 1992.

**E. Deutsch:** «Die Genomanalyse: Neue Rechtsprobleme», *Zeitschrift für Rechtspolitik,* 1986, pgs. 1 *et seq.*

**E. Deutsch:** *Haftung für unerlaubte bzw. fehlerhafte Genomanalyse,* Versicherungsrecht, 1991, pgs. 1205 and ff.

**R. Dulbecco:** «El País», October 7th 1992.

**G. Freire Falcâo de Oliveira:** *Legal status and general rules concerning genome analysis and its application in general,* Workshop on «Genome Analysis», Coimbra, June 1992.

**S. Grisolía:** Introduction to *Human Genome Project: Ethics,* Bilbao, 1991, pgs. 11 and ff.

**López Pina:** *Saber leer,* 1992, no. 58, pg. 10.

**R. Martín Mateo:** *Problemas legales de la genética* [*Legal problems in genetics*]. «ABC», August 8th 1992.

**J. Martínez de Pisón:** *El derecho a la intimidad en la jurisprudencia constitucional* [*The right to privacy in constitutional case law*], Madrid, 1993.

**J. C. Paz-Ares:** *La reforma del Registro Mercantil* [*The reform of the Companies Registry*] in «Homenaje a J. B. Vallet de Goytisolo», VI, Madrid, 1988, pgs. 480 and ff.

**A. E. Pérez Luño:** *Intimidad y protección de datos personales: del habeas corpus al habeas data* [*Privacy and the protection of personal data: From habeas corpus to habeas data*], «Estudios sobre el derecho a la intimidad», edited by L. García San Miguel, Madrid, 1992.

**P. Präve:** *Das Recht des Versicherungsnehmers auf gen-informationelle Selbstbestimmung,* Versicherungsrecht, 1992, pgs. 279 and ff.

**P. Präve:** *Genomanalyse and Lebenversicherung,* Zeitschrift für Versicherungsrecht, 1991, pgs. 82 and ff.

**C. M. Romeo-Casabona:** *Some implications of Human Genome research in Spanish Law,* Workshop on «Genome Analysis», Coimbra, June 1992.

**F. Sánchez Calero:** *Comentarios al Código de Comercio y Legislación Mercantil especial. Ley de contrato de seguro [Comments on the Commercial Code and special commercial legislation. The insurance contracts Act],* Tome XXIV, 1st volume, Madrid, 1984, pgs. 125 and ff and 162 and ff.

**J. Simon:** *Genomanalyse-Anwendungsmöglichkeiten und rechtlicher Regelungsbedarf,* Monatsschrift für Deutsches Recht, 1991, pgs. 5 and ff.

**D. Schwampe:** *Überlegungen zu einer Reform der vorvertraglichen anzeigepflicht im Vesicherungsrecht,* Versicherungsrecht, 1984, pgs. 308 and ff.

**F. J. Tirado Suárez:** *Comentarios al Código de Comercio y Legislación Mercantil especial. Ley de contrato de seguro [Comments on the Commercial Code and special commercial legislation. The insurance contracts Act],* Tome XXIV, 3rd volume, Madrid, 1989, pgs. 258 and ff.

**G. Wiese:** *Die Entschlüsselung des menschlichen Genoms Gegenwärtiger Rechtszustand in der Bundesrepublik Deutchland and Diskussion über gesetzliche Neuregelungen,* Workshop on «Genome Analysis», Coimbra, June 1992.

**G. W. de Wit:** *Genetic technology, insurance and the future,* Human Genome Project: Ethics, Bilbao, 1991, pgs. 299 and ff.

# THE CHALLENGE OF NEW GENETIC INFORMATION FOR THE LAW OF HEALTH AND LIFE INSURANCE

## Mark A. Rothstein[*]

Member of the Law Foundation. Counsellor of the Health Law and Policy Institute. Professor of Law, University of Houston, Texas. United States of America.

## Introduction

In many meetings at the national and international level, representatives of the insurance industry have been quite clear in stating that insurers have no interest in performing genetic tests. This is certainly understandable. For the foreseeable future, even assuming major developments in genetic testing technology, it will simply not be cost-effective to perform population-wide genetic testing, especially when the focus is on rare disorders.

This disavowal of interest in *performing* genetic testing, however, is not the same thing as disavowing interest in obtaining access to the results of genetic testing performed in the clinical setting. To avoid adverse selection, in which those who know they are at risk will seek the maximum amount of coverage, insurance companies demand access to the same information available to individuals. As genetic testing becomes more widespread in the

---

* Narrator.

clinical setting, applicants for insurance will have more knowledge of their genetic risks. If insurers cannot be confident that all medical genetic information has been provided to them, then insurers are likely to perform their own genetic tests to prevent the effects of adverse selection.

Another misunderstanding surrounding genetic testing in insurance is that the issue will not really need to be addressed until the genetic technologies develop to the point where testing is cheap and commonly available in the clinical or other settings. Nevertheless, genetic prediction does not necessary require the most sophisticated DNA-based technologies developed by the Human Genome Project. In many instances, a complete family health history, the ultimate «no tech» medical procedure, will reveal more than enough information to indicate that an individual is at risk of a genetic disorder.

It is always difficult to generalize about law and policy issues on a comparative law basis. For example, although the issue of life insurance underwriting is similar in many countries, health care systems and health insurance are quite different. Nevertheless, even in the area of health insurance there are lessons to be learned from studying different health care systems and their responses to the challenge of new genetic information.

## Health Insurance

In the US, with the exceptions of government programs for the aged (Medicare) and the indigent (Medicaid), health insurance funding has been left to the private sector. Today, 85-90% of Americans covered by health insurance are covered by group health insurance and 68% are covered by employer-provided plans. Although in recent years many employers have required their employees and retirees to pay a larger percentage of the costs, employers still pay the major share. In 1992, the average, per-employee cost of health insurance was approximately $4,000 and in many industries it was substantially higher, depending on the benefits provided.

The American health care system is currently the subject of much debate. It has one excellent feature. For individuals with substantial resources, it offers care that is as good as any to be found in the world, including the latest in new medical technologies. The deficiencies in the system also are well known. Because of a lack of emphasis on preventive care, and the lack of universal access to health care, in the US many measures of aggregate health, such as infant mortality and life expectancy rates, lag well behind other industrialized countries. The cost of the system is out of control, currently consuming nearly 14% of GDP, and with costs increasing much faster than the rate of inflation.

Approximately 37 million Americans have no health insurance, public or private. Two-thirds of these people are workers and the dependents of workers whose employers do not provide health insurance. The system also renders care of uneven quality. Low reimbursement levels of government programs (especially Medicaid, but also Medicare) means that many physicians are unwilling to treat these patients. Furthermore, there are perverse incentives built into the reimbursement system. For example, under fee for service systems, health care providers have an incentive to perform unnecessary surgery, diagnostic tests and other procedures; under some managed care plans, such as health maintenance organizations (HMOs), providers have incentives to forego using expensive but medically indicated procedures.

What are the implications of new genetic technologies for this already beleaguered system? According to a recent study, 5% of individuals consume 50% of health care resources; 10% of individuals consume 70% of health care resources. To an individual payer in the private sector, an employer or an insurer, if these high cost users can be excluded from coverage, then vast savings could be realized. Consequently, in the US there are frequent reports about entire industries (e.g. those with hazardous work, low-paying or seasonal work, higher rates of claims, and higher administrative costs) being unable to obtain group health insurance coverage. In addition, individuals who smoke, are overweight, ride motorcycles, have a chronic illness or have other risk factors (or if their dependents do), may be excluded from employment and, in effect, health insurance.

A 1990 law, the Americans with Disabilities Act (ADA), is a federal statute that seeks to prevent discrimination in employment against qualified individuals with disabilities. Because the law did not take effect until 1992, it is still not clear to what degree health insurance-based discrimination by employers will be prevented or reduced. Nevertheless, the ADA only applies to decisions regarding employment. It does not apply to underwriting activities of insurance companies (whether employment related or otherwise) or self-insured health benefits plans of employers, where claims are paid directly by the companies.

In the much-discussed case of *McGann v. H & H Music Co.,* 946 F.2d 401 (5th Cir. 1991), cert. denied, 113 S. Ct. 482 (1992), an employee was covered under an employment-based, group health insurance contract that had a $1 million maximum payout for all illnesses. After Mr McGann became ill and submitted his first medical bills for treatment of AIDS, his employer canceled the policy, became self-insured, hired its prior insurance company as claims administrator and reduced coverage for AIDS to $5,000, while leaving other illnesses at $1 million. The employer's action was upheld by the courts because another federal law (the Employee Retirement Income Security Act-ERISA) provides, in effect, that self-insured plans are not insurance and can be modified by the employer at any time.

Because of our increasing ability to predict future risk of disease by using genetic tests, a major premise of any new health insurance system in the US must be the elimination of risk-based health insurance. Community rating (where all policy holders pay the same rates regardless of age or medical condition), noncancellable coverage at standard rates (where, after an illness, insurers could neither cancel coverage nor increase rates), abolishing preexisting conditions clauses (where no coverage is provided for the recurrence or additional treatment of any past illnesses), prohibiting exclusions (where certain conditions will not be covered) and other major reforms would be essential just to preserve the viability of private health insurance as the primary source of health insurance coverage in the US. To avoid the risk that discrimination based on health status will simply be shifted from insurers to employers, if employers are to have any role in a new health care finance system, it must be limited to a flat, per capita assessment in the form of a tax or standard premium contribution.

There is one additional issue, already of significance in much of the world, that is likely to be of significance in the US as well. The issue is, whether in a system in which a basic package of health care is guaranteed, it should be permissible for a private insurer to use genetic information in deciding whether to offer a supplemental health insurance policy providing additional benefits. In my view, the ethical and legal issues involved in these policies is more like those related to life and disability insurance than in those related to access to a minimum level of health care.

## Life Insurance

The purpose of life insurance is to provide for income replacement and the peace of mind that comes from knowing that income replacement is assured. While the need for financial security is important, it is less essential than the allocative function of health insurance. There are few alternatives to health insurance, but there are various investment alternatives to life insurance.

The concern about adverse selection discussed earlier is especially pronounced in the setting of life insurance, where coverage limits may be virtually unlimited. The insurance industry's concerns about adverse selection for life insurance are certainly legitimate, even though the exent of the problem is unclear. While it would be unethical for a society to deny access to health care to an individual with Huntington's disease, it also may be unethical for an individual identified as presymptomatic with Huntington's disease to purchase $5 million of life insurance at standard rates. The insurance companies either would have to go out of business or charge substantially higher rates to all policyholders. It may be reasonable for a society to require that healthy people subsidize the health insurance or health care of those who are ill, but it is unreasonable to require that healthy people subsidize the estate building of people with current or future lethal illnesses.

The life insurance industry has long used medical information and examinations in underwriting. Should they be permitted to use *genetic* information as well, or is there something different about genetic information, as opposed to medical information about the risk of stroke, cancer, and heart disease? I would argue that there are four reasons why genetic information is different.

First, at least as to single gene disorders, there is nothing the individual could do to avoid inheriting the gene. Regardless of the moral weight of the reasoning, much of society would regard individuals with genetic diseases as powerless to avoid their fate and therefore more deserving of societal support than individuals whose medical conditions are attributable to behaviors such as cigarette smoking or substance abuse.

Second, a family stigma may be associated with genetic disorders. The use of genetic criteria could have the effect of excluding entire families from societal opportunities and in stigmatizing them as being less worthy citizens and humans.

Third, genetic traits sometimes fall along the lines of race and ethnicity. In the US, and in other countries as well, any policies that have the purpose or effect of disqualifying individuals on such bases are legally and morally suspect.

Fourth, given the history of eugenics in the first half of this century, we should have great reluctance to embrace any program of systematic application of genetic criteria. Thus, the proponents of genetic testing should have a heavy burden of proving a clear need for the testing, that no other methods of medical underwriting are feasible, and that extraordinary measures to protect privacy and confidentiality are in place.

What public policies should be implemented to deal with genetic information in life insurance? The Canadian Privacy Commission has recommended that no medical underwriting of life insurance should be permitted for any life insurance policy under $100,000. In the Netherlands, ordinary life insurance for under 200,000 guilders may not include genetic information. This general approach is commendable for two reasons. First, it strikes a reasonable balance in protecting access to insurance without creating irresistible pressures for adverse selection. Second, by prohibiting all medical underwriting, it avoids the definitional problem of deciding which medical tests are genetic, although it still must be decided which other inquiries (e.g. smoking, drinking, family history) are medical.

Even under this approach, some additional issues need to be resolved. Individuals should be entitled only to a total of $100,000 of life insurance from all insurers. In addition, there must be some limitation placed on the timing of insurance applications. It would be ridiculous to permit individuals near death to submit application forms from the intensive care unit of hospitals. One possible solution would be to impose a one-year waiting period before a life insurance policy was in force, except in the case of accidental death.

## Conclusion

Although a strong case could be made that genetic information ought not be used in private health insurance, at least in the US, the issue merely addresses one part of the overall problem of access to health care. Accordingly, the principle of excluding genetic and other health risk assessments in health insurance must be a part of more fundamental reforms.

The issue of life insurance is a closer case, but a reasonable balance might be struck by prohibiting all predictive medical underwriting for insurance policies below a specified amount. The same approach also could be used for disability insurance and supplemental, private health insurance policies.

In some respects, the health care systems of the US and many other countries are beginning to converge. The US is likely to become a more public system at the same time that other countries are increasingly relying on private insurance. It is certainly an appropriate time for all countries to confront the new challenges raised by genetic information in insurance.

# PAPERS

# GENETIC INFORMATION AND SECTION 89 OF THE SPANISH INSURANCE CONTRACT ACT

## Luis M. Almajano Pablos

Government Attorney, Madrid. Spain.

How far will knowledge of the human genome go? That is the question I, as a lawyer approaching this field for the first time, ask myself, and I assume to also be on the minds of the people directly involved in human genetics research and in the field of ethics or other social sciences, including the world of law, who are in «one way or another» interested in the possible significance of human genome knowledge for man.

For the purposes of the following analysis, I understand human genome to be, in the words of E. Deutsch (also cited in the talk on «The genetic code and insurance contracts» given by professor Menéndez) «the hereditary substance of an organism or the sum of hereditary information existing in a cell», such that «we may affirm that it is now possible to speak of obtaining information on inheritance from genome analysis, including information on the hereditary predisposition to certain diseases». While this knowledge is still limited, the extraordinary pace at which investigation of this field is advancing allows us to foresee that a very thorough understanding will be achieved in the not too distant future.

It was precisely for the purpose of addressing the consequence of such knowledge that the Fundación BBV organized last year's meeting on «Human Genome Project: Ethics» and the present

«International Workshop on the Human Genome Project: Legal Aspects». One of the various legal areas affected by the genome project is the law of insurance contracts, which was the subject of Professor Menéndez's paper. My paper will cover a very specific aspect of these questions: the implications of actual or possible human genomic knowledge on the duty to declare relevant health circumstances prior to making a life insurance contract.

Three basic ideas will be investigated.

## Genetic information as a right of the person

The first thing jurists do when taking up some new phenomenon is to try and rechannel it into already existing juridical categories and, only when this is not possible, create a new entity that, through a set of more or less complex legal relations, resolves the problems raised by the said phenomenon.

It is my understanding that we are not in the latter situation, since genetic information is fully within the scope of the so-called rights of the person. Thus, there already exists an adequate legal framework (the most complex of all) with its component rights and obligations which requires deeper study but nonetheless serves as a starting point.

### 1.   The so-called «rights of the person»

Professor Lacruz Berdejo has pointed out that if man is the subject of law and of all rights it may be contradictory to speak of the «rights of the person» as if they were the object of law or integral attributes of the subject himself. It may therefore be more appropriate to identify them with a terminology that has also been employed in reference to the same rights but met with less fortune, that of «innate rights».

In any event, regardless of the expression used, what matters is to define an area in which «the individual is recognized and protected by the law, not only as the beneficiary of legal rights but also as a being whose humanity is per se fundamentally worthy of protection. The interests and attributes of the person are defended, not because they are each, independent of and simultaneous with their status as a component of the person, the object of law, but as part of the very person» (Lacruz Berdejo).

The characteristic features of these rights of the person are:

– The person has limited possibilities for waiving such rights. They are normally considered as inherent to the person and not as property thereof. As such, they are inalienable, cannot be renounced and cannot expire, and their exercise is sometimes even compulsory. They are neither property nor personal rights, but attributes of the person himself, inseparable therefrom and almost always born therewith. This is particularly true insofar as genetic information is concerned.

– As with the case of absolute rights, there arises for the other subjects of law a general obligation of respect which transcends the scope of private law and fully enters the realm of public law. In effect, protection exclusively through individual initiative proves to be inadequate for the purposes of the law in those cases where the inequality between the power of the victim and that of the infringer is too large. The means of individual reaction must then yield to public instruments of social control, particularly in the form of preventive measures, be it by the attribution to the government of protective powers or through imperative or prohibitive norms.

Thus understood, the rights of the person are essential to all legal systems. Specifically enshrined in the Spanish Constitution are the right to life and to physical integrity (article 15), to ideological and religious freedom (article 16), to freedom of thought and expression (article 20), and others, amongst which of special relevance here are the right to honour, to personal and familial privacy, and to one's personal reputation (article 18).

## 2. Genetic information forms part of the right to privacy

The right to privacy, as a right of the person, is protected by article 18 of the Spanish Constitution and, insofar as it is inseparable from «human dignity», also by article 10. This scope of protection is further elaborated in the Organic Act 1 of May 5th 1982 for the Civil Protection of Honour, Personal and Familial Privacy and Personal Reputation and in the recent Organic Act on the Automated Treatment of Personal Data. In particular, section 1.3 of the Organic Act 1/1982 provides that «The right to honour, personal and familial privacy and personal reputation is inalienable and inextinguishable. Waiver of the protection provided hereunder shall be null and void, without prejudice...». This inalienable aspect of the rights of the person was already mentioned above. In the above-cited section and in others, the Organic Act sets down a series of provisions, as manifestations of social control by public powers, in which certain conducts are considered as «illegitimate intrusion» into those rights and the attorney general's office is authorized to participate in their protection.

The Organic Act, however, does not define what is meant by the right to privacy, so we must turn to the doctrine of our Constitutional Court, which in its Judgement 231 of December 2nd 1988, held that:

«The rights [...] to personal privacy [...] recognized in article 18 of the Constitution arise as fundamental rights closely linked to personhood. They are no doubt derived from the «dignity of the person» recognized under article 10 of the Constitution and imply the existence of a domain that is proper to and reserved to the person, and which others may not act in or know. They are necessary, according to the standards of our society, to the maintenance of a minimum quality of human life. These rights thus prove to be extremely personal and closely tied to the individual's very existence».

If the human genome is the hereditary substance of an organism or the sum of hereditary information existing in a cell, it evidently lies completely within the scope of the reserve to which the individual is entitled with respect to knowledge by others. And if human genome investigation can now provide information as to hereditary predisposition to certain diseases, such information obviously has great bearing on the individual's health and very existence, depending on the nature of the disease in question.

In short, the human genome forms part of the right to privacy as a right of the person («extremely personal» rights the Constitutional Court calls them) and for that matter, in my opinion, the most intimate part, as it constitutes the biological essence of the human person.

It remains to be said then that extending the right to privacy to embrace the human genome implies, naturally, the right of the person to know his own genetic information and to keep it intimately reserved, and, moreover, the right, also, not to know said genetic information. Indeed, since it belongs to the most intimate realm, nobody can be obliged to know their own genetic information.

### 3.  Qualitative difference and differences of degree

The human genome is not the only means of knowing a person's real biological condition. Medical science has made great progress in its capacity to ascertain the state of peoples's health through checkups, clinical analyses and the use of high-tech apparatuses. The information thereby obtained also affects the rights of the person and should be eligible for protection as private information. But there is undoubtedly a qualitative difference between these methods and the human genome. Knowing a person's state of health, for all the sophistication of the means used for such purpose, is not the same as knowing the person's genetic information. This qualitative difference warrants an «extra» protection for the human genome, the legal protection of which must be especially as the only reliable means for safeguarding the dignity of the human person. Put into other words, the protection of privacy with respect to information on a person's state of health is sufficiently assured under current legal provisions, but protection of privacy with respect to human genome information necessarily requires greater oversight and protection. Our present-day legislation must therefore be amended accordingly.

So, on the one hand, we have a qualitative difference between examining a person's genome and evaluating a person's state of health. On the other hand, differences of degree arise within the study of the human genome and the scientific advances that permit us to obtain ever greater and more reliable genetic information. Partial genomic information indicating predisposition to certain diseases is not the same as hypothetical complete information that would allow us not only to know hereditary predisposition to any given disorder, but also the person's entire lifelong behaviour (I do not believe in this last possibility because, irrespective of hereditary predisposition and greater or lesser degrees of freedom, man is essentially free and, therefore, the relevance of such hereditary information would be limited to physical but never the ontological aspects of the person). Leaving aside the question of the reliability of the information acquired (scientific certainty could only be achieved after a longer period of experimentation) and the possible errors which may be committed in the investigation, the differences between the levels which could arise here are clearly quantitative in nature, and as such, they should all be afforded identical protection, irrespective of the level attained by scientific advances in human genome understanding. Or, stated differently, at least from the present standpoint there should be a single uniform legal treatment of genetic information, regardless of any quantitative differences in the content of the information.

## No obligation to provide genetic information as precondition for taking out a life insurance policy

Having thus introduced the general legal significance, we may now take up its relation to the area of law dedicated to regulating insurance contracts. This analysis will specifically consider the obligation of prior information provided for in section 89 of the current Insurance Contract Act in connection with life insurance contracts.

Applying the legal principle derived from the foregoing analysis to section 89 of the Insurance Contract Act implies that the insurer should in no case be able to require genetic information as a precondition for entering into a life insurance contract. I will now give the reasoning behind this conclusion and examine the consequences of its application for legal duty of prior disclosure set down in the aforementioned section.

## I. Grounds for and scope of the non-requirement of genetic information

If genetic information belongs to the most intimate sphere of the rights of the person, then a condition *sine que non* for the policyholder to be able to provide the insurer with the insured's genetic information prior to the contract being executed is the consent of the insured. This begs the question as to whether such consent is sufficient for us to understand that the right to privacy has not been left unprotected. Although legal opinion generally shares the premise that consent of the interested party (except in the case of inalienable attributes) eliminates the illegitimacy of invasions into the private sphere, I agree with Rodota that consent is overvalued. As said author has stated, «shifting our inquiry away from the formal plane and to actual practice, we immediately see the illusory nature of protection based on consent. What desperately ill patient would deny his consent to experimenting with a new drug? What bank customer would deny consent to the free use of his account information if this were the sole condition for obtaining a loan». What insured, I might add, will deny consent to supplying genetic information to the insurer if the latter so demands as an indispensable requisite for taking out a life insurance policy?

In insurance law the person's consent should be accompanied by legal guarantees such that denial of consent cannot be used by the insurer as grounds for not entering into the life insurance contract. Or put in positive terms, it should be possible to execute a life insurance contract without the prior disclosure requirement necessarily applying to the insured's genetic information. This is even further supported by the fact that the insured's privacy rights also include the right to not know his own genetic information.

What is more, in light of the qualitative aspect previously described (genetic information affects the most intimate realm of the person), there should be absolutely no connection between the insured's real, possible or hypothetical knowledge of his genome and the duty to disclose relevant information prior to taking out a life insurance policy. This means that in cases where the insurer has not received permission from the insured to know the latter's genome, it is irrelevant whether or not the insured already has such knowledge of his genome and, where so, of any attendant hereditary predisposition to specific diseases. Therefore an insured cannot be deemed to be acting fraudulently or in bad faith when concealing possible diseases of which he is only aware by means of his genetic information. Only where they are known to the insured or knowable to the insurer by clinical or medical means other than genetic information will failure to inform in the insured's precontract statement be considered as concealment.

This radical separation constitutes the only guarantee of respect for the insured's right to privacy with respect to genetic information, not only *ad extra* (the possibility of the insurer misusing the information with third parties, irrespective of the possible liabilities of all kinds, including criminal, it may thus incur) but also, and fundamentally, *ad intra* (where the insurer uses knowledge of the insured's genetic information to not fulfil legal obligations to the policyholder, the insured or the beneficiaries, as the case may be, because they will not be able to offer any resistance to the insured's dominant position).

In conclusion, the non-obligatory nature of genetic information disclosure in the duty to declare prior to making an insurance contract has two ramifications. First, the insurer is absolutely prohibited from making access to the insured's genetic information a precondition for a life insurance policy. And second, in life insurance contracts made without the insured consenting to insurer access to his genetic information, the question of whether the insured knew or did not know said information is of no relevance, such that even when that genetic information gave the insured prior knowledge of some pre-existing condition or hereditary predisposition, he cannot be considered to have acted in bad faith so long as he did not obtain (or the insurer, through the pre-contract declaration or clinical examinations, could not have obtained) that knowledge through some means other than genetic information.

## 2. Need for amendment of section 89 of the Insurance Contract Act

Section 89 as it stands today provides:

«In the event of any reticence or inaccuracy in the policyholder's statements which affects the appraisal of the risk, the general provisions of this Act shall apply. Nevertheless, the insurer may not challenge the contract after the expiry of the term of 1 year, reckoned from the date when the contract was made, unless the parties have established a longer term in the contract and, in any case, unless the policyholder acted fraudulently.

This provision shall not apply to inaccurate statements in connection with the insured's age, which case is regulated in the following section.»

Leaving aside the question of the insured's age, which does not affect this analysis, section 89 provides a normative mandate for deference to section 10 of the same Act with certain particularities. We must therefore examine the latter section in order to fully comprehend that normative mandate:

«It is the duty of the policyholder, before the contract is made, to declare to the insurer, in accordance with the questionnaire submitted by the latter, all circumstances known to him that may affect the appraisal of the risk. [The following sentence was introduced by operation of Act 21 of December 19th 1990 in order to adapt Spanish law to EEC Directive 88/357] He shall be relieved from such duty if the insurer does not submit a questionnaire to him, or where, despite submitting the same, circumstances are involved which may influence the valuation of the risk and are not included therein.

The insurer may cancel the contract by means of a declaration to the policyholder made within the term of 1 month, reckoned from the time the reservation or inaccuracy on the part of the policyholder is made known. The premiums for the period in course at the time when the insurer makes this declaration shall be payable to him, unless there exists any fraud or serious fault on his part.

If the loss occurs before the insurer has made the declaration referred to in the preceding paragraph, his payment shall be reduced in proportion to the difference between the agreed premium and the premium that would have been applicable had the true nature of the risk been known. If there existed any fraud or serious fault on the part of the policyholder, the insurer shall be released from the payment.»

Section 10 is included among the general provisions applicable to all insurance contracts, whereas section 89 comes under Title III, dedicated to «Personal Insurance», specifically Sub-Section Two thereunder, regulating «Life Insurance». Comparative examination of both sections allows us to establish that the current legal regimen is characterized by the following:

– The insurance policyholder's duty of truthful declaration prior to making the contract: Since the enactment of Act 21/1990 this duty is limited by the questionnaire submitted to the insurer in that if a determined question does not appear on the questionnaire, the policyholder does not violate the duty of truthful declaration with respect thereto. The particularities set out in section 89 are therefore not applicable to this duty.

– Possibility of the insurer cancelling the contract within 1 month's time from discovering that the policyholder provided incomplete or inaccurate information. Although section 89 uses the term «challenge» instead of «cancel», the legal mandate is the same, but with the introduction of a restriction: the cancellation may not take place later than 1 year (or earlier, where so provided in the policy) from the date on which the contract was made, whereas under the general insurance provisions the insurer maintains the right to cancel for the life of the contract.

– Proportional reduction in the indemnity if the insured loss occurs before the insurer cancels the policy. Section 89 is silent as to this point but, given that cancellation can only take place within 1 year's time from the date when the contract was made, the said proportional reduction shall likewise only apply during that same period. Otherwise we would have the absurd conclusion that the Insurance Contract Act puts a time limit on the insurer as to the action of greater consequence (cancellation) while indefinitely maintaining the lesser consequence (proportional reduction in the indemnity). In any event, and allowing for the possibility of interpretations holding that the possibility of proportional reductions in the indemnity remains in place indefinitely, this aspect should also be contemplated in the proposed amendments to section 89.

– Fraud or serious fault by the policyholder frees the insurer from the indemnity payment obligation. However, section 89 provides such exemption only for fraud or bad faith and hence not for cases where the policyholder is at fault, even serious fault.

This legal regulation of the duty to declare and its consequences, as succinctly expressed above, does not envisage, as it obviously could not have done, the possible impact of genetic information. Actual experience in Spain –in particular, the Claims Service of the Directorate General for Insurance– demonstrates that section 89 is the source of numerous problems with insurers which will be compounded by the lack of any reference to genetic information. If to said problems we add the many and varied negative consequences of not amending section 89, and its lack of specific protection for genetic information, with respect not only to the insurer's disclosure of genetic but also to the insurer's dominant position under the insurance contract in the conflicts which could arise from such disclosure, we arrive at the conclusion that the aforementioned section must be modified to provide rigorous protection of genetic information and thus avert, or at least forestall, the danger in question.

Along these lines, I understand that the factors which should be considered in amending section 89 of the Insurance Contract Act are as follows:

– No amendment of section 10 of the Insurance Contract Act.

I should first point out that section 10, as the general insurance regulation of the pre-contract duty to declare, has in practice proven to be effective and, particularly as amended by Act 21/1990, has established an adequate system of «balanced benefits».

Genetic information is not only of relevance for life insurance. It may also affect other forms of personal insurance and may even have significance, albeit remote, on certain types of property damage insurance (for example, in civil liability automobile insurance, with respect to certain predispositions of the driver). But the remaining types of personal insurance allow for a relatively easy solution: including section 89 among the other sections referred to in section 100 of the Insurance Contract Act. If such a provision were included in accident insurance, taking into account that section 106 for health insurance defers to the provisions on accident insurance insofar as they are compatible, inclusion among the aforesaid references would permit coverage of all types of personal insurance.

– Basic reference to section 10 of the Insurance Contract Act.

If, as we have just seen, the regulation provided by section 10 is considered adequate, the general principle of section 89 should be to defer to section 10, adding as special rules the refinements needed in the latter section.

– Regulation of special rules applicable to the specific problems of life insurance.

The specific provisions suggested by the foregoing analysis of the significance of the human genome for life insurance should be added to those already contained in section 89. These new provisions can be summarized as follows:

First, disclosure of genetic information shall not be required as part of the duty to declare prior to making an insurance contract.

Second, the genetic information known to the policyholder shall always represent an absolute limit. This, in turn, implies, stated negatively, that in no case (even when known to the policyholder) shall concealment of genetic information be considered as constituting a case of «incomplete or inaccurate» information; or, in a positive sense, in order for material risk-classification information to be deemed «incomplete or inaccurate», such information must have been knowable through other scientific means in the insurer's questionnaire filled in by policyholder.

### 3. *Proposed alternative wording*

On the basis of the foregoing, a possible alternative wording of section 89 of the Insurance Contract Act, to reflect the requirements imposed by the need to protect genetic information, is given below:

«The insurance policyholder's duty to declare prior to making an insurance contract shall be regulated as set down in section 10, with the following specific provisions:

*a)* The insurer may not include in the questionnaire the insured's genetic information.

*b)* The provision of paragraph 2 of section 10 for cancellation of the contract by the insurer due to the provision of incomplete or inaccurate information by the policyholder and of paragraph three of the same section for the proportional reduction of the indemnity shall only apply for 1 year from when the contract was made.

*c)* The insurer shall only be released from payment if there was fraud in the policyholder's declaration.

*d)* Failure to disclose genetic information shall not be considered as fraud, as deliberately incomplete information or as inaccurate statement by the policyholder and shall not be grounds for proportional reduction of the indemnity.

This provision shall not apply to inexact statements as to the insured's age, which is regulated in the following section».

## Toward a dual system of life insurance contracts

Now if we were to stop here, our conclusion might be somewhat frustrating. Indeed, if the availability of genetic information truly represents an advance and yet is completely blocked from entering into the insurance contract, we must ask the question: Then of what use is genetic information in the life insurance contract?

We therefore must not stop our analysis here, but further examine how genetic information can be treated within the obligation of pre-contract disclosure.

For this purpose two apparently contradictory principles have to be reconciled. One holds that the law cannot oppose or hinder scientific advances, or ignore them, and must instead embrace them in order to be, as professor Legaz Lacambra has defined, a «form of social life». Although justice should be «blind» it cannot close its eyes to social reality. The second criterion sustains that the right to privacy is, in all cases, inviolable and that as such even the smallest of infringements represents a grave threat. Hence, the more science advances, the more exquisite care we must take in defending privacy as an «extremely personal» right (as it was deemed by our Constitutional Court). This is not new and is consistent with the very notion of law as an equilibrium or balance of principles which, taken to their ultimate consequences, are contraposed (for example, those of freedom and legal certainty).

There are widely different systems for reconciling both of the above criteria. They run from the search for eclectic solutions that combine and adequately contrapose both principles to –and this is my leaning– a dualist system that presents two alternatives, both of which can nonetheless embrace both freedom (the right to privacy) and legal certainty (including the obligation to disclose genetic information in the pre-contract phase). This duality of legal regimens as to questions of genetic information turns on whether such information can be included in life insurance contracts or, on the contrary, such inclusion is prohibited.

The two regimens comprising the dualist system would be:

## I.  Classic regulation

Its point of departure is the currently applicable regulations but with the addition of normative elements to specifically preclude genetic information from being incorporated into the structure of life insurance contracts without the insured's consent.

Briefly stated, this would mean maintaining the current legal provisions but amending section 89 of the Insurance Contract Act in the sense set out above.

By way of example, the respect for «the principles of equity and sufficiency founded on the rules of insurance practice», which is imposed on premiums by section 23.3. of Act 33 of August 2nd 1984 on Private Insurance Regulation, would be maintained through the traditional system of basing premium rate calculations on the so-called «mortality and morbidity tables», irrespective of advances in the methods for elaborating said tables, and even if they include consequences derived from genetic information (proving, as mentioned previously, that the separation can never be absolute).

## 2. New regulation

This is the alternative to the foregoing system and incompatible therewith. The essential difference is that this regimen allows for the insured's consent to the inclusion of genetic information within the pre-contract duty to declare, necessarily requiring a different legal regimen than the one described above.

This regimen would obviously not be exclusively circumscribed to the pre-contract duty to declare, but touch on other aspects of insurance contracts and even on insurer regulatory provisions. Thus, taking the premium rates example alluded to above, the reference to «insurance practice» cited in section 23.3 of the aforementioned Private Insurance Regulation Act must obviously be modified. Otherwise it could be improperly construed so as to allow the insurer to incorporate all the consequences of the insured's disclosed genetic information into its premium rate calculations. In certain circumstances, genetic information can transform uncertainty –the essential element of insurance contracts– into certainty, whereupon the notion of risk, regarded by section 1 of the regulatory act as the defining, characteristic element of the insurance contract, could even disappear.

Focusing solely on the subject of this analysis, that is, the pre-contract disclosure duty, this proposed alternative would imply the addition to the Insurance Contract Act of a new provision (which we could hypothetically cite as «section 89 bis»). The main features of this new provision would be as follows:

– Voluntariness.

In the first place, the consent of the insured. Election of this system must be voluntary on the part of the policyholder and must in all cases be accompanied by the insured's express consent, supported by the necessary safeguards for avoiding any coercion or intimidation by the insurer. Framing the pre-contract duty of disclosure within what in legal doctrine is known as the «preparatory phase» (professor Díez Picasso), the insured should be entitled to withdraw his consent, even after having issued it, up until such withdrawal ceases to make sense, that is, until his genetic information is revealed to the insurer. Along these lines the first paragraph of this hypothetical provision could read as follows:

«The insurer shall not use as grounds for denying a life insurance contract the policyholder's refusal to furnish the insured's genetic information when declaring circumstances known thereto which could influence the risk classification.»

– Restriction of the rights of the insurer arising under section 89.

Secondly, disclosure of the insured's genetic information to the insurer should necessarily restrict the scope of section 89 of the Insurance Contract Act only to aspects not connected with genetic information. This applies to the insured's pre-contract duty of disclosure, as well as to the right to cancel the contract for incomplete or inaccurate information, and to the proportional reduction of indemnities. The second paragraph of the provision proposed herein could thus read as follows:

«If in the pre-contract questionnaire the policyholder provides the insured's genetic information to the insurer, the insurer shall not include in the said questionnaire circumstances already reflected in the genetic information, or cancel the contract, or proportionally reduce the indemnity on the basis of the circumstances encompassed in said genetic information.»

– Prohibition on disclosure.

Lastly, the insurer's knowledge of the insured's genetic information should be circumscribed to the strict limits of the insurance contract and not surpass those bounds for any cause. The prohibition should be as rigorous as the insured wishes. For example, even where the insured's genetic information is known to the insurer, the right of the former not to know such information should be respected if he so states, irrespective of the effects it may have on the insurance. The last paragraph of the proposed provision would thus read as follows:

«The insurer shall safeguard the secrecy of the insured's genetic information known thereto and shall disclose said information or use it for any purposes other than authorized by the insured.»

This system may strike some as overly cautious and as not offering advantages that encourage the insured to grant the insurer access to his genetic information. But caution is necessary when dealing with a new area of problems of such enormous potential impact on the right to privacy. The untold injurious consequences of any excessive intrusion into the most intimates sphere of a person warrants caution. In conclusion, that cardinal virtue, prudence, should also preside the elaboration of laws.

# ENLARGEMENT OF RISK UNDERWRITING IN LIFE INSURANCE WITH REGARD TO GENETIC TESTS?

## Kerstin Berberich

Institute of Insurance Science at the University of Mannheim.
Federal Republic of Germany.

## Introduction

The development in molecular biology concerning the detections of genes and their functions will quickly proceed. The data below give a first impression of this development:

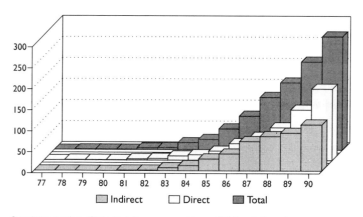

Cumulative number of inherited diseases amenable to DNA-based diagnosis.
SOURCE: Cooper/Schmidtke (1992), pg. 40.

In January 1993 there were 440 genes amenable to direct or indirect DNA diagnosis [1]. With this increasing knowledge of course the number of DNA-based tests for genetic disorders and predispositions will certainly expand by an order of magnitude. It should be mentioned that in this context we restrict the term «genetic test» to DNA analysis and exclude cytogenetic tests for chromosome abnormalties and tests for specific gene products.

With a genetic test it is possible to detect a certain gene on the genome of an organism. One gene may be responsible for the outbreak of a certain disease (monogenetic diseases) or at least can provoke in interaction with other factors the outbreak of a disease (multi-factor monogenetic or polygenetic diseases).

This increasing disposal of genetic tests will strengthen the conflict of interests of insurance companies and applicants for insurance contracts which is described appropriatly as follows: «While customers fear how insurers may use genetic testing to deny coverage or invade privacy, insurers fear how consumers could use genetic testing to forsee coverage needs and exploit the insurance system» [2].

The following article will briefly explain these different interests and their possible protection by law (according to the German law).

## Genetic tests as an instrument of diagnosis

Using genetic tests as an instrument of diagnosis within the underwriting process means that certain symptoms of the physical condition of the applicant which might indicate a certain disease can be proved or excluded by genetic tests.

The application of genetic tests as an instrument of diagnosis is not controversially discussed in literature [3]. Apparently in this case they are evaluated as any other medical examination to determine a disease.

---

[1] Verbal communication in January 1993, by Dr M. Krawczak, Institut für Humangenetik, Medizinische Hochschule Hannover.
[2] Cf. ACLI-HIAA (1991), pg. 8.
[3] Cf., f.e., German Federal-Land-Commission «Genome Analysis» (1990), pg. 117. The commission already permits genetic tests in this case for health insurance.

## Genetic tests as an instrument of prognosis

Using genetic tests as an instrument of prognosis means that certain −particular monogenetic− dispositions that cause a nearly definite realization of the claim can be detected by genetic tests before the conclusion of the contract.

### 1. Potential interests of life insurance companies in genetic tests

1.1. *Symmetrical distribution of information*
Symmetrical distribution of information of material circumstances on the side of the applicant as well as on the side of the insurance company is necessary to prevent adverse selection.

Adverse selection is a process in insurance by which an applicant who is uninsurable, or is a greater than average risk, seeks to obtain a policy from a company at a standard premium rate. A nicer description of a premium calculation that renounces individual calculation criteria is the follwing: applicants who are uninsurable or are at a higher than average risk are given a present and they will hurry to get it [4]. Life insurance companies carefully screen applicants for this reason, since their premiums are based on policy holders in average good health and nonhazardous occupations [5].

Sect. 16 VVG (German Insurance Conract Law) provides the legal basis for the person-related questions. But furthermore it constitutes the obligation to the applicant to disclose all circumstances known to him that are material for the assumption of the risk. Circumstances are material if they are of a nature to have an influence on the insurers decision whether to enter into the contract at all, or whether to do so under the agreed terms.

Economic consequences of adverse selection in life insurance are illustrated on the following example.

A collective of 1,000 policyholders is based on a group of 20-30 year-olds. One part of this group is at average risk with an expected disease rate of one thousandth a year. In another part of the collective everyone has the knowledge of his genetically caused disease which is a material circumstance according to sect. 16 VVG. The mortality rate of this group is 50%. This higher risk is not recognized by the insurer. Therefore the latter group is insured under normal conditions, too.

---

[4] Cf. Hax (1949), pg. 80.
[5] Cf. Rubin (1987), pg. 10.

The cost increase of the insurer because of adverse selection within ten years does depend on the composition of the collective: if there were only one policy holder who antiselected within that collective, the insurer would have to pay 5% more benefits. If there were 10% antiselected 14.9 cases of death have to be expected. This would equal an increase in cost of ca. 50% for an insurance company. If adverse selection is reaching a level of 50% the insurer would be hit by an increase in cost of 245%.

For preventing such an adverse selection the insurance companies ask in the life insurance application forms also for person-related data of the insured person: e.g. age, sex, details about occupation, possibly hazardous sports and naturally questions concerning the health status. These application forms aren't subjected to a legally prescribed form to meet the requirements set up in the principles for Life Insurance Application Form Formats by the BAV (German Federal Supervisory Office for Insurance Companies).

A right of the insurer to demand a medical examination does not exist (sect. 160 VVG). If the applicant, however, refuses a medical examination, no German insurance company will conclude a contract with him.

If this duty to disclose material circumstances is violated by the policy holder or if he fraudulently avoided knowledge of the circumstance (sect. 16 par. 1 VVG) or if he has given incorrect information about a material circumstance (sect. 17 par. 1 VVG) the insurer may rescind.

If the rescission takes place after the insured event has occurred the insurer's obligation to perform continues unaffectedly, if the circumstance with respect to which the duty to inform was breached has had no influence on the occurrence of the insured event and on the extend of the insurer's obligation to perform (sect. 21 VVG). The burden of proof for all circumstances being the basis for a rescission from the contract such as notice of risks, substantiality of the risk, incorrect answers etc. is –according to the prevailing view– subjected to sect. 16 par. 1, cl. 3 VVG placed to the insurer. The burden of proof for all circumstances cancelling the rescission is placed with the policy-holder [6].

The insurer's right to avoid the contract on the ground of fraudulent deception about circumstances of the risk remains unaffected (sect. 22 VVG).

In case of rescission or avoidance, received premiums have to be refunded in accordance with sect. 20 par. 2 VVG, especially those

---

[6] Cf. Prölss/Martin (1988), sect. 16, 17 VVG, anotation no. 9.

policy reserves built for an endowment insurance (sect. 176 VVG). The risk and cost parts of the premium payments payed by the policy holder, however, do not have to be refinded by the insurance company (sect. 40 par. 1 VVG).

*1.2. Realization of a premium calculation as risk adaquate as possible*

By striving for a premium calculation of risk as adequate as possible the attempt is made to fulfill the principle of equivalence as exactly as possible. The principle of equivalence is a stochastic calulation principle of the premium; the expected mean value is the equivalent to the expected compensation payment. Better risk classification could translate into lower prices for future applicants and higher returns on investment for stockholders and policy holders [7].

In reality those causes of claim among the risk factors are chosen which offer the maximum contribution to explaining and prognosticating the claim regularity (rate factors). Besides age and sex, also job and special risks as well as health conditions serve as rate factors in life insurance. Therefore, in life insurance the basis of calculation is the decrement table.

By persuing the target of a premium calculation most appropriate to the principle of equivalence each applicant would have to be screened on certain disease dispositions without regard to the individual (family) anamnesis. This may exceed the limits of the postulate of symmetrical information distribution. The criterion of randomness is being examined here on the part of the insurance industry above the minimum level required because of the principle of equivalence

The criterion of randomness is one prerequisite for the insurability of risks: the events causing policy proceeds must be uncertain in advance for the subject taking decisions and are not to be influenced by his will and behaviour. The uncertainty must refer to the origin and/or the moment and/or the amount of the claim occuring [8].

This constellation would be economical if the tests were on late onset diseases which are very common and cause a higher mortality as the average.

The legal basis for a premium calculation as exact as possible according to the principle of equivalence using all or a part of all methods of gaining knowledge about genetic dispositions first also is given by sect. 16 par. 1, cl. 3 VVG in connection with sect. 160

---

[7] Cf. ACLI (1989), pg. 24.
[8] Cf., f.e., Helten/Karten (1983) pgs. 84/85 (208/209).

VVG. A legal restriction of the right of questioning and the right of health examinations which makes possible a symmetrical distribution of information on the part of the applicant and the policy holder as well as an adaquate control and situation of proof neither follows from sect. 16 VVG nor from any other policy regulation nor the contemporary legislation in Germany.

*1.3.    Statements of insurance associations towards genetic testing*
Some life insurance associations do not see any need for their branch to fall back upon or to postulate genetic tests at the moment [9]. The German association is of the opinion that the section 16 VVG (German Insurance Contract Law) provides a sufficient protection at the moment. However, it declines a general exclusion of genetic testing already because of fundamental considerations and recognizes the possibility of a better risk classification. The German association finally emphasizes that genetic testing can also be an advantage for applicants (i.e. those who are at higher risk because of a family anamnesis).

The English association has restricted the use of genetic tests up to 1995 since the situation does not change dramatically. The Dutch association renounces the active use of genetic tests. It even renounces the indication of genetic tests already made for applications of insurance sums up to less than 200,000 guilders.

Most of the associations point out their need to have access to any already existing relevant health information for underwriting purposes, including genetic test results.

## 2.   The applicants interest

*2.1.    The applicants interest in not knowing about his own genetic disposition (unrelated to insurance matters)*
The result of a prognostic genetic test can have a radical impact on the emotional and psycho-social constitution of a person examined. Additionally, genetic tests create facts that –to a substantial extent and mostly at the disadvantage of the concerned person– are noted and taken into consideration by the person's social environment [10].

However, the emotional and psychological reactions might be similar getting knowledge about a disease that already occurred.

---

[9] Association of Life Insurance Companies in Germany (LVV) (1988); The Life Underwriters Club (LUC), Great Britain (1992); McNamara (1992); The Dutch Life Insurance Association (NVL); The American Council of Life Insurance-The Health Insurance Association of America (ACLI-HIAA) (1991).
[10] Cf. Krahnen (1989), pg. 69.

One difference in knowing about a certain genetic disease disposition and an already existing one is the uncertainty. In the case of monogenetic diseases the uncertainty is about the time of the onset, in the case of multifactorial ones not only the time of onset is uncertain, but also if the disease actually occurs.

On the other hand, in the case of multifactorial diseases the gentically affected might actively do something to prevent the outbreak of the disease [for example, in changing some habits (nutritional/living ones)]. Concerning monogenetic diseases, the only active reaction possibility of the genetically affected is to make a kind of psychological preparation [11].

Legal protection of this interest may be offered with the right not to know [12]. This right not to know is construed from the general right to privacy which falls under «any other right», as defined by sect. 823 par. 1 BGB. By this general right to privacy as subjective civil law, constitutional values are introduced into the civil law [13].

The German Federal Constitutional Court has commented on the relationship of the individual to the «entire public power» as follows [14]: there is an area of private life decisions reserved for the individual citizen under the constitution; there is a final area of human liberty which cannot be infringed upon and is beyond any influence of the entire public power.

The general right to privacy of the civil law, however, is not protected in general but in its concret form gained by balancing interests [15].

Also suggested as a legal basis for not being forced to get knowledge about the own genetic disposition is the right of informational self-determination [16].

A «Right of informational self-determination» has been developed by the Federal Constitutional Court in continuation of its decisions passed down so far and pertaining to the general right to privacy from Art. 2 par. 1 GG (Constitution) and Art. 1 par. 1

---

[11] Nevertheless uncertainty may also be a reason for making a genetic test: such will be the case in a family where a severe genetic disease already has appeared. But this is not the subject of that paragraph.

[12] Cf., f.e., Donner/Simon (1990), pg. 913; Wiese (1991), pgs. 475-499.

[13] Cf. Wiese (1991), pg. 483.

[14] BVerfGE 6,32,42; 6,389,433; 27,1,6.

[15] Cf. Hubmann (1967), pgs. 156/157; Nipperdey/Wiese (1962), pp. 834/835; Schlechtriem (1975), pg. 65; Wiese (1989), pg. 2279; (1990), pg. 359.

[16] Cf. Wiese (1991), pg. 484.

GG as a defense law regulating the relationship of the individual with the state [17].

Under the modern conditions of data processing, the right of the free development of one's personality necessitated the protection of the individual against unrestricted collecting, storing, use and transmitting of his personal data. This protection is said to be incorporated in the basic right of Art. 2 sec. I in connection with Art. I sec. I GG. In this respect, the constitution guarantees the power of the individual to basically decide himself on the release and use of his personal data. This «Right of informational self-determination» has its bounderies in a person's belonging and obligation to a community [18].

As to the applicability of the right of informational self-determination within the civil law, the Federal Constitutional Court has not yet commented to that effect [19]; the direct applicability of the basic laws within the civil law is denied by prevailing opinion [20]. The opinion is held that this right also has to be recognized as a concrete form worthy of the protection of the general right privacy within the civil law in a scope yet to be developed [21].

In an extension of the interpretation of this Federal Constitutional Court ruling, this self-determination not only covers the exclusion of others from access to information on one's own sphere of privacy (here: your own genetic disposition) but also extends to the freedom of decision as to what extent each individual himself wants to have knowledge of it. Such a right of self-determination has to be granted to him in respect of his genetic disposition. In this sense, he has a right not to know [22].

2.2. *Minimizing the danger of misuse*
Another interest of the applicant is to minimize the danger of data misuse.

Some authors are of the opinion that genetic disposition data is extremely sensitive information of a most private nature. This would automatically increase the danger of data misuse [23]. Others do not contribute a new quality to those data compared with sensitive information gained from other medical examinations [24].

---

[17] BVerfG 65, I, 41 ff.
[18] Cf. BVerfG 65, I, 43.
[19] Cf. Zöllner (1984), pg. 246.
[20] Cf., f.e., Maunz/Dürig (1990), Art. 2 Abs. I, annotation no. 57.
[21] Cf. Wiese (1991), pg. 484.
[22] Cf. Wiese (1991), pg. 484.
[23] Cf. BMFT (1991), pg. 218.
[24] Cf. Karten (1991), p. 649.

The quality of the data differs from the normal health status data with regard to possible or sometimes certain severe diseases which might occur at the time aspect. And this time aspect might have the consequence of an earlier social stigmatization if data misuse is given.

This danger of an earlier social stigmatazation is due to the prognostic nature of genetic diseases that have not occurred yet: it is not due to a different handling in the insurance industry as compared with other health data.

Our point of view is that the danger of data misuse by the insurance companies concerning data flow between the insurance industry and its environment is not increased in Germany because of the good record insurance companies have with respect to the handling of other sensitive health data in the past. But of course the danger of data misuse is greater compared to the situation where no data of genetic dispositions exist.

The confidential handling not only of very sensitive data is laid down in the German Federal Data Protection Act (BDSG). A danger to the right to privacy is considered with the technical possiblities to process extensive data, quickly channel data, to combine data and to store data unrestricted by time and place. To protect this right to privacy from infringement is the target of the German Data Protection Act (sect. 1 BDSG). Infringement of the regulations of the BDSG is punished by a custodial sentence up to 2 years or by a fine (Sect. 43 BDSG).

According to the British Club of Underwriters the handling of genetic data will not lead to an increase of dangers because of standards already existing and the careful dealing with medical data [25]. Regarding the American situation, a subcommittee of the ACLI stated that the existing situation did not suggest the most appropriate framework for treating genetic test information. This subcommittee makes some recommendations to improve the situation [26].

As far as the data flow within the insurance business is concerned, the approval clause pertaining to passing on data of any life insurance contract has to be taken into consideration.

According to the approval of the applicant and policy-holder, the insurer passes on adequate data –which is gathered from the application documents or the performance of the contract (premiums, insurance events, risk/contract modifications)– to reinsu-

---

[25] Cf. McNamara (1992).
[26] Cf. ACLI (o.A.).

rance companies and to the Association of Life Insurance Companies eV for passing this data on to other insurers. Health data may be passed on to reinsurance companies and personal insurance companies only; agents may receive the data only if it is necessary for drafting the contract. Independent of the conclusion of the contract, this approval also applies to other examinations of (insurance) contracts applied for somewhere else and to applications in the future. Furthermore, it has to be approved of that the insurer of group X (with whom the present contract has been closed; annotation by the author), as far as this serves the orderly processing of the policy-holder's insurance business affairs, combines general data on contract, statement of accounts, and performance into one common data bank and passes the data on to its agents. This approval applies only if the policy-holder has the option –in an acceptable fashion– to obtain knowledge of the content of the insurer's leaflet on data processing made available by the insurer [27].

This means that health data which has been gathered in the process of closing a life insurance contract is also available to the health insurance company of the same insurance group. Thus, it is also true that information about genetic tests that have already been carried out and paid by a private health insurance can be made available to the life insurance company of the same group.

Associated life insurance companies will notify the information center for special risks about those life insurance contracts that have been accepted with a risk surcharge, deferred or denied or cancelled by withdrawl or avoidance. This data flow is in compliance with the Data Protection Authorization Clause and the release from confidentiality statement [28].

Through this information center, all member companies have access to certain health data of individual applicants and policy-holders. This gains importance as soon as the permissibility of genetic tests in life insurance and health insurance companies is treated differently [29].

### 2.3. Avoiding discrimination
Another interest of the applicants is the preventing of discrimination. One of the possible definitions of genetic discrimination is discrimination directed against an individual of a family based soley on an apparent or perceived genetic variation from the «normal» human

---

[27] Ver BAV 2/1990, pg. 75.
[28] Cf. Hagelschuer (1987) pg. 91.
[29] A different treatment is suggested by the Federal-Land-Commission «Genome Analysis» (1990), pg. 47.

genotype. This definition does not include discrimination against an individual who at the time of the discriminatory act was affected by the genetic disease [30]. We understand discrimination as a denial of insurance coverage not justified by the facts.

Discrimination within this subject can be subdivided in discrimination against the asymptomatic ill and in discrimination based on the disregarding of clinical variability of genetic conditions [31].

One example given of possible «discrimination» against an asymptomatic ill did happen in health insurance. An 8-year-old girl who was diagnosed of having phenylketonuria (PKU) at 14 days of age. An adequate diet was given immediately and her growth and development have been completely normal. She was covered for medical insurance by the company that provided group insurance for her father's previous employer. When her father changed jobs recently, she was considered to be a high risk patient because of her diagnosis and therefore ineligible for insurance coverage under the group plan of the new employer [32].

This could not happen within the German insurance system. It is true that in Germany compulsory health insurance is linked to a certain income level, but does not depend on the employer. The same applies to private insurance, i.e. when changing employers, the current health insurance can be kept with a new employer.

When changing the insurance company it is legitimate for the new insurance company not to assume a definitely bad risk. The high costs of a phenylalanine diet that have to be paid by the health insurer make this girl a bad risk. If this person she is co-insured with tried to change insurance companies in Germany she would have to face the same problems here. So in our defintion this is no discrimination. But the example illustrates that a different structure of health insurance can provoke different (more) problems in several countries.

Apart from the cases of the asymptomatic ill, there is a lack of knowledge of the clinical variability of many genectic conditions [33].

An applicant for a life insurance with Charcot-Marie Tooth (CMT), a nonfatal, clinically variable and genetically heterogeneous neuromuscular condition was denied insurance cover in spite of him/her having informed the insurance company that people do not die of

---

[30] Cf. Billings *et al.* (1992), pgs. 476/477.
[31] Billings *et al.* (1992), pgs. 478/479.
[32] Billings *et al.* (1992), pg. 478.
[33] Cf. Billings *et al,* (1992), pg. 479; refering to this context, they talk about a misunderstanding.

CMT. Another person with CMT has been turned down for auto-mobile insurance in spite of his not having had any accident or traffic violations within 20 years of driving [34].

The complaint is that the insurance company decided soley on a diagnostic label, without regard to the severity of the condition of each individual. In these and other cases, having a particular genotype is equated with the presence of a severe illness and the lack of effective treatments. The indivdual may suffer serious consequences as a result of the inaccurate and unfair simplification of genetic conditions. It illustrates a lack of understanding of the concepts of incomplete genetic penetrance, variable expressivity and genetic heterogeneity [35].

In order to prevent discrimination in the sense of an unjustified denial of insurance cover, the term substantial risk has to be defined. Only detecting the appropriate gene is insufficient. Criteria such as life style (eating habits, prevention of risk factors, etc.) or family history (e.g. diseases the courses of which show an intrafamilial consistency) could play a role in this.

If genetic testing is considered admissable there would be a lot of practical problems. The criterion of suitability represents one of them. On the one hand, the material genetic dispositions with respect to sect. 16 VVG have to be defined. On the other hand, it has to be examined to what degree genetic findings are secured and thus can be applied in life insurance business. A discrimination because of inappropriate application of genetic testing has to be prevented.

Because of the insurers having an interest in an appropriate use of genetic data themselves —rejecting too many applicants not justified by the facts means the renunciation of business— legal arrangements might not be necessary. The insurers might ensure that underwriting with respect for genetic results has to be made only by qualified staff members.

## Conclusions

### 1. Obligation to disclose results of genetic tests already made

In literature a restriction of the obligation to disclose test results with respect to material circumstances as defined in

---

[34] Cf. Billings *et al.* (1992), pg. 479.
[35] Cf. Billings *et al.* (1992), pgs. 479/480.

sect. 16 VVG is demanded, as far as genetic tests are concerned [36].

To evaluate the necessity of this obligation concerning results of genetic tests which represent material circumstances as defined in sect. 16 VVG, the phenomenon of adverse selection should be mentioned. As discussed above insurance companies have a justified interest in a symmetrical distribution of information.

If a symmetric distribution of information is not given, there may be an actuarial loss, which in the long run might endanger the workability of the insurance company. At least premiums which would have to be paid by future policy holders will not be calculated any longer on the principle of equivalence. These premiums would steadily increase until applicants will not be able and willing to pay such high premiums any more.

A symmetric distribution of information with respect to all material circumstances as defined in sect. 16 VVG –including the results of genetic tests– is urgently necessary [37].

To evaluate the reasonableness it should be mentioned that the applicant is neither directly or indirectly forced to get knowledge of his genetic disposition. His right of informational self-determination with regard to the knowledge of his genetic status is not being touched.

On the other hand, he has to disclose the core of his personality [38], a fact that may represent a restriction of his right of informational self-determination. In literature, the conclusion is drawn that a weighing of interests would favour the right of informational self-determination, and which is influenced by the constitutional law, and disfavour «the material interest of the insurance companies for a risk and cost restriction» [39]. Therefore sect. 16 VVG should be restricted so that the results of genetic tests do not have to be disclosed, even if they represent a material circumstance [40].

We hold the opinion that the adverse selection –because of fundamental actuarial reasons which are a precondition for the wor-

---

[36] Cf. BMFT (1991), pg. 220; Wiese (1992), pg. 60; BMFT (1985), pg. 39; BACDJ (1988), pgs. 105 and 107; Präve (1992), pg. 283; Simon (1992), pg. 20.
[37] This also represents the attitude of insurance companies concerning the question of application of genetic tests in life insurance; cf. chapter 3.1.3.
[38] Cf. Wiese (1992, pg. 60 (prior to fn 111).
[39] Cf. BMFT (1991), pg. 220; Wiese (1992), pg. 60, who later on nullifies the restriction concerning late manifesting diseases, which are certain to break out.
[40] Cf. BMFT (1985), pg. 39; BACDJ (1988), pgs. 105/107; BMFT (1991) pg. 220; Präve (1992), pg. 283; Simon (1992), pg. 20; Wiese (1992), pg. 60.

kability of private insurance– weighs more than possible dangers resulting from the partial disclosure of the core of the personality. Consequently, we consider the obligation to disclose all material circumstances as defined in sect. 16 VVG urgently necessary, including results of genetic tests [41].

This result represents the contrary of the dominant opinion in literature. In the discussions and evaluations in –at least German– literature, the phenomenon of adverse selection is not even realized [42].

There is also the question if the amount of the insurance sum might be a criterion for not having the duty to disclose results of genetic tests already made.

One –already mentioned– proposal from the Dutch is the rejection of the duty to indicate results of genetic tests which are material circumstances if the applicant applies for an insurance sum less than 200,000 guilders.

Another proposal wants to determine the rejection of duty to disclose by an insurance sum depending on the social and financial situation of the applicant [43]. This proposal clearly prejudices those who are at on a lower income level than others.

We reject this restriction of the obligation to indicate with the same arguments made above in this paragraph.

## 2. Genetic tests as precondition for a life insurance contract conclusion

As a precondition for the admission to a life insurance, insurance companies make genetic tests with all applicants to find out about diseases with a big influence (rate factors) on an early death. For this purpose, genetic tests appear appropriate for diseases with multi-factor and monogenetic causes.

### 2.1. General remarks
At first sight it seems that this scenario only corresponds to the original interest of the insurance company: By getting knowledge of the applicant's genetic disposition it would be much easier to calculate on the basis of the equivalence principle.

---

[41] Another opinion is that of Billings, who realizes the phenomenon of adverse selection but judges it as follows: «It is a type of loss, but it is controlable.» in: Chase (1992), pg. 9.

[42] Cf. BMFT (1991), pg. 220; BMFT (1985), pg. 39; BACDJ (1988), pgs. 105 and 107; BMFT (1991), Präve (1992), pg. 283; Simon (1992), pg. 201; pg. 220; Wiese (1992), pg. 60.

[43] Cf. Kohnstamm (1992) Art. 5.

This original interest is –as already mentioned– legally protected by sect. 16 par. 1, cl. 3 VVG in connection with sect. 160 VVG, or at least is not restricted. That is the insurer is allowed to ask any question on the genetic disposition concerning a material circumstance as defined in sect. 16 VVG and demand the presentation of a genetic test as a part of the health test.

The questions on certain genetic dispositions –especially the diseases with a late onset and a high mortality– represent an appropriate instrument to find out a fair risk charge system according to the equivalence principle.

To evaluate the necessitiy of genetic tests as a precondition for a life insurance contract conclusion, it is mentioned that a general application of genetic tests is incompatible with the nature of an insurance, that is to insure people in order to prevent negative financial consequences deriving from a dangerous development [44].

Indeed, with the above mentioned general application of genetic tests, which are made regardless of the genetic disposition of the applicant and therefore are nonspecific, one exceeds all bounds of the postulate of the symmetric distribution of information –to prevent the danger of adverse selection– for both the insurance company and the insured party. The criterion of chance, demanding that the events to cause the insurance benefits must be uncertain in the beginning and not influenceable by the will of the *decisive subject,* is examined by the insurance to a degree that exceeds the required minimum.

The postulate that regular medical examinations would also be sufficient, which could be proved by the workability of the existing private insurances, is so far correct [45]. Consequently the prohibition of such screenings only prevents a more precise calculation of charges.

But of course the nature of private insurance is also to calculate on the basis of the principle of equivalence. A fact which is protected –as already mentioned– by sect. 16 VVG.

## 2.2. *Dispersion degree of genetic tests as a decision criterion*
However, it should be taken into consideration that the evaluation of the necessity criterion depends on the dispersion degree of genetic tests beyond the insurance business. Therefore the notion of henceforth making tests for certain genetic dispositions as a matter of routine in the medical range, similar to the medical check-ups for cancer in Germany, is quite realistic. Furthermore

---

[44] Cf., f.e., Hagelschuer (1990), pg. 15.
[45] Also cf. Wiese (1992), pg. 57 (prior to fn 9).

the development of genetic tests being offered by private laboratories should be taken into consideration. In such cases the application of genetic tests by screening can be considered a safety measure for a symmetric distribution of information for both the insurance company and the insured party.

However, this case construction presently is merely a theoretical one.

### 2.3. The kind of a genetic disposition as decision criterion

Possibly the question about the admissibility of genetic tests has to be judged with regard to the kind of genetic disposition.

With regard to serious diseases caused by monogenetic factors with a high mortality rate, the applicant has to face this threatening disease all of a sudden.

In this case, that is if such a test is not absolutely necessary for actuarial reasons (guarantee of symmetrical information distribution), genetic tests on such dispositions by screening should not be admitted, regarding the serious consequences caused by the knowledge of such a disposition. The right not to know has to be evaluated as more important as the contractual freedom of the insurer.

The reasonableness of confronting the applicant with such a disease is to be judged differently if dispositions with a high probability to cause widespread diseases with a high mortality (multifactor caused diseases) are concerned. In this case the applicant may possibly delay or even prevent the outbreak of the disease by changing his living habits.

Genetic dispositions (monogenetic and multi-factor) associated with increased mortality which may be proved at the DNA level and which also indicate a high spontaneous mutation rate could be interesting for a life insurance company carrying out screening.

The findings concerning multi-factorial hereditary dispositions are not yet completely proved. A large proportion of genetically caused disorders and those partly due to genetics can be traced to the mutation of several genes rather than just one. Risk figures established for this are confused because it is –not yet– clear how many genes are responsible for the materialization of the relevant feature [46].

So at the moment we have very little knowledge on a molecular level about multi-factorial diseases. Knowledge about the interde-

---

[46] Cf. Witkowski/Prokop/Ullrich (1991), pgs. XXII-XXIII.

pendence of such genetic dispositions with the effect of external factors which finally lead to the outbreak or degree of severity of a disease is just as vague. Therefore genetic tests to prove a disposition of multi-factorial diseases presently do not represent an adequate means of risk analysis for insurance companies.

Most genome and chromosome mutations show –if a spontaneous abortion does not occur during pregnancy– a phenotype which deviates from the normal type at birth. These mutation forms are –as long as they do not cause a disease which manifests itself later– not relevant for life insurance.

Presently the screening for diseases caused by monogenetic factors with a high mortality would represent an inefficient measure. Such diseases are extremly rare. Moreover, the rate of spontaneous mutation is too low to get an asymmetric distribution of information by a greater amount of the applicants [47]. Therefore testing anybody just as a measure of prophylaxis will not be efficient.

## 3. Voluntary presentation of results of genetic tests

Of course applicants who are considered an above-average risk group because of their individual health data or the family anamnesis and are therefore either accepted for insurance with an extra risk charge or denied as uninsurable should be allowed to make genetic tests and present the results voluntarily to the insurance company.

Another scenario is that applicants can prove by results of genetic tests that they have no genetic disposition for certain diseases with a higher mortality, this may lead to a lower premium. It is up to the insurance company if it makes use of such information.

If there are only a few applicants who present such results, it will have no influence on the premium of those who do not want to make such tests. If there will be quite a number of applicants presenting such results, the premium of those who do not want to make such tests will increase. This may lead to pressure on other applicants to do such tests.

At the moment, there do not exist genetic tests for many monogenetic disorders that lead to a higher mortality. The amount of multi-factorial late onset genetic diseases of course is higher and genetic tests for such diseases will increase relative rapidly.

---

[47] Cf. Berberich (1993): *EC Research Project* (forthcoming), appendix.

To achieve a remarkable reduction in premium there would have to be quite a lot of genetic tests for genetic dispositions that have a definitive higher mortality or that lead with a high probability to a higher mortality.

Making genetic tests just for the reason to lower the premium would only be efficient for relative high insurence sums: Only for high insurence sums there would be a profitable reduction in the insurance premium. Further the costs of genetic tests are relativly high at the moment (US $188-5,000). But this argument is only a temporary one, because costs for genetic tests will decrease by the invention of new methods and further amelioration of the existing technical possibilites.

The –from the actuarial point of view– legitimate interest of the applicant to get a premium reduction has to be opposed to the interest of an applicant not to make such tests and so not to get any knowledge of his genetic disposition (this interest may be protected by the so-called right not to know or the right of informational self-determination).

The presentation of such genetic test results is appropriate to lower the insurance premium. Also it is essential for a premium reduction. Also such a premium reduction according to the principle of equivalence does correspond to the nature of private insurance.

In order to guarentee the functionability of a life insurance the presentation of such genetic test results is not necessary. However, this criterion has to be examined within the principle of reasonabless.

It has to be assumed that only for high insurance sums (and a great number of different genetic dispositions) the voluntary presentation of genetic test results will lead to a relevant premium reduction.

So it can be concluded that the right to have a premium reduction according to the individual risk situation in the case of high insurance sums is to be evaluated as more important than the so-called right not to know or the right of informational self-determination. Particularly because these rights are not infringed upon directly: Applicants who do not want to make such tests would either have to pay a higher premium or have to renounce on insurance coverage at all.

As far as smaller insurance sums are concerned the amount of the reduction of the insurance sum would be less than in the case of high insurance sums. Here the avoidance of the possible indirect pressure –and also the costs which would arise– for the applicants who do not want to make such tests can be evaluated as more important than the right of other applicants to get a premium that is calulated more precisely on the principle of equivalence.

However, should the premium reduction be relative low even in the case of contracts with high insurance sums, one could renounce at the voluntary presentation of those genetic test results. In this case one can evaluate the interest of the applicant not to have the indirect pressure to make such genetic tests as more important than the –relatively small– restriction of a calculation that is closer to the principle of equivalence.

On the other hand, it is possible to permit the voluntary presentation of genetic test results in exactly these cases –high and small insurance sums with only a low reduction in premium– because the increase in premium for those applicants who do not want to do such tests only would be small. Therefore there would not be a strong indirect pressure for making such tests for those applicants who do not want to know anything about their genetic disposition.

At the moment not only genetic tests are relative expensive but also the assumed amount of genetic dispositions with the relevant attributes for such a presentation to life insureres for which genetic tests exist is small. Therefore it is the technical and economic argument that implicates that the voluntary presentation of such genetic test results with the aim of a premium reduction –at least at the moment– is a rather theoretical scenario.

## Summary

Enlargement of Underwriting With Regard To Genetic Tests in Life Insurance?

Illustrated on the example of the German law and insurance regulation.

The attitudes towards genetic tests within the course of the application for an insurance contract naturally differ between the applicant and the insurer: The applicant fears the denying of insurance coverage and the invasion of privacy, the insurer fears an exploitation of the insurance system.

However, genetic tests as an instrument of diagnosis seem not to be controversially discussed. They are regarded as any other medical examination.

With regard to genetic tests as an instrument of prognosis, the most important target of the insurers concerning this subject is to have the same information on material circumstances as the applicant by the time of the contract conclusion, including results of genetic tests already made. Concerning the actuarial view it is absolutely neces- sary for the functionning of the private insurance system to prevent adverse selection. This is guarenteed by sect. 16 German Insurance Contract Law (VVG). Another interest of the insurance company is to calculate the premium most appropriate to the principle of equi- valence. This interest also is guarenteed by sect. 16 VVG.

The attitude of the applicant towards genetic testing in private insurance of course is of another nature. The knowledge of one's own genetic disposition might have severe consequences –similar to being affected by an already existing disease– on the psycho- social situation. Therefore the applicant might not want to know anything about his genetic disposition. This interest is protected by the right not to know [sect. 823 par. 1 German Civil Code (BGB), derived from Art. 2 par. 1 in connection with Art. 1 German Constitution (GG)].

Another fear of the applicant is a possible misuse of genetic data. The target of the German Data Protection Act is to prevent such a misuse.

After evaluating the controversial interests we present the follo- wing demands to meet by a legal regulation on the subject of the enlargement of underwriting with regard to genetic tests:

1.  A statutory regulation should ensure at least the symmetrical information distribution about material circumstances at the time of the conclusion of the contract, including results of genetic tests already made.

2.  Concerning the active use of genetic tests for severe mono- genetic late onset dispositions with a high mortality rate, insurance companies should renounce on their application in the case with a screening of each applicant.

3.  In order to prevent adverse selection and to guarantee an equal treatment of each applicant in the Common Market, there should be made a standard regulation within the EC.

## References

**ACLI (O. A.):** Genetic Test Information and Insurance: Confidentiality Con- cerns and Recommondation.

**ACLI (1989):** The Potential Role of Genetic Testing in Risk Classification, Report of the Genetic Testing Committee to the Medical Section of the American Council of Life Insurance, 1989.

**ACLI-HIAA (1991):** *Report of the ACLI-HIAA (The American Council of Life Insurance– The Health Insurance Association of America).* Task Force On Genetic Testing, Washington, 1991.

**BADCJ (1988):** *Arbeitskreis-Christlich-Demokratischer-Juristen, Leitsätze zur Genomanalyse,* Teil 4, These 10 und 11, in: Seesing, Heinz (Hrsg.). «Rechtspolitische Grundsätze von CDU und CSU zur Gentechnik am Menschen», München, 1988.

**Berberich (1993): EC-Project (forthcoming):** «On the Permissibility of Genetic Tests in Life Insurance».

**Billings et al. (1992), Billings, Paul R./Kohn, Mel A./De Cuevas, Margaret/Beckwith, Jonathan/Alper, Joseph S./Natowicz, Marvin R.:** «Discrimination as a consequence of Genetic Testing», in: *American Journal of Human Genetics* 50; 476-482, 1992.

**BMFT (1985):** *Bundesminister für Forschung und Technologie (Hrsg.): In-Vitro-Fertilisation, Genomanalyse und Gentheorie: Bericht der gemeinsamen Arbeitsgruppe des Bundesministers für Forschung ung Technik und des Bundesministers für Justiz,* München, 1985.

**BMFT (1991):** *Die Erforschung des Menschlichen Genoms, Ethische und soziale Aspekte.* Hrsg.: Bundesminister für Forschung und Technologie, Frankfurt/New York, 1991.

**Cooper, David N./Schmidtke, Jörg (1992):** «Molecular Genetic Approaches to the Analysis and Diagnosis of Human Inherited Disease: An Overview», in: *Annals of Medcine* 24: S. 29-42, 1992.

**Donner/Simon (1990):** *Genomanalyse und Verfassung DÖV 90, 907ff.*

**Federal-Land-Commission «Genome Analysis» (1990):** «Abschlußbericht», in: *Bundesanzeiger* 1990, Jg. 42, Beilage zu Nr. 161a vom 29.8.1990, S. 1 ff.

**Hagelschuer, Paul (1987):** *Lebensversicherung, 2., überarbeitete und erweiterte Auflage,* Wiesbaden, 1987.

**Hagelschuer, Paul (1990):** «Medizinische Fragen der Privaten Lebensversicherung», in: Henke, J./Kömf, J./Diesel, A. J. (Hrsg): *DNA-Polymorphism in Forensic and Medicine,* 4th Annual Meeting Arbeitsgemeinschaft für Gen-Diagnostik e.V., S. 7-15.

**Hax (1949):** *Die Betriebsunterbrechungsversicherung, zit. nach Lochmaier,* VersArch 1955.

**Helten, Elmar/Karten, Walter (1983):** «Das Risiko und seine Kalkulation», in *VWStud,* 3. Aufl., 1981/83; Studienplan VBL V, S. 1-151.

**Hubmann, Heinrich (1967):** *Das Persönlichkeitsrecht,* 2. Aufl.; Köln, Graz, 1967.

**Karten, Walter (1991):** «Risiken der Gentechnologie für die Asseku-ranz», in: *Versicherungen in Europa - Heute und Morgen, Geburtstagsschrift für Georg Büchner,* Hrsg.: Hopp, Franz-Wilhelm/Mehl, Georg, Karlsruhe, 1991, S. 645-651.

**Kohnstamm, J. (1992):** *Wet keuringen, voorontwerp initiatief-wetsvoorstel,* Tweede Kamerfractie D66, 20 augustus 1992.

**Krahnen, Kai (1989):** «Chorea Huntington. Das Recht auf Wissen ver-sus Das Recht auf Nichtwissen», in: Schroeder-Kurth (Hrsg.): *Medizi-nische Genetik in der Bundesrepublik Deutschland, Reihe Gentechnologie Chancen und Risiken,* Nr. 18, S. 66-103, Frankfurt/Main, 1989.

**Maunz/Düring (1990):** *Grundgesetz, Stand: 28.* Lieferung München, 1990.

**McNamara, Jack (1992):** *Brief an den Life Insurance Council,* Association of British Insurers, London vom 26. März 1992.

**Nederlandse Vereniging van Levensverzekeraars NVL (1991):** *Brief der NVL an den Leiter der Vaste Commissie voor de Volksgezondheid uit de Tweede Kamer vom 29.* August 1991.

**Nipperdey/Wiese (1962):** In Bettermann/Nipperdey, *Die Grundrechte,* Bd. VI, 2. Hbd., 1962.

**Präve, Peter (1992):** «Das Recht des Versicherungsnehmers auf gen-informationelle Selbstbestimmung», in: *VersR,* 1992, S. 279-284.

**Prölss/Martin (1988):** *Versicherungsvertragsgesetz,* 24. Auflage, München, 1988.

**Rubin, Harvey W. (1987):** *Dictionary of Insurance Terms,* New York/London/Toronto/Sidney, 1987.

**Schlechtriem (1975):** «Inhalt und systematischer Standort des allge-meinen Persönlichkeitsrechts», in: *Deutsche Richterzeitung,* 1975, S. 65.

**Simon, Jürgen (1992):** «Genomanalyse bei Versicherungen», in: *Medi-zinische Gentik* 3/1992 S. 17-20.

**Verband der Lebensversicherungsunternehmen (1988):** *Stellung-nahme des Verbands der Lebensversicherungsunternehmen e.V. vom 15.4.1988 auf die Anfrage des Justizministeriums eines Bundeslandes.*

**VerBAV 2/1990:** «Einwilligungsklausel nach dem Bundesdatenschutzge-setz –BDSG–» in: *VerBAV* 2/1992, S. 75-78.

**Wiese, Günther (1989):** «Verbot wegen der Benachteiligung des Ges-chlechts bei der Begründung eines Arbeitsverhältnisses-BAG», in: *Der Betrieb,* S. 2279 ff, JuS 1990, S. 357 ff.

**Wiese, Günther (1991):** *Gibt es ein Recht auf Nichtwissen?* in: *Festschrift für Hubert Niderländer zum siebzigsten geburtstag am 10.* Februar 1991, Hrsg.: Jayme, E./Laufs, A./Misera, K.-H., Reinhart, G./Serick, R., Heidelberg 1991, S. 475-488.

**Wiese, Günther (1992):** *Die Entschlüsselung des menschlichen Genoms-Gegenwärtiger Rechtszustend in der Bundesrepublik Deutschland und Diskussion über gesetzliche Neuregelungen,* Landesbericht, vorgelegt für das Expertengespräch (ESLA) in Coimbra, Portugal, im Juni 1992; erscheint demnächst.

**Witkowski, R./Prokop, O./Ullrich, E. (1991):** *Wörterbuch für die genetische Familienberatung,* 4. Auflage, Berlin 1991, Bd. 1.

**Zöllner (1984):** «Die Nutzung DV-gestützter Personalinformationssysteme im Schnittpunkt von Datenschutzrecht und Betriebsverfassung», in: *Der Betrieb,* 1984, S. 241 ff.

# HUMAN GENOME AND INSURANCE LAW

## *Bronwer Loder*

Commission of the European Communities, Brussels. Belgiun.

Professor Capron drew attention to certain reasons for the interest in this particular topic, genetic testing and life insurance, and although those are compelling, I think it was Dr Murray who gave us the real reasons for this and that is the unsatisfactory nature of health care insurance and provision in the United States.

In Europe, at least, it is essential to disentangle these different forms of insurance. To separate the social benefits like pensions, health and disability insurance from the private contracts like life insurance. In Europe, at least, in theory, we generally accept the idea of equal access to things like education, training, work and general well being. Therefore, we also accept an obligation to attempt to remove any differences of a social or health related nature which present an obstacle to access to these things. It follows that we agree to make social provision, generally through taxes for pensions, for health insurance and things like unemployment benefits. And it also follows, quite obviously, that we avoid differential treatment on the grounds of hereditary attributes as we do on other grounds.

Life insurance and term insurance, are, however, a very different matter. These are private contracts between an insurance company and an individual, they are not a social benefit, or at least not generally seen as such. And again, there usually exist alternatives, other ways that one can actually make the provision that one makes through life insurance or through term insurance, although these may be less effective.

As Dr Berberich has pointed out, the characteristics of life insurance are that the premium reflects the risk, that there is a symmetrical distribution of information between the insurance company and the person wishing to be insured, that one is allocated to a group which reflects actuarial risks on the basis of age, life style, medical history and perhaps of medical examination. Most of us, I think, in Europe have come to expect that there will be variations in our premiums which reflect certain specific risks. For instance, there are very few nonsmokers now who would expect to pay the same premium as smokers for the same insurance policy, and in the UK at least, young single males now have to pay an enormously increased premium for life insurance unless they're willing to take an AIDS test. The increase has been something like 500% over the last 5 years.

But, nonetheless, alongside these differential premium policies, there generally exist policies which do not attempt subdivisions of this sort. However, you can usually only insure yourself for a lower sum, you pay somewhat higher premiums, and some risks may still be excluded. In the UK, it is generally usual to exclude diabetics. So, there is no doubt that insurance companies interested in obtaining any information that makes allocation to a certain risk group more accurate, and they are, therefore, interested in gaining access to the results of genetic tests.

We, therefore, have to look at the consequences of allowing genetic testing or not. There are certain problems about allowing genetic testing as far as those wishing to obtain insurance are concerned. The first is very serious problems of confidentiality, there is no doubt about it that information is already becoming more available throughout hospitals, say, between hospital departments. If you also have insurance in a rather unrestricted fashion in insurance companies, there are bound to be problems. There are also ethical problems about late onset genetic disease for where there is no cure or treatment possible. It is clearly unethical to require people to undergo a test for this sort of thing.

So, what are the consequences of banning genetic testing? The Danish Council of Ethics considered this recently in the light of a Danish bill which would actually ban genetic testing for life insurance in Denmark. They concluded that it was already possible, without recourse to DNA tests, to determine and I quote: «the likelihood of future disease, susceptibility to environmental influence, or possession of certain genes» in the instance of $\alpha_1$-antitrypsin, for instance, for which you can test by simply testing for the presence of the protein in serum. The Danish Council of Ethics concluded that prohibition of DNA tests was not sufficient to safeguard a quality of access to insurance if that was the intention. That the logical consequence would be to prohibit all examinations, and that was, of course, neither possible nor desirable. And this, of course, is in a country which probably contains the archetypal European welfare state.

So in summary, for pensions, health and disability insurance, there is no possible reason in Europe for discrimination on genetic grounds. The life insurance situation is quite different and as long as certain safeguards are applied, particularly to the confidentiality of information, there's no *a priori* reason to exclude DNA tests as long as we include other forms of medical examination. Thank you.

# GENOME KNOWLEDGE AND INSURANCE LAW

# Guilherme F. De Oliveira

Professor of Law, Law Faculty, University of Coimbra. Portugal.

## Life insurance

In Portugal, as in other European systems, life insurance contracts are based upon a declaration by the insured about their sanitary history. This declaration is taken as true by the insurer, who does not impose the performance of any medical exam in cases where the amount implied in the insurance contract is considered normal.

If the amount involved is higher, insurance companies require progressively more exams, e.g. if the amount is over 25 million escudos the list of clinical tests imposed will be considerably long.

However, these tests do not use DNA techniques and are not therefore addressed to the detection of genetic diseases. This does not prevent them from detecting diseases with a genetic component, such as diabetes. This case has been incidentally taken into account for a long time by insurers, who translate diabetes into a shortening of life expectancy, thus demanding from the insured a higher premium.

Given the present state of development of medical genetics, Portuguese laboratorial conditions and especially the economic situation of insurance companies in Portugal, relevant and rapid modifications are not to be expected in this matter. Private insurance used to be very defficient until a few years ago; nowadays there is a tremendous expansion in the activity of insurers accompanied by enormous competition. These conditions seem to be leading insurers to concentrate mainly on increasing the number and volume of contracts and not on too rigorous a screening of candidates, which might prove expensive and socially unpleasant.

In a future I cannot for the moment foresee, it is to be expected that insurers will include in their demands the detection of genetic diseases, at least of those whose testing might be relatively inexpensive and well known in Portuguese laboratories.

I do not know of any discussion of these matters in Portugal. But the choice of the legislative attitude will probably be made from the following posibilities:

1.  Insurers should not have the right to require genetic testing or to inquire about results of previously performed tests as a precondition for the conclusion or the amendment of a contract.

2.  Insiously conducted in competent medical institutions; it seems less acceptable to allow new tests to be conducted as a condition for the conclusion of a contract, unless there be very serious evidence that candidates suffer from a genetic disease that they know or should reasonably know of.

If the contract is within the normal values practised in that branch of activity it does not seem acceptable that insurers may demand submission to any test or the disclosure of previously conducted tests as a condition for the conclusion of the contract.

The economic activity of insurers is based upon an estimate of risk distribution and the probabilities of verification of the damages. If it were possible to foresee the damages exactly and to eliminate the candidates with a strong probability of becoming onerous to the company, insurers would actually eliminate risk – the very basis of their own activity. Neither can it be said that the victims of genetic diseases will ruin insurance companies since these companies already have the charge of paying insurances to people affected by genetic disturbances and do not therefore acquire a new charge simply by not being allowed to exclude these bad clients.

On the other hand, the simple rejection of candidates who carry genetic anomalies creates what has been ciously conducted in competent medical institutions; it seems less acceptable to allow new tests to be conducted as a condition for the conclusion of a contract, unless there be very serious evidence that candidates suffer from a genetic disease that they know or should reasonably know of.

If the contract is within the normal values practised in that branch of activity it does not seem acceptable that insurers may demand submission to any test or the disclosure of previously conducted tests as a condition for the conclusion of the contract.

The economic activity of insurers is based upon an estimate of risk distribution and the probabilities of verification of the damages. If it were possible to foresee the damages exactly and to eliminate the candidates with a strong probability of becoming onerous to the company, insurers would actually eliminate risk – the very basis of their own activity. Neither can it be said that the victims of genetic diseases will ruin insurance companies since these companies already have the charge of paying insurances to people affected by genetic disturbances and do not therefore acquire a new charge simply by not being allowed to exclude these bad clients.

On the other hand, the simple rejection of candidates who carry genetic anomalies creates what has been called «the new class of the uninsurable», who are further sacrificed as the State withdraws from activity in the area of social security.

Besides, the systematic demand for genetic tests could cause the neglect of the imperative need for medical counselling. And it would be an extreme violence, because of a common insurance contract, to make a serious or even mortal disease known 10 or 20 years before the development of any symptoms!

These restrictions should not, however, eliminate the basic rule on which the insurance contract stands – good faith. In these terms, the moment insurers are called upon to pay the insured capital, even when the contract involves a common amount, they should have the right to question the insured and those who detain their medical files on whether, at the time of conclusion of the contract, the insured knew or should have known that they suffered from a specific disease that they omitted from their declaration and that was later revealed. It seems convenient that this inquiry be made by decision of a court of law and only when the court thinks the inquiry is justified. The protection of the privacy of individuals cannot justify bad faith; and insurers, in spite of their social function, should not be forced to tolerate any lie. Besides, the Commercial Code establishes that all omission of relevant and known facts by the insured determines that the insurance contract be void (Art. 429).

## Illness insurance

The preliminary considerations made in relation to private life insurance apply basically to private illness insurance. That is to say, insurers are in a period of expansion of clients and are not likely to disturb this growth with particular requirements such as genetic tests.

Besides, private illness insurances are expanding as group insurance and this precludes specific inquiries into the health of each member of the group. On the other hand, the lower prices and the greater number of insured will allow insurers a better distribution of the costs caused by the insured that will suffer from genetic diseases. Finally, insurers will be able, in many cases, to share with the State the charges of patient assistance.

For all those reasons this will not be the field where insurance companies will be the most aggressive in their attempt to know more personal data.

I think that insurers should not have the right to require genetic tests or to inquire about results of previously performed tests as a precondition for the conclusion or the amendment of an insurance contract.

However, I do not think that the principle of good faith in the conclusion of contracts should be abandoned; I would therefore admit that insurers should have the right to question the insured and those who detain their medical files on whether, at the time of conclusion of the contract, the insured knew or should have known that they suffered from a specific disease that they omitted from their declaration and that was later revealed. It seems convenient that this inquiry be made by decision of a court of law and only when the court thinks the inquiry is justified.

# ROUNDTABLE

# ROUNDTABLE

**Paul R. Billings.**   Several of the speakers in this afternoon's panel have defended the use of underwriting and genetic tests in life insurance contracts. In the United States, this is common, but there are other factors which relate to genetics which are also common to the life insurance industry. For instance, there are certain genetic conditions which are treatable and which thus become of no significant actuarial impact and which remain uninsurable in terms of life insurance. And this has to do with the principle that life insurers don't believe that people are compliant and don't wish to engage in the monitoring of preventive practices as part of their activities in forming insurance contracts. I wonder if this issue will, obviously, become more common as we discover more genetic conditions and also more treatments, effective treatments for those genetic conditions. If people who continue to be interested in the use of genetic tests in life insurance wish to address this issue.

**Alexander Capron.**   What I fail to see in the comments that Dr Billings has just made or in the suggestions that Mark Rothstein has put forward is the point that I thought Bronwer Loder underlined very nicely for us about the difficulty of distinguishing genetic from other conditions. If a person has tuberculosis, which is for the most part still a treatable condition, an insurance company will take the same attitude towards issuing a life insurance policy for the person with tuberculosis. And there are several solutions for that. One is to give a policy that provides for death from anything else other than the tuberculosis and another is to give such a policy provided that death does not occur within the next X number of years. And the premiums can be adjusted to reflect an adequate payment during those years so that the premium becomes standard to the risk of the pool in which the person is placed. But, why is it that we single out genetic diseases? The same with Rothstein's suggestion that somehow we have genetic diseases and we have cancer, heart diseases and so forth. It is only going to be a matter of time before Dr Vogelstein and his colleagues point out to us the genetic predispositions, either in an inherited form or through mutation that becomes discernible in a person's life, for all of our diseases, and that there are going to be combinations depending upon a mixture of genetic and environmental factors. Let me just complete the point now. We have run a system of life insurance which we could discard and I'm not sure I understand my Spanish colleagues because I'm not sure I understood all the translation, but it sounds as though they are proposing to do so because of the unique personality aspects of genetics. But we have run a system which up until now has, in effect, been using surrogates for genetic factors. We ask about personal medical history and we ask about family history with the intention in large measure of discovering whether a person is an elevated risk because of some inherited factor which makes it more likely that the person will die of cancer or heart disease or stroke at a premature age. Why is it that we prefer the use of these surrogate markers over tests, not necessarily DNA tests. Returning to what Bronwer Loder has said on this, we may be testing a lot of these things once we understand the DNA. We'll go back to testing metabolites and enzymes and other proteins and so forth. Because they'll be simpler tests to do. Why should we prefer the surrogates of family history and our own medical history over that? Right now, there's a discussion going on about homosexuals in the military and it looks as though the United States Congress is about to adopt a policy that is called «Don't tell and don't ask». We seem to be adopting a policy that says: «Don't test, just guess». I don't see why that is preferable to a policy which says if we have information which is both reliable on a medical basis and which is linked with enough probative information about the effect on life span, which may take 20 or 30 years to go, to develop, we may not have it right away. Why would we not regard that as fitting well within our model of life insurance?

**Paul R. Billings.** Your answer though, Mr Capron, doesn't address my question.

**Alexander Capron.** I think I did address your question by saying policies can be crafted. We now have disallowance of insurance for people who have «non» genetic conditions, and obviously tuberculosis susceptibility is going to be found to have some genetic element too. Let's call it a nongenetic infectious condition. People are complying in different ways and the insurance company is likewise going to be concerned that if it issues a policy to someone who has active tuberculosis, that person may not take adequate measures and may die of a disease which is preventable in your words.

**Paul R. Billings.** But we're not talking about people who have manifested illness, but people who have predisposition to illness and engage in activities to prevent the onset of that illness and thus eliminate their actuarial liability. That's a different situation.

**Alexander Capron.** Why is it different?

**Paul R. Billings.** I just wanted to finish by saying that for conditions like hemochromatosis, for instance, where it's already been published in life insurance literature that treated hemochromatosis has no actuarial impact, this remains a situation where individuals cannot get life insurance for hemochromatosis who have the genetic underpinning for hemochromatosis in the United States. So the life insurance industry treats genetic disorders differently. You can get insurance for treated hypertension, but you can't get life insurance for treated hemochromatosis.

**Thomas H. Murray (Moderator).** Let's see if we have another question in the audience.

**Question.** I'm very surprised by what the panel member just said, because it is one thing to carry out an investigation on the basis of a person's medical history, which is public and known, and quite another to intrude on that person's privacy, in their intimacy, by investigating their genes, something which is an invasion of the personal, private realm. But there is yet another question: an individual obliged by insurers to submit to such an investigation could find, for example, that he has 5 years to live. This could create a very tense situation or additional, psychological problems for many people. Quite another situation is that where a person knows he or she only has 5 years to live and does not disclose that fact.

**Thomas H. Murray (Moderator).** In the report of the task force on genetic information and insurance, there is a box on page 10 with the title: Basic health services vs. supplementary services. I will read only the last sentence in that box: «It cannot be emphasized too firmly that the programme of basic health services must respond adequately to the health care needs of the American people, or the ethically troubling features of our current system will reappear in the market for supplementary coverage».

**Question.** I just want to ask a question and make a very utopian proposition. I don't know if it would be possible to forbid any question in tests, clinical and so on, and that the rate of the price of the insurance would only be related to the age of the people so that there will be solidarity between the society. It is probably impossible, but I don't know.

**Thomas H. Murray (Moderator).**   Your proposition is less radical than our insurance report. We didn't even make age a factor.

**Question.**   Age is a factor, only.

**Thomas H. Murray (Moderator).**   In life insurance, you would have to. We dealt with life insurance. Any last question? I would respond to that by saying that's very attractive, but it only really makes any sense if you make it into a form of social insurance in which everyone participates, because as long as you have a standard rate, frankly, if the Spanish changes that I understood Professor Menéndez to be speaking about were to occur, I would advise every sick person in the world to come and buy his life insurance in Spain. Because the result would be that on that even rate, they have to be winners on average. They would have to die soon because soon all the insurance policies would be bankrupt. But if you have social insurance, so you don't have only people at high risk buying the policies and everybody else foregoing them, then you can make the rate standard and you're probably talking about a taxation system.

# LEGAL LIMITS ON GENETIC EXPERIMENTATION

# PRESENTATIONS

# INDUCED GENETIC ALTERATIONS AND CRIMINAL LAW

# Enrique Ruiz Vadillo *

President of the Criminal Chamber of the Supreme Court and of the European Institute. Spain.

## Introduction

It is not easy to explain and justify the raison d'être for this paper. If I say, as I probably should and hereby do, that I have no authority whatsoever to address these issues, then the blunt response from anyone hearing or reading me would have to be: Do not spend your time on it, go off in other directions where you perhaps have knowledge and experience.

The truth is that the problem, or better said, the problems arising from genetic engineering and assisted reproduction and other cutting-edge questions such as sex selection, for example, are so broad and complex that, for reasons which I will discuss later on, only a very few are able to attain a relatively complete overview of the subject and, at the same time, a sound understanding of the practical applications and the inevitable limitations thereupon.

The jurist cannot know everything; that is absolutely impossible. With the collaboration and ideas of specialist from other fields, he must translate human and technical solutions into legal provi-

---

* Moderator.

sions, that is, to make law regarding certain social needs. This is the case in matters of urban planning, the environment, epizooties, enrichment from narcotics trafficking (laundering of money), societies, and of course, of genetic engineering and assisted reproduction techniques.

At the same time, if we are to effectively contribute to a harmonious and well balanced criminal justice system, judges engaged in the study and practice of criminal law have a special need for the contributions of experts from a varmety of fields –biologists, chemists, physicians, psychiatrists, psychologists, social workers, genetic engineers, etc.– and from other sectors within the legal world: students and practitioners of administrative, commercial, tax and fiscal law, etc. Hence, as has so often been pointed out by Professor Beristain, interdisciplinary study is indispensable for achieving the requisite levels of effectiveness and justice needed to maintain peace and social order, according to the parameters appropriate to each place and moment in time.

Today we are in the midst of a veritable revolution. Alberto Arnedillo and Alejandro Sacristan have said that robotics, virtual reality, telecommunications, electronics, computer animation, automata, digital audio, algorithms, interactive laser disks, holography, autonomous sculpture, digital photography and computer programmes are the brushes and chisels wielded by the artists of the end of the 20th century.

In the field of research we find ourselves on the threshold of what the French Nobel Laureate Jean Dausset termed «predictive medicine», in which prevention will be more important than curing. Investigation advances: United States scientists have taken a major step forward in our understanding of osteoporosis with the discovery in chromosomes 4, 8 and 20 of three genes involved in bone formation. The finding was the result of studying the genetic links between certain proteins fundamental to bone growth and a rare degenerative disease. The fractures associated with this disease represent a very serious health problem. Various experts hold that the true importance of osteoporosis lies in its close relationship with bone fractures, some 70% of which in persons over the age of 45 are caused by this disorder.

These examples are not offered as a demonstration of erudition, something which would be absurd given their availability to anyone who reads the press, but as an indication of how much reflection is needed by legal thinkers (labour agreements, insurance, criminal liability, etc.) if the system is to maintain its equilibrium.

At the legal level, and with the greatest of respect for all other relevant ideas, I think a certain amount of healthy relativism should prevail in this respect and in so many others. Dogmatization should be avoided as false and counterproductive. It is useless. Conversely, if we proceed with a tolerant and conciliatory spirit, profoundly respectful of those who dispute our assertions, and if our interlocutors receive our reflections with a kindred disposition, then we will have well-founded hopes of successfully serving the cause of the human person, which is the same as saying of society, the goal pursued by all of us. It is in this sense that we should cite the Recommendation on biomedical investigation in human beings (18th World Medical Assembly, Helsinki 1964, revised by the 29th Tokyo Assembly in 1975 and amended in 1983 at the 35th meeting in Venice). Principle five of the recommendation sets out: Concern for the interests of the individual shall always prevail over the interest of science and society. Here then is what strikes me as central to the entire subject: the interests of the human person, which should be present not only in the problems studied here but in all others as well, such as, for example, adoption.

Judicial activity marks the character. Although in a democracy the judicial activity is, as stated by a November 19th 1992 editorial in *El Correo Español-El Pueblo Vasco* newspaper, unstoppable and untouchable, as judges we well know that our decisions, even when final, are fully consummated only when they are accepted by the majority of the people. Judges, after all, are servants of the people, who are sovereign over the state and thereby all powers, as laid down in article 117 of the Spanish Constitution.

In this paper I aim to reflect out loud on issues of genetic information and the possible genetic manipulation or engineering it allows, as well as on legal aspects of assisted reproduction. Perhaps what I will express herein is of little or no value; many of my opinions will likely be mistaken. But as my purpose is not to strive for exactitude, and much less to pontificate, but to carry out a simple intellectual exercise, I am less concerned with the content of this study than with whether or not it serves as a vehicle for serene discussion of these transcendental and often passionately debated issues. I first approached this subject years ago in a Liège, Belgium meeting of the Council of Europe, called under the general name «Scientific research and the law», which I attended as the Spanish representative. I have since then tried to keep abreast of developments by reading the leading scientific contributions that have come into my hands and even general interest magazines which do the magnificent job of reaching the general public with simpler, more general versions of this spectacular field and arousing their concerned and responsible interest. Thus, I believe, as I said in another paper presented at the Menéndez Pelayo University in Santander, during the course of a programme directed by Dr Zarraluqui, and in a similar paper which I defended in the Honourable Association of Lawyers of Madrid, overseen by the same director, that it might be useful for me to convey to you these developments and concerns.

My aim is therefore to recount the problems and their possible solutions in order to then take up what the position of statutory law should be in this respect. I will concentrate on criminal law (as mentioned in another one of my studies, I have devoted relatively little time to civil and administrative law implications, with respect to which some very valuable studies are already available) with a specific view to what should be envisaged under democratic Spain's new Criminal Code.

In this sense I believe that future lawmakers would be very well served if they were to take into account the no doubt highly useful opinions brought forth in these colloquiums, if they occur and are documented, before deciding on the inclusion in the new criminal code of genetic manipulation and assisted reproduction offences, and others of a comparable nature. During my time of service as a lawyer in the Ministry of Justice, one of my frequent responsibilities was, following the instructions given me, to draw up preliminary drafts (then and now called «monsters») that served as a starting point for discussion by lawmakers. Sometimes little or nothing survived of the initial outline, sometimes a substantial part was left intact, but in all cases it helped others pursue their difficult work, which is what mattered. Hence, I have written this paper with a similar purpose, as a possible aid to reflection alongside other drafts and outlines.

Before continuing I would like to express my very cordial gratitude to the Fundación Banco Bilbao Vizcaya, of such national and international prestige despite its relative youth, for the invitation to participate in this workshop, and to its President Mr José Angel Sánchez Asiaín, to whom Spanish culture is so indebted, an illustrious and dear friend and associate in the Department of Economics and Business Sciences in Bilbao, where we both gave undergraduate and doctorate courses in a time that is unforgettable for all of us who actively participated in so fecund and appealing an idea as was the launching of the first official faculty in the Basque Country, seed of what would later become its University. I must also express my gratitude to my admire friend and colleague Mr Rafael Mendizabal Allende, Supreme Court Chamber President and currently a Magistrate on the Constitutional Court, from whom I directly received the assignment to prepare this paper. I also worked with him when he was Undersecretary of Justice during the gestation of a democratic and social Spain, under the rule of law, while the outstanding jurist Mr Landelino Lavilla served as minister. The rule of law which we today enjoy was one of the greatest satisfactions of my long judicial and university career, for we were all convinced that our work was contributing –some with greater authority and weight and others, such as myself, much more modestly– to the birth of a new social and legal order grounded in justice, equality, liberty and solidarity.

A few days ago an association was formed in Barcelona under the high significant name «Law and Health». I am a member of its scientific committee. I hope that from the association we will be able to contribute to health-care improvements in the living conditions our fellow citizens and of all persons in general, as we now seek to do from this platform. The law as an instrument of justice and peace has much to say in this terrain. Material and intellectual techniques, as Professor Delmas-Marty has observed, no doubt influence the evolution of criminal policy. Above all, in tandem with the scientific process, they can provoke the emergence of new values; for example, current developments relating to genetic manipulation have set off the beginning of movement toward criminalization tending toward explicit recognition of the right to genetic heritage completely free of any manipulation whatsoever.

The values at stake are of decisive important and the law must set down the necessary provisions, including criminal statutes, for their protection and their corresponding ranking, where appropriate. Research and its practical applications, as stated above, must always and unconditionally serve the human person. In the 1988 Valencia Conference it was stated: The Conference participants believe that the knowledge arising from the mapping and sequencing of the human genome can broadly benefit society and produce wellbeing for humanity. Toward such end the participating scientists assumed the responsibility of assuring that genetic information only be used for the enhancement of human dignity, encouraging public debate over the ethical, social and legal implications of the use of genetic information.

When summing up the conclusions of the 3 days of the international workshop on the Human Genome Project, James Watson, director of the project in the United States, was called on to summarize the main consequences to be derived from genetic investigation. He singled out one for special consideration: its major influence in medicine. The Human Genome Project, he asserted, will allow us to study what we are both in sickness and in health. Genetic research will enable us to study ourselves, will allow man an idea of his own future, to know if he has life-threatening genes, as well as providing a better understanding of diseases like cancer, thus allowing us to one day forget terms such as breast cancer.

Jean Dausset stated: Thanks to science man has progressively acquired a certain mastery over nature. But if all conquests relieve man of many burdens, if proper precautions are not taken they can also enslave him. The understanding of the genetic code, that is, mastery of the DNA molecule (desoxyribonucleic acid), which transmits life on earth, is one of the most beautiful conquests in the history of mankind. Its immense benefits are still as difficult to gauge as are its dangers.

To reinforce those benefits and avoid the dangers is one of the great challenges of law. We still do not know how. The law will act, minimally in the case of criminal law, in several directions: impeding degradation of the human person, who since the very beginning of law that has always been the end, not the means, and research may never proceed contrary to this essential principle; and, perhaps also, in the more complete understanding of man's reality and in the proper handling of criminal activities. Crime, Professor García-Pablos has said, is not a tumour or an epidemic, but a painful interpersonal and community «problem»; a nearby, daily, almost domestic reality, a problem «of» the community that is born «in» the community and which must be solved «by» the community. A «social problem», in short, with everything this characterization implies for its diagnosis and treatment.

## Basic assumptions

Without a doubt we must begin with an essential idea: respect for human dignity. Without this any jurisprudence worthy of the name would be inconceivable. The basic platform of jural society is the individual man and woman as transcendent beings and around whom the entire legal system must revolve, as is set down in our Constitution, with absolute and unconditional priority, as Professor Hernández Gil has shown. In keeping with this principle, as Professor Martínez Cal has said, are arguments favouring respect for genetic identity and privacy, on the one hand, and for human dignity, on the other. There evidently may and in fact do arise conflicts between different basic interests or values commanding legal protection, for example, in the donation of semen, the right of the donor to maintain his identity secret and the right of all persons to know their progenitors. Such conflicts are inevitable, and the law exists precisely to resolve them. In criminal law, certain cases will require the invocation of general criminal law constructs and concepts concerning *inter alia* culpability, legitimate defence, state of necessity, legitimate exercise of one's rights, occupation or office, the non-exigibility of a different conduct, etc.

According to Zarraluqui there are three essential factors that oblige the law to address the issue of the legal nature of genetic elements: (i) the vertiginously accelerating advance of science which has lately multiplied the possibility of sustaining the functions of the different organs and components of relevance to genetics beyond their normal time and spatial framework; (ii) the increased possibility of manipulating these elements, contorting their natural purpose and destinations; and (iii) the transcendent importance of the unique procreative and hereditary effects for life-transmitting elements and the acts which affect them.

Against this backdrop Zarraluqui examines the following problems:

1. Legal possibilities of manipulation, of dead and living human bodies.

2. Patient consent, in cases involving living and deceased patients.

3. Consent of the recipient.

4. Use, assignment, removal, conservation, exchange and transplant.

5. Purpose, in live subjects, implantation in the person for purposes of improving life expectancy or conditions, and in the deceased, in addition to the above, for purpose of scientific research.

6. Anonymity.

7. Gratuitousness.

8. Principles: altruism and human solidarity.

And the following may serve as summary of his conclusions:

1. Components of the human body may be the subject matter of legal provisions.

2. Cadavers also.

3. Certain specific considerations exist as to blood, eyes, tissues and organs.

He has studied other extraordinarily interesting topics as well and I defer to his work: possible human rights repercussions; genetic elements, ie, gonads, gametes, uterus, zygote, genome; psychological, emotional, biological and legal aspects of procreation; the issue of human dignity to which I have already referred; genetic heritage; prohibitions, sex selection (to which I will devote a separate section further ahead), etc, as well as the civil and criminal law implications of all these issues.

As we can see, the problems are many but none are insoluble. The advances registered over the last decade in certain aspects of the biology of human reproduction, according to Professor Juan José Lacadena, have confronted a perplexed and startled society with de facto situations and issues which must be studied in depth and without delay. It is obvious that this needed debate must be interdisciplinary, as has already been stated, given that the fundamental problem, the «status» of the human embryo, embraces biological (genetic), philosophical, ethical, religious and legal aspects. The aforesaid author states that, acting together, all the experts (biologists, doctors, philosophers, moralists, theologians and jurists) may perhaps arrive at the truth. Yet it is absolutely certain that truth can never be attained if each one acts alone within their limited and partial vision.

When undertaking studies such as the present paper, I also like to refer to the mass media, notaries of the workaday social reality and vehicles for hearing the people whose concerns we are obliged to take into consideration. The broader the intake of such news, the more effective the ultimate result.

Leaving the discussion of sex selection by the parents for further ahead, there are a great many issues concerning the unborn child which are of great concern here. The French government has studiesd the possibility of passing a law to control the boundaries of bioethics. The debate was opened by the President of the Republic, François Mitterand, who declared that in our age science advances faster than morals. Such diverse personalities as Jean Dausset, Nobel Laureate in medicine, Michael Blasse, director of the first American company specializing in genetic therapy, and Jean Bernard, Chairman of the National Commission on Ethics, concur in the need to establish new legislation for the «life sciences», which encompass an ever broadening spectrum of activities, from artificial insemination to genetic engineering.

Just as in adoptions, what matters is the wellbeing of the child to be adopted, who is often incapable of giving an opinion, much the same holds with respect to genetic engineering and assisted reproduction. Take the case of lesbian mothers, for example. It is argued that there exists no historical experience or moral antecedents with which to judge, no clinical experience. Nothing is known about the development of children conceived and raised in these unprecedented conditions. And all this must be weighed in relation with the child, although it is true that his or her development will be strongly marked by the society in which the child is raised. Something similar occurs with the unwed couples referred to by the *ABC* newspaper commentator, Jorge Trias Sagnier, in a recent and interesting article on «living together out of wedlock».

The Human Genome programme, explained the headline of a story in the February 6th 1991 issue of *El País,* must wait; accompanied by this subheading: «Current technology can only sequence bacteria, fish or flies», according to Wilhelm Ansorge. The Swiss newspaper *Journal de Genève* touched on ethics and politics in a May 5th 1988 article. It stated that artificial fertilization must be legislated, and classifies the process referred to above as amazing. Artificial insemination has been known for two centuries; *in vitro* fertilization, on the other hand, since 10 years ago. It is necessary to demonstrate that politics has an ethical bearing insofar as concerns abortion and artificial insemination.

Santiago Grisolía believes that a sound understanding of the human genome will produce profound changes in medicine, with prevention becoming predominant over curative treatment. Some diseases will be diagnosed even prior to birth, with the attendant possibility of recourse to therapeutic abortion if the mother so decides. It will also be possible to diagnose the onset of certain diseases years before they appear. These and many other possibilities opened by genetic investigation bring ethical problems to the forefront. The scientific community, Grisolía asserts, must develop a consensus as to a set of ethical guidelines to avoid reenacting what happened with research into atomic energy.

Thus, the problems appear in all their dire force, sometimes, and always with their enormous bluntness and realism. That is why I believe it to be of utmost importance that we all face up to the ensuing difficulties, sincerely and honestly, and, above all, with love for others. Love of life, of our life and that of others, of life replete with humanity and also dignity and humility at the same time, which is the same as saying with liberty and solidarity. Love of life, Carlos Gurmendez tells us, is to submit ourselves to successive rebirths, for if we mourn what has already been lived and can never be relived, we will sink into the deep abyss of days without a dawn, verging on agony.

Here, too, balance and proportion are indispensable to prevent the law's oft-denounced inertia from becoming total paralysis and ineffectuality. Happily, science continues its advance and does not stagnate, as unfortunately sometimes occurs with the legal framework. It is intrinsically wrong for outworn ideas to hinder the discovery of new forms of sustaining and strengthening life, just as it is right to prevent transgression of the inalienable rights of person (including, of course, those of the unborn) and the most elementary ethical norms under the pretext of pretended scientific investigation. Scientific advances outpace the law and thus the Statement of purpose of Act 35/1988 rightly speaks of the «asynchronism between science and the law».

Hence the need, according to Paula Bradish, German molecular biologist and geneticist, for achieving a system of weights and counterweights that permits the establishment of effective and severe checks on scientific investigation in biotechnology and genetic manipulation, if genuine aberrations are to be avoided. And, I might add, this must be done in such way as to not hinder or block the work of true, concerned and responsible scientists. Science is not a neutral process, pursued in isolated ivory towers. It takes place in a specific social context requiring, as stated above, a severe and flexible system of checks and balances, including adequate mechanisms whereby the same can be continuously revised.

But the constant reminder of Galileo Galilei should spur us to reflect. He was one of the towering figures of western civilization and culture and should at the same time serve as a stimulus to and defence of scientific investigation and free thought. Never again should works be sequestered, or subjected to arbitrary and unjust condemnations, as with the famous *Dialogo sopra i due massimi sistema del mondo telemaico e copernicano* written in the style of a Platonic dialogue. We must throw open the doors which shut out genuine investigation and prevent the latter from undermining the inviolable ethical principles of the human person, his essential nature, and inseparable dignity.

In this respect, Professor Martín Mateo recalls the eternal reluctance of the conventional wisdom alluded to by Gilbraith to assimilate innovations. Galileo and Server, among others, have left us dramatic testimony of their personal experiences. The professor recounts how years ago, while visiting the old port of the city of Panama, he found a blackened wall on which one could read a fragment of a letter sent by Philip II to the Governor of those lands prohibiting the execution of a design submitted by Dutch engineers at his service for the construction (400 years ago) of the canal which today exists. The message was laconic and pointed: «What God has united let no man separate».

## Legal considerations

It is far from easy to address the problem of the legal aspects —and here the criminal law aspects in particular— of genetic engineering in general, and of the many issues directly or indirectly involved therein. According to Professor Castán, by deductive reasoning official investigation shows that law is the consequence of the principle of order which presides all things. Such order is indispensable for people to live in society, the existence of which, as Professor Albaladejo points out, would be impossible otherwise. The essence of law, Professors Díez Picazo and Gullón tell us, is nothing more than an organizing regulation of the human community, prescribing conducts and imposing sanctions with the aim of making justice a reality. That is how I began a study on «Legal aspects of artificial insemination with donor semen» years ago, one of the papers presented at a congress held in the Cruces Hospital, Faculty of Medicine of the Basque Country, directed by Professors Simón Marina and José Angel Portuondo, and that is how I will begin this chapter in memory of the latter, a dear friend and colleague who lost his life too soon while flying back from Madrid precisely after having given one of his magnificent talks on these questions.

The problem is there and I will defer to the said paper in full, for I have no substantial modifications to make with respect thereto. Here I will treat the problem from a different perspective, both as concerns the importance of its content as well as the focus, for here I will refer to criminal law.

It is said that the background to Nobel Laureate James Watson's resignation as director of the Human Genome Project was the bitter battle dividing researchers and governments over the patenting of new life forms. Meanwhile, the August 23rd 1992 ABC newspaper reported that genetic engineering techniques were already registering spectacular practical results such as genetic screening for hereditary diseases, the solution of problems of genic identification and the experimental design of the «oncological mouse» which renders plausible the disturbing possibility of altering the genetic heritage of species. The social and legal impact of these procedures demands new statutory regulation, in Europe and ultimately throughout the entire world.

The expected benefits of this genetic revolution, says Jean Dausset, are remarkable. What it in fact involves is the mastery of life. Man has never been able to imagine such power. A single generation will bear witness to the emergence and development of this new power. Humanity will thus receive a marvellous and at the same time disturbing tool; marvellous because it opens the doors to effective prevention and a rational management of its health capital, disturbing because it may reveal a less appealing destiny. The marvellous facet is undeniable all knowledge is liberation and, inversely, all ignorance a constraint. For millennia mankind has been toyed with by a destiny beyond its control, notwithstanding the unending efforts and attempts to know the future by means of fortune-tellers, the trajectories of birds or tarot cards. Today, at long last, a window has been opened, which, though still narrow, stands on solid scientific ground and must be used. Is it not better to prevent than to cure? And to prevent, it is said, it is necessary to foretell.

Thanks to the spectacular progress of molecular biology, it will be possible in a few years, say 10 (continuing with the thinking of the aforementioned scientist), to know most of the genes of our pathological states and calculate the probable risk of an individual becoming afflicted with diabetes, a cardiovascular disorder, a given type of cancer, or even, perhaps, neuropsychological disturbances. This knowledge will permit a new, predictive medicine, a truly personalized medicine, more satisfactory, perhaps more economic, and certainly more effective.

The disquieting aspect is both psychological and social. From the psychological standpoint, there are people who prefer the ostrich policy and choose not to see. Others, however, will heed these breakthroughs as a notice and see in them a means of struggling for a better destiny. The power of genetics will be such as to make plausible the detection not only of pathological predispositions, but of a person's future characteristics and behaviour as well. This is still far off, Dausset points out, but the time may come when the temptation to practice human selection may loom large, with all its attendant risks. What criteria will operate in such selection? Who will make the selection? What controls will be in place?

To believe that in such circumstances the law can remain indifferent to these problems is tantamount to denial of the possibility of constructing a system grounded in justice (which is at the same time proportionality and equilibrium) and capable of leading to genuine social harmony on a human basis. To investigate is one thing and to destroy the very essence of human beings is quite another. To eliminate the handicaps of a future being, or relieve them, is absolutely legitimate; not so to construct beings destroying their unique and untransferable personality.

This leads to other topics which cannot be properly taken up here. On the one hand, there is the problem of how those holding such powers should act, what limits should they have to respect and what are the basic characteristic features of abuses in this area, a question which has been generally examined by the Institute of Criminology in the Basque Country, under the direction of Professor Beristain. And on the other, we have the immensely profound issue of the normal evolution of the human species (recalling Darwin and his theories, and the question of evolution with or without selection).

The legal system –and here as in so many fields international cooperation is imperative– will have to carry out an extremely delicate operation: without hindering research, to place limits on its practical applications relative to the due respect for the individual genotype and facilitate the detection of pathologies and, if possible, their elimination or alleviation.

As Juan Ramón Vidal has said, it has been known for millennia that genetic inheritance is transmitted from parents to offspring, from like beings to like beings, in the different species of living creatures that exist on Earth. Albeit empirically our ancestors engaged in gene manipulation when they grafted plants and crossbred animals. Today we speak of the biological «chip» which contains the menu and programme to be followed by every living thing on the planet. In fact, until well into the 20th century the way in which life is transmitted continued to be a puzzle. The first to unravel the mystery was Gregor Johann Mendel (1822-1884) with his famous plant experiments.

Here we may turn our attention to ethics and the law as a bridge to the following sections. As Professor Santiago Grisolía has said, without entering into definitions of ethics, the latter represents and answers to the accepted customs of a society. Now the almost logarithmic development of science and of its impact on society modifies and will keep on modifying ethical conceptas. He goes on to say: fear and mistrust no doubt exist as to leaving human genetics in the hands of a scientific elite. Grisolía observes that «someone has said –I believe it was the astronomer Hoyle and I'm afraid he was only half joking– that in a few years we will see the nuclear physicists free and the genetic investigators behind bars».

Professor Viser of Rome delivered a talk at the X Colloquy on European Law held in Liège in September 1980, to which I have already referred, on mechanisms and instruments for the control of scientific and medical investigation. No scientific progress, he said, is possible without lengthy painstaking research work. In this sense the recent progress of medicine and genetics have been spectacular (discovery of genetic disorders, molecular medicine, *in vitro* fertilization, etc., new surgical and therapeutic methods, transplantation, resuscitation, discovery of new medicines, etc.). All this, he stated, demands special precautions and multiple testing, and no medical procedure or drug may be put to use without the authorization of the public authorities, notwithstanding which grievous failures sometimes unfortunately occur, such as the case of thalidomide. When the regulations are set out by the authorities, sanctions (even penal sanctions) must be established for any eventual violations.

The problem, in my opinion, lies in the how and when of this legal intervention and in its effects, but I will discuss that in my detailed examination of the problem from the standpoint of criminal law, which is guided by the criteria and principles of minimum intervention, culpability, proportionality and, of course, legality, that is specificity and concreteness.

That is probably why Jack McConnell proposed the Human Genome Project be presented to society, along with the relevant ethical considerations, in order to avoid future rejection. Toynbee's laws of cultural penetration would thus not be forgotten. Claude Rosenfeld concurs that most scientists agree it would be highly desirable for the Genome Project to be a genuinely worldwide enterprise open to participation of scientists from all nations, including the developing countries.

Once again, balance is needed. Modern biomedical techniques, observes Professor Barbero Santos, allow a woman to be fertilized by means other than intercourse, and the genetic structure of a human being to be modified, thereby affecting essential components of his or her life and origin. That is why I believe the law's response to these problems cannot be monolithic or unitary, but should be plural and highly diversified.

## Establishment of some of the principal concepts

Professor Grisolía has stated that the human genetic map will be known within 5 years but that it will be 15 years before the human genome is completely sequenced. According to him the human genome initiative is a worldwide research effort aimed at locating all genes of the human organism. The Genome Project will help doctors to understand, and in the not too distant future, treat many of the four thousand genetic diseases which afflict humanity.

In this section I will offer some cursory ideas on the most elemental concepts up-to-date knowledge of which will allow us to conclude this study with an understanding of what stance criminal law can and should adopt with respect to these crucial issues.

*Gene.*   Hereditary factor, principal unit in the transmission of the hereditary traits considered to be an ultramicroscopic particle occupying a fixed location on a chromosome. In Spanish it can be called «gen» or «gene» and it constitutes the elemental genetic unit of biology. The name is due to United States geneticist T. H. Morgan, who deduced that each chromosome is made up of certain linearly arranged material entities which determine hereditary characteristics. Their individuality makes them capable of being interchanged between two homologous chromosomes, changing their position in one of them, and undergoing mutation, which processes affect hereditary traits. Chemically, the gene is a portion of the deoxyribonucleic acid helix made up of thousands of nucleotide links whose function consists in directing the synthesis of a structural or enzymatic protein and properly ordering the necessary amino acids (see also deoxyribonucleic and ribonucleic acid, genetic code, chromosomes, inheritance and genetic information).

*Genetics.* That part of biology dealing with problems of inheritance and studying phenomena relating to hereditary transmission and variation in biological species. The scope and study of genetics may be said to comprise two distinct aspects:

1. Observed facts which man has been able to contemplate since remote times, such as those relating to inheritance types, distribution of traits in hybrids and the fixing of specific types by hereditary transmission.

2. Investigation into the essence of all these phenomena with the aid of experience and the use of microscopy and statistical methods.

Today it is recognized (this information is gathered from the Espasa Dictionary published in Spain by Salvat and the Medical Dictionary published by Teide) that human, animal and plant organisms grow and develop under the simultaneous influence of two forces: the genetic inheritance from ancestors and the influence of the external medium or environment. The former is enclosed in the chromosomes, in the so-called genes or hereditary units, which we may represent as groups of atoms fixed in the chromosome. The fundamental genes of each species are constant in number and location within the chromosome, but at certain times, and under special circumstances, new genes may appear. This phenomenon is called mutation.

Genes do not necessarily manifest themselves at birth, but are instead closely linked to stages of development and growth and are affected by environmental inputs, which in some cases may trigger their manifestation and in others reduce or block it. Birth, it is said, does not mark a definite boundary but a mere accident in the life of an individual; whereas some morphological deformations may appear at birth (polydactylism), others appear later, such as hip deformity, a cause of arthrosis which does not appear until old age. The forerunners of genetic investigation were Naudin and Mendel, with later noteworthy contributions by H. de Vries, Delage, Correns, T.H. Morgan, Zeninger and others.

*Genome.*   The whole of the genes which make up the characteristic hereditary patrimony of each being.

*Genotype.*   The whole of the hereditary factors contained in the chromosomes of an individual and which, in conjunction with the medium, determine the characteristics the individual will develop throughout his or her life.

I will expand on some of these concepts further ahead where appropriate.

## Ethics, genetic engineering and the law. Disease. Scientific investigation

This is the central preliminary question to this specific study –the implications of these extraordinary discoveries for the field of criminal law. Before going on, however, we must still examine other collateral problems.

Here, as seen before, we come across certain contradictions: scientific investigation and its limits; what arguments may be used to restrict the advance of science. Scientific investigation cannot be limited without reason, according to Barbero Santos; hence, it can be limited if there are weighty reasons for so doing. Biomedical techniques have biological, ethical, social and legal implications. They are applied throughout the world but we have to know what the role of criminal law is to be in this sphere.

One preliminary determinant emerges (in my opinion a decisive one): the therapeutic or non-therapeutic nature of the manipulation. Bubble children, haemophilia, diabetes, cancer, Aids and so on are situations in which such interventions should be accepted even when involving risks. Conversely, much more debatable is the question of whether such techniques are admissible for determining the sex of the future person (I will return to this further ahead), save where such determination falls into one of the above-indicated categories, say, haemophilia.

In the Valencia workshop Albert Jonsen, Professor of Medical Ethics at University of Washington discussed the coming changes. Now, he explained, one goes to a physician when some symptom of a disease is felt. In the future, in 10 or 15 years when all genetic information has been sequenced and mapped, and our understanding of specific genes and how they act advances step by step, people will become patients before they actually fall ill. The justification for the physician's role will have to be viewed from different standpoints because the *lex artis* will have undergone substantial change.

But there are values which must be defended. The revolutionaries of modern medicine and biotechnology have themselves achieved appreciable success in the fight against disease and in the enhancement of human wellbeing, according to the *Revue de Droit Penal,* but undesirable side effects have also arisen, posing dangers to the individual and humanity. These new problems, of an individual and social magnitude, demand reexamination of traditional ethical principle and, where appropriate, the adoption of new legal statutes.

We must therefore, in my opinion, carry out a very rigorous, complete interdisciplinary study of the correlation of ethics and morals with law from a modern social perspective, in order for lawmakers —who must ground themselves in society if they wish to be effective— to then adopt the needed legal measures, including where appropriate, in the most extreme cases, criminal law measures. Obviously legal statutes must never constitute an obstacle to the development of science and its practical applications which benefit human beings. If the law is, as it is, an instrument, the only possible one, at the service of a just and peaceful social harmony, it makes no sense to place obstacles, difficulties and restrictions on, instead of promoting, the personal and material resources which can exalt the human person. And scientific investigation must likewise be placed at the service of human beings, human dignity, human ennoblement and freedom. To do otherwise would be to convert scientific activity into something spurious and harmful. That is why it is absolutely correct for the law to place limits on investigation, even though such constraints will only be legitimate to the extent they obey the above-cited ideals and aims.

Ethics is the basis for human intercourse. Ethics is that part of philosophy which treats of morals and the obligations of human beings. It is the science by which are regulated the actions of human beings (rational and free beings) in accordance with a criterion (moral law) and with a view toward an end (good). Rational and free acts are the stuff of ethics but its formal objective, according to the Salvat Dictionary, is the order which should preside over those acts. Ethics does not study the ordering of human acts as they are, but as they should be, that is, according to an ideal moral order. Medical ethics is the set of professional rules governing the physician's conduct with his or her patients and colleagues, and ethicotheology is, in Kantian terminology, the theological system in which the existence of God is demonstrated by means of evidence taken from the moral sphere. To me, ethics is the rule which fixes human behaviour according to the rules of reasons and the rigorous respect for others. In his most recent Christmas message, His Majesty the King referred to the need for ethical renewal in politics and a new respect for moral values and the dictates of law.

As recalled earlier, Professor Martínez Val says that ever since Galileo's trial and conviction all authority and institutions labour under a kind of guilt complex. Curbing freedom of investigation is not considered, and indeed is not, an easy task. In this sense, the 1966 International Rights Agreement sets down in its article 15.3, that the signatory states undertake to respect the indispensable freedom of scientific investigation and creative activity, as a matter of participating in and promoting the scientific process (article 15.1; see article 27 of the UN's Human Rights Declaration). But, as I have just said, there is no such thing as unlimited or absolute freedoms (article 20.4).

Professor Esteban Domingo (as cited by Martínez Val) stresses that somatic cell manipulation aimed at remedying defects or curing or preventing diseases must be regulated differently than manipulation of germinal cells, which raises problems concerning not only the person involved but his or her offspring as well. Regulation of the former should be analogous to that for organ transplants. Eurodeputy Willy Rothley has said that we must have the courage to prohibit, with no exceptions whatsoever, the production of human embryos for scientific purposes. We cannot fabricate human beings solely to investigate them. The dispute as to when human life begins has dissipated and it is now known, he argues, to commence before the embryo, which as a potential human needs legal and political protection.

Hence the need for legislation, preferably with international backing.

As Martínez Val says, the genetic code is universal, that is, unique for all living organisms, and genome is the particular, distinct and individualized genetic code of each person. Genetic engineering has wide experience, proven experience (Cohen 1976 and Murray 1976), in «cutting DNA segments, interrupting their individual chain and leaving a segment attached, where it is connected to another DNA fragment cut from the same enzyme». This is how the so-called cloned genes are produced, which could serve to obtain millions of exact copies of a single being.

Along these lines, Professor María Dolores Vila Coro states that it is of utmost interest to determine at exactly what moment the product of fertilization, or what in our legal system is termed *nasciturus* (unborn child), is recognized to be a human being. If a pre-embryonic stage is admitted, discussion could centre on whether it may be object of scientific experimentation during that period. But we must bear in mind that gene manipulations are irreversible and have a permanent effect on the person. Furthermore, the consequences of placing a human being in a psychological and social environment different from the one which would have resulted by virtue of his genetic parents will influence the formation and development of his personality. Man is more than just nature, he is history also, and the humanization process depends on the philogenetic causality relation that is broken when his generational roots are torn away and he is inserted in a different parental atmosphere.

In this regard it is of utmost relevance to summarize the basic principles set out in the Valencia Declaration on Ethics and the Human Genome Project:

1. A civilized society entails respect for human diversity, including genetic variations. We acknowledge our responsibility to help ensure that genetic information is used to enhance the dignity of the individual, that all persons in need have access to genetic services, and that genetic programmes abide by the ethical principles of respect for persons, beneficence and justice.

2. We believe that knowledge obtained from mapping and sequencing the genome will have great benefit for human health and wellbeing. We endorse international collaboration.

3. We urge coordination among nations and across disciplines.

4. In addition to discussion in professional circles, public debates on the ethical, social and legal implications of clinical, commercial and other uses of genetic information are needed.

5. We support efforts to educate the public (press and schools) about genome mapping and sequencing, genetic diseases, and genetic services.

6. In light of the great increase in prognostic and therapeutic information that will arise from the genome project, we urge greater support for training of genetic counsellors and genetic education of other health professionals.

7.  General principle: genetic information about an individual should be ascertained or disclosed only with authorization from the individual or his legal representative. Any exceptions to this principle require strong ethical and legal justification.

8.  Somatic cell gene therapy may be used for the treatment of specific human diseases. Germ-line gene therapy faces technical obstacles and does not command ethical consensus.

It has been documented that the French government, according to Jean François Girard, has undertaken a national programme on the human genome that covers aspects such as coordination of activities, DNA sequencing and mapping, development of data processing systems, and training and education, and information transfer. He then goes on to say that the French already have a certain amount of experience in ethical debate at the official level. Questions concerning human dignity and rights and human genome ethics, however, are not sufficiently clear.

According to Hans Martin Sass, «the German federal government and the federal parliament support the Human Genome Project. The first draft of the EC Predictive Medicine Project [COM (88) 424 final SYN 146, July 20th 1988], however, caused a stormy debate in the federal parliament as all positions had problems with the semantics of the project and its possible eugenic consequences. In particular, the wording "Predictive Medicine seeks to protect individuals from the kinds of illnesses to which they are genetically most vulnerable and, where appropriate, to prevent the transmission of the genetic susceptibilities to the next generation" was interpreted as introducing a eugenic public health policy for entire Europe».

«The meaning of ethics», Tony Vickers tells us, «is not univocal and by shielding themselves behind it, many could deprive mankind of the most important benefits the Human Genome Project could contribute, a project which on the other hand poses no more risks than any other human activity».

And Paolo Vezzoni reports that «an agreement has been reached in Italy, by which genotherapy of somatic cells is permitted, but not that of germinal cells».

Demmer says that theological thought on current moral issues is beginning to admit the principle that actions to modify the genetic code are legitimate when the intention is entirely therapeutic. Years ago Pius XIII was amenable to the negative eugenic projects then under way designed to eliminate hereditary diseases. The current pope's thinking follows along much the same lines, i.e. explicit approval of genetic engineering for therapeutic purposes.

The Catholic Church, according to Angelo Serras, «recognizes the value of basic scientific research and gives great importance to progress derived from applied research in general and from the Human Genome Project in particular. However, the Church is against selective abortion» in connection with prenatal diagnosis, which will facilitate the detection of a greater number of genetic diseases. «Likewise, it considers germinal therapy and *in vitro* production of embryos to be morally unacceptable».

I agree, provided the appropriate reservations are noted, with J. David Smith, as to «how erroneous it is to attempt to reduce human life to biology, disregarding ethical and social considerations on which human rights are based: by this I mean that life and health doubtless constitute basic human values, for without life there can be no person and, sometimes, a life deprived of a minimum quality also negates the person. I defer to the insightful observations this author makes on genome information and on the word genome itself.

No doubt that is why John Fletcher poses the question: «...is it technology that dictates ethical norms or is it ethics itself that governs the application of science and technology?», and goes on to say, «logically, an international ethical code should be set up for geneticists that takes into account problems such as free choice in the matter of abortion, confidentiality, respect for privacy or the use of parental diagnosis, among others».

An exhaustive study of the problems is impossible. In a magnificent work, to which I will defer, on «The Human Genome Project and Labour Relations», Professor Tomás Sala poses a series of questions of utmost interest concerning the possible implications of these investigations for employment contracts.

We are no doubt in the presence of a momentous development in the history of humanity. A thorough understanding of the human genome is the most important project in modern biology, Professor Grisolía has asserted, as in addition to embracing medical aspects it also covers the evolution of species and the clarification of determinism. It will also have profound influence on industry, agriculture and other technologies. He believes that genomic knowledge will produce profound changes in medicine by enhancing prevention. Certain serious diseases will be capable of being diagnosed even prior to birth, with the ensuing possibility of recourse to therapeutic abortion if the mother so wishes. It will also be possible to diagnose the onset of certain diseases years before they appear.

The subject could hardly be more complex. Professor Rafael Oliva explains that the human genome is composed of three billion fundamental units of information, called bases or «nucleotides». The specific sequence of these bases is what forms the genes which determine all human characteristics.

Hence the question: Can/must we wait? Some say the Human Genome Project must wait. Current techniques can only sequence bacteria, fish or flies, according to Wilhelam Ansorge. There are more than 100,000 genes in the human genome, some 3,000 or 4,000 of which are known, and many sections appear to have no function. Scientists refer to these segments as scrap DNA, not daring to call them junk.

In my modest opinion I have to say any delay could be unfortunate. The legal system must strive for science to advance as much as possible on this dynamic, changing platform, provided the law's view be ever fixed on the human person, his integrity, spirit and body, his dignity, liberty and wellbeing.

The genetic differences observed between persons are the basis of human evolution, according to James Watson, and can determine the existence of everything from serious disease to the quintessential capacities and aptitudes of man. Yet it is very difficult to show what is due to genetic determinism and what is environmental heritage.

The Human Genome Project aims to identify the DNA of organisms with genomes of very different dimensions, says Walter Gilbert. At present, he continues, the sequencing of DNA enables us to attack human illnesses, even to tackle economic problems and study evolution.

Further ahead we will see other important consequences that DNA knowledge could produce in the field of law, specifically in the investigation of certain offences such as rapes, murders, etc. The human genome is made up of 23 chromosome pairs, with each chromosome containing from 50 to 250 megabases of DNA. The total human genome is $3 \times 10^8$ base pairs of DNA, all this according to Norton D. Zinder. But all this will be covered later on, although in this subject it is inevitable that problems and difficulties spill over into each other, at least for this author.

## A world full of spectacular innovations

We have now made a preliminary approach to the essential problem explored in this paper: scientific investigation, on the one hand, and limitations on its practice, on the other. To find the proper equilibrium –that is the difficulty. In this respect, part of the foreign press has recently spoken of meetings and meetings and yet more meetings seeking solutions to the problems of genetic engineering and related issues. In France, as has already been seen, there exists a Higher Council for Biotechnique presided by the President of the Republic. Numerous deontological problems are raised and there is continuous discussion of the ethical problems to which I have referred rather extensively. On the September 13th 1988 a Report was presented in the Council of Europe on scientific investigation involving human embryos and fetuses (Document 5,943), and in 1989 Recommendation 1100 was published on the use of human embryos and fetuses in scientific investigation. All the Council of Europe documents are of useful reference in this respect.

The Council of Europe held a scientific session in Liège on the central theme of this paper, which I had the honour of attending as the Spanish representative. Then, and now, the question in the air was: what is to be done?

In my judgement what is called for is a very profound, serene, rigorous and interdisciplinary study to ascertain which offences entail the greatest gravity, and decide which of these should, subject to international agreements, be included in criminal codes, where such conducts represent serious transgressions of public policy in view of their importance, gravity, value or interest harmed by the offence, inadequacy of other legal means for protection of such values, parallels with already existing offences, etc. The principle of minimum intervention must always be present in criminal law, along with the principles of culpability, proportionality, and, of course, as I have already mentioned, the «legality principle» [1].

This is compounded by a particularly serious problem: the confidentiality of genetic findings. Employers, personnel managers and insurance companies could perhaps reject those persons having genetic traits which make them susceptible to certain diseases, premature death or physical incapacity; for example, the serious bone disorders to which I referred earlier. There exists a potential conflict between genetic discoveries and the consequences such findings may produce in the individual. Something similar occurs with the exceptionally valuable diagnostic means currently available and yet nobody is greatly disturbed by this. It is a matter of assimilating new realities and orienting them on the basis of certain principles which should always govern life in society, precisely the reason why the law exists.

---

[1] No crime without a law, no punishment without a law.

It is therefore indispensable that the response to these truly spectacular innovations be a seamless legal framework that is flexible and rigorous at the same time (which, contrary to what may appear, is not a paradox), affecting genetic investigators, biologists, chemists, pharmacists, physicians, genetic engineers, etc., in terms of civil, administrative and employment liabilities, which I dealt with in a previous study, and, where appropriate, of criminal liability, always with maximum respect, as indicated above, for the legality principle. This principle is of unconditional application to all law, but even more so in the criminal law, where its full significance is attained, owing to the specificity and precision required in criminal law, that is, the exactness with which criminal offences and their corresponding sanctions must be laid down.

Study of the intellectual process which necessarily precedes the legislative process has been recently accelerated by the proliferation of ever more complex and difficult cases. I have already referred to many of these cases: the widow who wishes to be artificially inseminated with semen from her husband who had died with Aids; lesbian couples wishing to be mothers by means of artificial insemination, male homosexual couples who wish to become fathers by using the womb of an adoptive mother, sex selection, etc.

There has been an almost absolute legal vacuum in many areas. Today the situation has improved but we are still lacking in historical experience and in many cases our ignorance is almost total. I have already expressed my view: the law must favour everything that makes existence more gratifying, eliminating or alleviating diseases or their more harmful effects, looking after the health and wellbeing of the future child. But while discourse is easy, effective action is difficult.

A fairly recent editorial in the *El País* newspaper said: public powers should intervene as little as possible in cases where these techniques are use to solve problems between people and, on the other hand, be extremely severe with anything involving possible deviation toward other unspeakable objectives of social domination or economic profit.

In any event, it is most important that the law advance in step with technical advances, not faster, and that is not lag behind the social dynamic of the age. With an open and tolerant spirit it must set down the boundaries of permissible investigation and practical applications beyond which the person and humanity, which is nothing but all persons taken as a whole, run the risk of losing the transcendental meaning of human life, of untransferable individual personality and human dignity, of genetic identity and personal self-realization. This must be done within a broad framework of liberty in which clear distinction is made between that which affects these undeniable and universal principles and everything that entails legitimate, albeit painful and dangerous, struggle against physical and mental diseases, deficiencies of all kinds. To do so we should, insofar as possible, place ourselves in the place of the affected person, who, after all, whether already born or not, is in general best defended by his parents.

In this regard I will defer to the magnificent works of Professor María Dolores Vila Coro.

Lastly, I want to take note of other problems such as the search for the genuine meaning of the words normal/abnormal, so relative and arbitrary, labour aspects, and insurance, and the important role society must necessarily play in such momentous issues.

## Sex selection

A concrete manifestation of the general subject of this paper is sex selection and its legal implications. The expression itself, says Professor Martínez Calcerrada, one of the most brilliant essayists in this field, clearly refers strictly to selection and must therefore not be confused, as sometimes occurs, in conventional language with «sex change», or with the more or less real possibility of an adult of a determined sex being able to employ scientific know-how to attempt to, and even succeed, to change that sex.

Martínez Calcerrada gives a precise recounting of the different positions. The positive position aspires to justify fulfilment of the mother's desires, and, in general, to recognize that in circumstances comparable to those of the so-called «Mataró mother», such a desire is perfectly acceptable and genetic sex selection can be perfectly well carried out. The issue involves popular and familial notions regarding families where all the offspring are of the same sex, the legitimate aspiration of the parents to diversity and the protection of such aspirations. The decision, moreover, entails no harm to any specific person.

The negative opinion, on the other hand, attempts to demonstrate that there are countervailing social, ethical and scientific reasons which override the legal arguments for allowing such practices. Arguments of a medico-scientific nature are invoked: personality in crisis. Professor Dexeus says he believes problems of anxiety and obsession in these cases are due to personality crises of varying degrees, and that the proper answer is psychiatric treatment. Health care budgets, he adds, should cover priority needs such as early cancer detection in women or care for the chronically ill. Physicians, he believes, should wage constant battle against futile medicine, against all unnecessary health care practices. He views sex selection *a la carte* as such a practice. In addition, there is the risk of failure: apparently genetic experiments have a 70 to 80% success rate.

In my opinion, it is important not to generalize. First of all, there are types of cosmetic surgery which seemingly do not qualify as being vitally necessary, yet they may be subjectively so regarded by the person requesting them. What, after all, is necessary or indispensable? Another and quite different question is whether or not such operations should be government funded, weighing the public health care system and its economic possibilities against a scaling of priority needs according to the currently prevailing social parameters.

I also feel it is important to distinguish between decisions by couples, man and woman, woman and man, considered in isolation, and those other decisions which may be adopted, albeit indirectly, by persons in power. Here is where the truly unacceptable risks lay. The former are seeking, rightly or wrongly, to respond to their family gender balance, something which to the majority may be unimportant or relatively unimportant (much could be said on this point) and could even pass unnoticed, but which to others, a minority, can represent a serious obstacle to a happy family life.

I believe the crux of the problem is to know whether a genetically engineered sex change may bring about an alteration in the person of such nature as to rupture the harmony which should preside, as much as possible, over the existence of all persons. As is known in certain areas there exists the belief that the likelihood of the future child being a boy or a girl could be greatly influenced by the day, or even the position, in which sexual intercourse took place. In this sense, I think further reflection is needed before a decision can be taken. The issue remains open. Nor should we overlook the relevance for haemophiliacs, for example, which is not disputed. As we well know, public awareness of the controversy has been heightened after the woman's request to one of the Mataró judges in this respect.

Martín Pallín has said in this regard that until it is not shown that the decision has brought about harm to some group, there is no need to be dogmatic or to see immovable obstacles.

Martínez Calcerrada, on the other hand, asserts that selecting the sex of a child is illegal. Following the logic of its proponents, he argues, a black woman could demand to have white children. It is only acceptable when the only means of avoiding disease in the unborn child. According to this professor, modifying the genetic code implies the risk of creating handicapped children. There are many happy couples which have had only sons or only daughters.

Santiago Dexeus believes that according to this view, the solution appears clear, keeping in mind that while a great number of diseases of genetic origin are believed to exist, medical knowledge embraces no more than 200. In only a few of these is the transmission of the pathology sex related. Perhaps haemophilia is the one best known to the public.

Thus the determinant would be the therapeutic or non-therapeutic nature of the manipulation. For «bubble children», haemophilia, diabetes, cancer, Aids, such intervention would be acceptable in these cases, but not for sex selection purposes, except in the case of the onset of a serious disease. In this sense the United States has given gene therapy in human beings a green light.

Can familial equilibrium be decisive in sex selection? The Mataró mother said: «I am not mad or capricious. Having a girl is my greatest dream». In Santiago Dexeus' opinion, sex selection for mere caprice is reproachable as a use of medicine for interests possibly different from the patient's health.

In my opinion, the question, I repeat, should be left open until the specialists, including psychologists and sociologists, make further progress in the important subject of familial gender balance.

## Criminal law

Having thus outlined the general problem, it is time to set down the norms which should govern the central subject or subjects of this paper, and then, define the relevant criminal offences and their corresponding sanctions.

Investigations in human beings (born or unborn), organ transplants, procreative medicine and genetic manipulation, according to the aforementioned issue of *Revista de Droit Penal* published in connection with the Congress of the International Association of Criminal Law (IACL), constitute the main trouble areas needing new statutory regulation. In these aspects, more than those classically treated by the law, we find opposed and contradictory interests. On the one hand, the biomedical sphere essentially strives to protect the human being as subject of experience: to protect his freedom of decision, appealing to his unequivocal consent, to protect his life and physical integrity from unjustifiable risks, and, what is more, to protect his human dignity against humiliating tests or against exploitation of his particular vulnerabilities. Modern reproductive medicine can disregard the interests of the future child while at the same time endangering the institutional protection of marriage and the family. This requires national (and I think international) controls of health care services.

We all agree with the principle of minimum intervention but also with the principle that scientific freedom cannot be limitless (in this regard, see the already cited Professor Barbero Santos, among several others).

On the one hand, the field under study here is essentially concerned with biomedical demands that the human as the subject of experience be protected (returning to the IACL study), that his freedom of decision be protected, as we already saw, and that limits be set. Criminalization of medical activities and the threat of penal sanctions must be *ultima ratio*. The primary criterion to be used must be of a moral nature, even though the protected legal interest is particularly worthy of criminal law safeguards, as with human experimentation, organ transplants and the use of artificial organs, medically assisted procreation, investigations with living embryos, interventions in the hereditary substance itself, genome analysis and genetic therapy, etc.

Professor Barbero Santos refers to the problem of defining criminal offences, included among which are: fertilizing human ovules for purposes other than procreation, maintaining fertilized ova alive *in vitro* beyond the 14th day after fertilization mixing of semen of different donors in order to inseminate a woman, disclosing donor identity in cases other than the exceptional circumstances provided for by law, cloning identical human beings, and other procedures designed for racial selection, the fusion of pre-embryos or any other procedure aimed at producing chimeras, human genetic interchanges or recombination with other species in order to produce hybrids. Criminal law is largely silent as to these conducts, he says. In this sense, the Swiss newspaper *Journal de Genève,* in a May 5th 1988 article, stated that artificial fertilization must be legislated. Maria José Varela Portela recently spoke out against quality control for offspring, asserting that the law does not permit use of the new techniques for determining the child's future, and it is not advisable to attempt to alter the course of nature (I do not agree with this opinion; sometimes epidemics and cataclysms could be thought to be nature's way of recovering lost equilibriums). Luis Martínez Calcerrada has made some very important observations with respect to genetic identity, sex and human genome, to which I will defer.

Maria Dolores Vila Coro, after citing Constitutional Court judgements of April 11th and June 27th 1985, states that all living beings, in principle, enjoy the right to life. When this right clashes with other rights, she adds, and the latter are of higher ranking, than that right must be graduated. It is one thing for the right to life of an embryo to decline or weaken due to its lesser viability vis-à-vis the mother's, and quite another for the embryo's right to life to considered as some lesser right. Its life expectancy may be less, and its right may thus have to yield to other prevailing interests. In cases of legitimate self-defense he explains, the aggressor's right to life yields to the right to life of the victim, but not because the aggressor has less right to life per se than the victim.

Human life is the hub and focus of everything. Article 15 of our Constitution pronounces itself in this sense. Nothing makes sense without the right to human life. The expectation of human life is, in some way, human life and therefore an object of protection. Barbero Santos holds that life is the fundamental legal interest; the nucleus from which all the others derive. That is why all international statements concerning the rights of man grant it preeminent importance.

Let us now return to the conclusions of the last Congress of the IACL:

1. The right to inherit unmanipulated genetic traits should be protected by law.

2. Limits to interventions on hereditary patrimony should be the subject matter of legal regulation. Guarantees must be set down for the protection of the individual against the non-therapeutic implementation of such practices, safeguarding public health interests and environmental protection against the risks of contamination from genetic experimentation.

3. Prenatal genetic testing should be limited to those cases where there are grounds for suspecting a genetic disorder representing a serious threat to the embryo's development before or after birth.

4. With respect to genome analysis, specific legal provisions should be set down including, if necessary, criminal sanctions.

The use of genetic testing methods in legal medicine should also be subject to legal regulation. Gene transfer in human gametes for non-therapeutic purposes is prohibited without exceptions and should continue to be so.

Deontological and policy guidelines of a restrictive character should be put in place. All attempts to clone human beings must be illegalized, as should all experiments aimed at generating hybrids or chimeras (or monsters) by fusing human cells with animal cells. Violations of statutes regulating the use of embryos, gene manipulations intended to determine specific traits in the offspring, of a capricious, non-therapeutic nature (although the distinction between caprice and utility is not easy), unjustified alterations of the genotype, the right of all human beings to their own, untransferable personality, genetic identity, etc., can be subsumed under administrative law and, depending on the circumstances, criminal law.

One of the difficulties to be resolved is the issue of whether it would be best to define criminal offences by means of a «blanket» criminal law, that is, one in which the content of the offence is given by a non-criminal law, in this case the special Act 35 of 1988, or, what would no doubt be better although much more difficult, to continue along the path of a specific precise description of each of the conducts meriting penal sanction. The first solution would be regulation by reference to other statutes, albeit adding certain criminal ingredients: seriousness and intent. For example, only certain very serious administrative infractions shall be considered as criminal offences. The second option would imply providing something like the following (this wording is only very preliminary): Persons who for purposes other than the elimination or diminishment of serious disease or disability intentionally manipulate genes so as to alter the vital constitutional type of a person's genetic heritage, shall be liable to a sentence of *prisión menor* [imprisonment of from 6 months and a day to 6 years] and specific disqualification from the exercise of that type of activity. Persons violating the provisions of the laws relative to assisted reproduction and genetic manipulation, with a view to... (here there would following the corresponding description) shall be liable to a sentence of *prisión menor* in the lowest degree and specific disqualification also in the lowest degree.

Also requiring study would be whether manipulations that are substantially in compliance with the law but which generate some harm as a consequence of serious negligence or in violation of regulatory standards should or should not be subject to criminal sanction as negligent offences. In any event, only conducts involving reckless or serious negligence should be included.

After studying Act 42 of December 28th 1988 on the donation and use of human embryos and fetuses or their cells, tissues or organs, which complements the October 27th 1979 Act on organ extraction and transplant, professor Barbero Santos says: Injuries occasioned to the woman, even with her consent, in connection with amniocentesis or a karyonic biopsy performed in order to determine the sex of the unborn child and cause abortion if so desired, are already *lege data* conducts, for sex cannot be considered as a serious physical handicap that would exculpate abortion (section 417bis of the PC), nor can consent eliminate the illegality of the behaviour. Other conducts meriting penal sanction (for example, disclosing the donor's identity) could perhaps be included under the offences of disclosure of secrets.

What is not admissible in the criminal code, he goes on to say, would be procedures aimed at race selection or artificial insemination achieved by means of violence, intimidation or deceit, nor injuries caused to the embryo or fetus (see article 12.2 of the Act).

Other issues, await our attention, such as the right to investigate paternity (which I have not previously addressed). The Commission recommended that certain conducts be categorically prohibited and considered as criminal offences. Lawmakers, according to Barbero, have lacked a vision of the system's harmony.

Faced with these situations criminal law must adopt a position of utmost caution. On the one hand, it must acknowledge and accept the great value of these investigations with respect to imputability, and, on the other, it must contemplate the phenomenon of genetic manipulation and artificial fertilization within the broader context in which human relations develop, and to which I have already referred.

Just as there is no doubt a correlation between the determinants of personality and the criminal world, the issues examined in this paper inevitably also have implications for criminology, the object of which, according to Rodríguez Devesa/Serrano Gómez is the study of the real forms in which crimes are committed and of the fight against the same. On the other hand, in the opinion of Professor García-Pablos de Molina, criminology is more than just the accumulation of data. It transforms information into a means of understanding, by systematizing and interpreting the data and integrating them into a general theory or framework. That is why, according to Puig Peña/Ortiz Ricol, special mention should be made of the application of this science in the last stage of the concrete criminal phenomenon, that is, in the enforcement of the punishment; especially when considering that genetic research can help us attain a better, more effective understanding of the person. The limits of investigation, Barbero Santos has said, are precisely the human being, his development, his immediate future. This must not be forgotten by creators of men, of hybrids, of chimeras. Nor by society... Hence, according to the deontological code of the Organization of Colleges of Physicians of Spain, the physician is bound to respect human life, all human life, including in gestation.

A more profound understanding of the criminal could help bring rulings in criminal cases into line with the general purpose of justice, according to Alexander and Staub, for whom Michael Kohlaas's legal philosophy is to be seen, behind the mask of the ideal defender of absolute rights, as a form of the pleasure principle, restricted to a large extent by raw reality or by the individual's desperate observation of the remainder of his enormously limited personal liberty. In this sense, Wittels takes note of the important deterrent effect of punishment.

The prevailing genetics, says Seelig, rejects the possibility (always questionable) of the hereditary transmission of acquired traits and explains the individual novelty of each person's genotype by means of the countless gene combination possibilities. Specific psychic «properties» are not hereditary per se, but rather the product of the evolution of dispositions, which, in turn, are a combination of root dispositions inherited independently from one another. That is why people may have inherited dispositions not found in any of their ancestors. These dispositions develop from the moment of birth according to their intrinsic possibilities under constant input from the surrounding world, which Seeling calls the surrounding development world. Said input is in turn determined in many ways by the dispositions; the latter condition the person's sensitivity to the surrounding world, which can be greater or lesser, such that one's personality represents a filter which allows different stimuli from the outer world to pass to varying degrees —an event which has a profound impact on one person may go relatively unnoticed by another.

Everyone agrees as to the need for new legislation concerning life sciences, which embrace an ever vaster terrain, from artificial insemination to genetic engineering. We must not forget that nobody chooses their genes and that, therefore, nobody can be held accountable for the genes they carry. Genetic information, on the other hand, must be confidential because it affects the most intimate and personal realm of a person's existence. Nobody should be analysed without their consent and the information thus obtained must not be disclosed to anyone to the detriment of its owner, unless required to avoid serious harm to others, such as, for example, with the genetic characteristics of an anonymous semen donor.

The differentiation between the ego, id and the superego, with this or with some other denomination, continues to be essential. The carriers of unique genetic information (genes) are the chromosomes, as we have already seen, that is, formations which join together to form rods around the cell nucleus and of which humans have 24 pairs in each female cell and 23 pairs plus an odd one in each male cell. When germ cells mature, the chromosome pairs

separate, such that the woman's mature ovum has 24 chromosomes and the mature spermatozoon has 23 or 24 chromosomes.
Hence when the ovum and spermatozoon fuse there either arise
24 new pairs of chromosomes (female embryo) or 23 chromosome
pairs plus one odd chromosome (male embryo). Thus sons received 23 isolated chromosomes from the father and 24 from the
mother, while daughters receive 24 from each parent. If in this
situation a hereditary characteristic of the chromosome pairs formed from the chromosomes of each parent is of the same class,
then the characteristic is transmitted to the child. If genes of different classes are brought together there then arises a mixed property (intermediate) or only one of the dispositions stands out in
the child (dominant trait), such that the other disposition is transmitted as well but does not manifest itself (recessive trait). But
when two individuals with the same recessive trait are crossed, the
recessive trait again stands out in part of the descendants of the
following generation (recall Mendel's experiments). Criminal law
can only act upon the free part of human beings and this, owing to
a lack of adequate information, is unfortunately very often not
realized by those who must pass judgement.

Thus we arrive at positive criminal law. We must, as always, draw
the fundamental principles from our Constitution. The preamble
thereto lays down the need to assure the welfare of the citizenry,
article 10 the dignity of the person, man's inviolable and inherent
rights, the free development of his personality, respect for the
law and for the rights of others as foundations of political order
and social peace.

Article 15 provides: All have the right to life and to physical and
moral integrity, and in this sense I defer to the paper I presented
at the 1990 conference organized by the Ministry of Justice's
National Legal Service.

Article 20.1 recognizes and protects *inter alia* the following rights:

The right to literary, artistic, scientific and technical production
and creation.

4.   These freedoms are limited by respect for the rights recog-
     nized in this Title, by the legal provisions implementing it, and
     especially by the right to honour, to privacy, to personal
     reputation and to the protection of youth and childhood.

I will now review just some of the opinions offered in this connection.

Professor Barbero Santos concludes that the following represent
serious offences: to provide human ova for other than human

procreative purposes, maintaining fertilized ova alive *in vitro* beyond the 14th day after fertilization, mixing of semen of different donors in order to inseminate a woman, disclosing the identity of the donor in cases other than the exceptional circumstances provided for by law, cloning identical human beings, and other procedures designed for racial selection, the fusion of pre-embryos or any other procedure aimed at producing chimeras, human genetic interchanges or recombination with other species in order to produce hybrids.

Professor Zannoni argues that the conducts listed below should be considered as crimes and that the sanctions in respect thereof should include professional disqualification of the physician, biologist and other participating personnel:

1.  Experimentation with human embryos for eugenic or other purposes which alters or modifies the original genetic components thereof or which involve selection of genetic characteristics.

2.  Artificial insemination or heterologous extrauterine fertilization of a married woman without the written consent of her husband.

3.  The public offering, in any form, of fertile sperm for insemination, of ova for fertilization or embryos for implantation.

4.  In cases of artificial insemination and heterologous extrauterine fertilization, all practices that involve breach of the semen or ova donor's anonymity or of the anonymity of the recipient thereof.

With respect to a) Zannoni proposes that only insemination and heterologous fertilization performed without the husband's consent be defined as crimes, and not those done with such consent. Even though the latter is also questionable from an ethical standpoint, we do not dare to impose criminal sanctions thereon. He says that the operative principle should be article 19 of the national Constitution. He nevertheless recognizes that the conclusion is debatable.

The currently applicable Spanish Criminal Code makes no provisions with respect to these problems.

## Criminal Code Organic Bill

We thus come to the 1992 Bill and its important novelties. The statement of purpose, somewhat puzzling, contains the following extremely brief reference: «In the sphere of crimes against sexual freedom there appears a new category, unconsented artificial insemination, a situation which is fortunately still rare, but the potential seriousness of which obliges legislative provision». I can find no explanation for the lack of reference to genetic manipulation of human embryos and fetuses, the regulation of which strikes me as acceptable notwithstanding the numerous difficulties entailed in its criminal law definition.

The proposed 1992 code, in general, follows this basic pattern:

*Basic offence:* Manipulation of human genes with alteration of the vital constitutional type for purposes other than elimination or diminishment of disability of disease. It consists of two fundamental elements: the core verb is the manipulation of human genes and the teleological element is negative: any purpose other than a therapeutic one is sufficient to constitute an offence. As a result this condition which could have served as a circumstance excluding illegality is incorporated into the criminal offence and forms part of its content (see article 19.8 of the Bill).

*Complementary offence:* Any manipulation other than the above-described one, involving violation of legal provisions. That is, this is a «blanket» legal provision drawing on other laws. I believe it could not have been otherwise. We all know that the system of «blanket» criminal laws is, in principle, not desirable, but we all likewise know that on many occasions, and this is one of them, there is, in principle, no other option. The advance of scientific research could mark the contours of this criminal law provision. It would in any case be appropriate to distinguish between offences of a purely administrative nature, which should not make up part of the criminal law provisions, from those others which define the essential border between the permitted and the prohibited.

*Culpability:* Here the draft could have opted for one of two paths: maintain the crime only where wilful misconduct is involved (direct or indirect wilful misconduct, leaving those involving negligent fault to the purview of administrative law. But in light of the protected legal interests involved, practically the human person himself, I think it correct for the criminal law to encompass both types of culpability, considering that the proposed Code only includes serious offences, that is, reckless negligence.

*Determining the sex of the future child:* Application of genetic technology to sex selection (male or female) is only considered a criminal offence if done without the consent of the progenitors. As this is not specified any further, I will assume that the consent of only one of them is not sufficient to legitimate the genetic operation or intervention.

*Other conducts:* Included by lawmakers in this category is the donation, use or destruction of human embryos and fetuses or their cells, tissues or organs, other than in the cases authorized by law. Here the offences involve wilful misconduct, keeping in mind that the Bill generally requires offences involving negligent fault to be specifically defined. The conducts thus envisaged are widely varying in significance and seriousness but all entail violation of non-criminal laws, in the terms examined above. The criminal law judge is to apply the sanction in the form he deems just depending on the circumstances, within the parameters set down by the Code.

*Artificial insemination of a woman:* This offence requires the lack of consent by the woman and, in this sense, I understand that cases where consent has been obtained by fraud or deceit will be included, even though the Act does not so state and should have specifically provided in order to avoid extensive constructions, such as, for example, when a woman gives her consent but has not yet reached the age of 12. The Act says nothing with respect to the child born of unconsented artificial insemination (see section 153.3 of the Bill on abortion, where provision is made for cases of unconsented artificial insemination; and also section 181.3 with respect to rape of minors below the age of 12).

From the foregoing it is clear that this offence can only involve wilful misconduct. Bringing criminal action in respect of this offense will require an accusation by the aggrieved person. Charges may also be brought by the parent and the attorney general's office. Criminal prosecution and liability is not extinguished by the victim's pardon.

In my opinion a statement analogous to the one contained in section 195 is needed with respect to aggravated penalties for parents, custodians, guardians, etc., the possibility of imposing specific disqualification, declaration of filiation and indemnification.

The penalties it sets down are as follows:

| | |
|---|---|
| Artificial insemination with alteration of the vital constitutional type for other than therapeutic purposes. | Imprisonment for 2 to 6 years and disqualification for 1 to 4 years (section 167.1). |
| Any other manipulation in violation of applicable legal provisions. | Imprisonment for 6 months to 2 years and disqualification for 1 to 4 years (section 167.2). |

| | |
|---|---|
| Serious negligence causing damage to the vital type. | Fine for 6 to 15 months and disqualification for 7 months to 3 years or suspension for 1 to 3 years (section 167.3). |
| Donation, use or destruction of human embryos. | Imprisonment for 1 to 5 years and disqualification for 1 to 4 years (section 169). |
| Unconsented sex selection. | Imprisonment for 1 to 3 years and disqualification for 1 to 4 years (section 168). |
| Artificial insemination of a woman without her consent. | Imprisonment for 2 to 6 years and disqualification for 1 to 4 years (section 170). |

Jaime M. Peris has pointed out several shortcomings in the draft Bill. For purposes of illustration, special attention should be paid to the technical defects it displays. There are criminal categories in respect of which equal conducts and sanctions are provided irrespective of whether the genetic materials «donated», «used» or «destroyed» are embyros, human fetuses, cells, tissues or organs. As I have already indicated, I believe the sanctions should be individualized by the criminal law judge on the basis of the specific circumstances, and a regulatory description of the conducts should be avoided.

On the other hand, this same author states, the punishment for artificial insemination of a woman without her consent is disproportionate with respect to other crimes against sexual liberty, such as statutory rape of a minor compounded with deceit or misuse of authority resulting in impregnation of the victim. What is more, if that is what the proposed Code's drafters actually intend, he asks whether they wish to reward «natural» insemination. On the whole, the text gives the impression that its drafter were desperately trying to stem the tide of the latest genetic advances.

The General Council of the Judiciary's Report on genetic manipulations states the following: section 184.1 (the reference to the proposed Code text is inaccurate, no doubt due to a typographical error or because a different version was reviewed) adequately respects the principle of minimum intervention within the meaning of this term as set out in the general part of the Report. More questionable is section 164.2. If the provision dispenses with the alteration of the vital constitutional type (genotype) and outlaws manipulations carried out for scientific purposes, there is an ensuing risk of curbing research in this field. Likewise debatable is the criminal negligent fault set down in section 164.3. A specific reference to indirect wilful misconduct in the form of a formula similar to «reckless disregard of scientific and legal norms for safe research» would perhaps suffice. Express reference is also made to cases involving pregnancy.

It is consequently indispensable, in my judgement, for the Code –as has been done in the Bill– to establish a normative framework or system setting down the basic principles for this area and affecting researchers in general, biologists, chemists, pharmacists, physicians, genetic engineers, etc., independent of the possible civil and administrative, and even labour and criminal, liabilities.

Hence the question in connection with genetic engineering and assisted reproduction techniques is to determine the conducts which at the present historical moment should be subject to criminal sanction. This debate is currently under way.

Criminal law should no doubt be governed by the principles of decriminalization and depenalization, that is, of minimum intervention, culpability and proportionality. This does mean that is should not be used against grievous new forms of criminality insofar as they threaten the principles of respect for human identity, indemnity, and dignity, including that of the unborn. I believe the drafters of the 1992 proposed Code have succeeded in doing this, although the actual text is of course improvable.

## Some brief considerations on artificial insemination

We do not have time to study this equally momentous subject beyond the general considerations already noted, and I will defer to the relevant legislation and the recent extensive analysis and construction thereof which have appeared.

Truly notable progress has been registered in this area. We come across the offences laid down by Act 35 of November 22nd 1988 on assisted reproduction techniques. An apparently sound initial methodology to pursue would seem to be close examination, with the aid of the relevant specialists, of the degree of seriousness (illegality) of each one, followed by a selection in which criminal law would only apply to those acts of greatest importance from a social standpoint and deemed intolerable by our community.

Along these lines, in what has been regarded as a historic ruling, a North American judge denied a surrogate mother the right to keep the child she carried to term in her womb during 9 months. The judge assured he was acting in defence of the child's interests, ruling that the baby belonged to the genetic parents. Any other solution, he stated, would be a monstrosity given the impossibility of living a normal childhood with two natural mothers.

The Special Commission for the Study of human «in vitro» Fertilization and artificial insemination, has not given equal priority to issues of different ranking. But this, according to Barbero, has not diverted attention from questions of special interest, such as surrogate mothers, gestation in single women, etc., which are not yet widespread in Spain but which will surely have to be regulated in the not too distant future. Consideration has been given, on the other hand, to issues defined as «undesirable deviations» derived from modern procedures –cloning, children of couples of the same sex, pregnancies produced by gametes from different species, etc.– although these deviations «should be the object of rigorous meditation and of strict legislation» (On April 10th 1987 the Report was approved by the Spanish Congress in full session).

## Final considerations

By way of provisional conclusions, I will offer these final considerations:

1. The legal system must not be an obstacle to the development of science or to those of its practical applications which do not run counter to human nature.

2. In section 3.1 the Civil Code sets down that social reality is to be the integrating reference when construing legal provisions. The legislature must always bear this mandate in mind.

3. Civil, administrative, employment and, of course, criminal laws must in each case clearly and unequivocally set down the boundaries of legality.

4. All persons are entitled to their own genetic identity. There can only be one justification for making any alterations therein: the elimination or diminishment of an existing pathological condition.

5. Criminal law is the last legal redoubt for the defense of the social order, and as such only those genetic manipulation conducts representing grave affronts to the natural order should be the subject matter of criminal offences.

Professor Martínez Val formulated these conclusions:

1. The right to an unmanipulated genetic heritage is essential, unless such manipulations are done for therapeutic purposes (Council of Europe Recommendation no. 943 of 1982; 7b).

2. Everything that could be defined as undesirable manipulation or deviation should be prohibited, including *inter alia* the cloning of human beings, and the implantation of a human embryo in another species or the fusion of human gametes with those of other species, (Recommendation no. 1046 IV and Warnock Commission no. 15, as well as the Palacios Commission no. 89, to which I will emphatically defer given its exceptional interest).

3. Prohibition of ectogenesis, that is, laboratory production of human beings (*ibid* Warnock Commission).

4. The creation of human beings from persons of the same sex, of identical twins, sex selection by means of genetic manipulation, and investigation and experimentation with human embryos, whether viable or not (*ibid* Palacios Commission no. 87).

5. Maintaining embryos alive «in vitro» beyond fecundation, after deducting the time of any cryoconservation (Warnock Commission no. 12 and Palacios Commission no. 77).

Martínez Val goes on to say: Even when having the potential to develop, so long as human gametes and embryos do not reach the stage of individualization in the biological sense, and especially when this stage is not reached because the entire process remains in the laboratory, they should not proceed in their «human» development, and references to genetic identity and privacy, and especially to human dignity, may be dispensed with for legal purposes. These values are in no way brought into question in connection with a specific human being who will never come into being or be born.

I believe that in the face of such spectacular scientific advances, jurists must be vigilant in continuously adapting the legal system to the changing social realities.

# LEGAL LIMITS OF GENETIC EXPERIMENTATION

## Jean-Louis Baudouin *

Judge of the Justice Court of Appeal of Quebec. Canada.

The extraordinary development of genetics has brought both hope and anguish to society in general. Hope, because for the first
time in human history, man can now envisage control over his
own destiny. Hope, because mankind now has the potential ability
to achieve some form of predictability and control over genetic
disorders that are still, as of now, impossible either to diagnose
or to treat adequately by conventional medicine. Hope, because
gene therapy may, in the near future, bring relief to some common illness like heart diseases and cancer. Hope, because genetic
engineering will, without doubt, help to improve considerably the
preservation and growth of plants, animals and food upon which
the human race depends for its survival. Hope, finally, of drasti-
cally transforming the classical structure of curative medicine into
a predictive and accurate one, allowing it to counter the potential
hazards of a deadly combination of environmental and genetic
factors.

From the discovery of the DNA structure by Watson and Crick in
1953 to the present Hugo Project, the pace of progress and the
acceleration of scientific knowledge have simply been outstanding.
However, this pace has sometimes also been too rapid and too
overwhelming for society as a whole to adjust to and digest without

---

* Keynote Speaker.

problems. Concerns by sociologists, ethicists, lawyers, various representative of other disciplines and the public alike, have been raised and voiced publicly [1]. They all have to do, in reality, with two different sets of problems; those touching directly or indirectly the protection of individual liberties and freedoms such as the right to monitor and control the gathering and disclosure of individual genetic information; and also those of a larger social impact such as the protection of the human community against potential permanent alteration of the human genome through germ-cell transfer therapy or the radical transformation of the human gene pool and, of course, the specter of a planned and deliberate, eugenic socio-political policy for mankind.

It is now well-known that some of the most common fears amongst the public (what I would call the Frankenstein and the Andromeda strain syndromes) have been greatly overplayed by the media. Yet, we all have to recognize for a fact that through genetics a bold, new social covenant is in fact proposed to mankind and that we have just barely started to try and adjust to concerns, problems, crises and ideas that will, in the future to come, profoundly alter the social fabric and the perception of humanity for generations to come.

One particular area of concern is, of course, the delimitation of the frontiers of genetic scientific research and experimentation, that is the process (be it biological, medical or social) through which genetic knowledge is gained and procedures on scientific hypotheses are tested. In the field of genetics, the classical and well-known parameters set by law and ethics as conditions precedent to the legality of experimentation on human subjects take on, however, a particular and special aspect. Firstly, the classical but difficult distinction between experimentation and therapy is perhaps more blurred than in other areas of conventional or even innovative medicine and biology. Although the term *genetic therapy* is now widely used, it is safe to say that most, if not all, the present *therapies* are still, for the time being, largely experimental by nature. Secondly, in the field of genetic research, unlike many other fields, experiments are not solely carried out on the person itself (as, for instance, is the case for new drugs), but in numerous instances simply on human cells. This, of course, raises both from an ethical and legal point of view, an important and somewhat new set of concerns and issues over the possession, ownership and right to dispose of, and to use human cells outside the human body [2]. The fact that only cells are used may also help

---

[1] See for instance, in the US, the various court actions brought by Jeremy Rifline in the area of genetic engineering and experiments on the human germ cells.
[2] See, for instance, the well-known Moore vs. Regents of the University of California, 249 Cal. R. 494 (1988); 252 Cal. R. 816 (1988) concerning the ownership of human cells and the commercialization of the human gene.

project the image to the public that the general rules concerning experimentation should perhaps be less restrictive in the case of genetics because cells, unlike individuals, do not suffer from experimental failures or mishaps.

Up to the present time, there is no general consensus on how genetic research and experimentation should be regulated. As we all know, several countries have attempted to address the problem by adopting laws or regulations prohibiting certain types of procedures or research deemed to be, at this time, either too risky or against a general social consensus of ethical admissibility. This is the case, inter alia, of France, Germany, the US, Australia, Denmark, etc. [3].

It would be totally improper for me today to attempt an exhaustive review of these rules. We are all gathered here as specialists in various fields related to genetics, and I take it for granted that most of these rules are already known or, at the very least, that this information is readily available to all of us.

What I would like to do, to stimulate our collective reflection and provoke debate, is to discuss briefly two main questions relating to the legal limits of genetic experimentation. Firstly, I would like to share with you my views on the role of the law in setting limits to experimentation. Secondly, I would like to discuss the models and forms of legal regulations that could be advisable in the area of genetic research and experimentation.

## The role of the law

For a long time in the history of medicine, no regulatory process governed scientific research and experimentation on human subjects. After the Second World War, however, the shock of Nazi atrocities created a political impetus for some general form of universal control. The Nuremberg Code, the Helsinki Declaration and other various international rules were put forward. Since then, all of our countries have adopted a series of legislative or jurisprudential rules that reflect, under one form or another, the

---

[3] See for France: *Science de la vie: de l'éthique au droit*, Paris, Doc. française, 1988; *avis du Comité national d'éthique de 1990 sur les recherches sur l'embryon visant àpermettre la réalisation d'un diagnostic génétique avant transplantation;* for Germany: the Benda Report (1987) and the *Report on the Prospects and Risks of Gene Technology* (1988); for the US: see in general the voluminous H.F.W. and M.M.S. *Regulations;* for Australia: see *inter alia* the *Victoria Infertility (Medical Procedures) Act,* 1984. See also: Council of Europe -Recommendations 1046 (1986) and 1110 (1989) on the *Use of Human Embryos and Foetuses in Scientific Research* (1989).

two basic fundamental conditions to the legality of experimentation on a human being: free and informed consent and an acceptable ratio and balance of risks and benefits [4].

I do not believe in general, and more particularly in the area of
genetics, that in 1993 one can seriously argue that law has no
business whatsoever in attempting to regulate research and experimentation [5]. However, neither do I believe that the role of
the law, in this respect, is to attempt and achieve total and complete regulation of the process itself. The classical opposition
between no control and full control is, in my opinion, a clearly
obsolete and unrealistic debate.

On the one hand, the promotion of scientific progress and discovery at any cost is not a legitimate social goal in itself. Medicine,
biology and genetics, as any other human activities, must be assessed by and through the values that society holds at a particular
moment of its evolution as a whole, and social relevance cannot
simply be measured by the unique standard of scientific promotion
and achievement. Genetic progress and discoveries, even when extremely valuable from a strictly scientific point of view, are not
necessarily good, valid and acceptable in terms of our present ethical and social standards. The benefits that they bring to scientific
knowledge are not necessarily compatible with those of society as
a whole. The vivid debates over experimentation on the human egg,
on the embryo and on the fetus are clear examples. One cannot
simply divorce research and morality. Likewise, one cannot divorce
research from the potential future of negative applications of the
knowledge gained through it. In other words, science is not and
can never be purely neutral in terms of ethics and social concerns.
Scientific experimentation must then be compatible with the general
standards of society and conform to what society, at a particular
moment of its evolution, regards as acceptable. Society cannot be
asked to sign a blank check to experimental medicine.

Yet, it does not follow that society through law must necessarily
attempt to regulate and settle, in detail, all aspects of scientific
genetic experimentation. This of course, would go a long way
toward stifling, or at least seriously impeding, scientific creativity
as well as probably seriously alter the march of scientific progress
and infringe upon the freedom of research by directly mixing
politics in it. Legislators must then resist the frequent call of the
public for stringent and detailed regulation of genetic experimentation. The public demand, at least the one that is often heard,

---

[4] See in general inter alia: Experimentation biomédicale et droits de l'homme,
Fondation Manangopoulos, Paris, Presses Universitaires de France, 1988.
[5] See: S. Stich, Le débat sur les manipulations de l'ADN, in Éthique et biologie,
Cahiers S.T.S., Paris, 1986, pg. 157.

is mostly a demand for criminalization of certain types of research. It is a fact, that law is to a certain extent a reflection of public morality and that by its action, law attempts to translate for science the limits between what is socially acceptable and what is not. However, law cannot go much further than that. It cannot attempt to dictate to the biologist in his or her laboratory, how to experiment and define with precision the various steps of the research process itself. Law is a tyrant and over-legislation of the scientific world, in my opinion, can only lead to disaster. Moreover, law can only truly attain respectability and social consensus if it achieves a certain degree of enforceability. A piece of legislation that is not enforced, or worst one that is not enforceable, is a caricature of law and defeats its goals. Law has a much more modest role and can only hope to set general standards for the protection of individual liberties, rights and freedoms, as well as (and this is certainly more important in the area of genetics), for the protection of society as a whole, of the environment we live in, and of future generations.

If, on the one hand, total and uncontrolled freedom of genetic experimentation cannot be condoned and, on the other hand, the role of the law is to set only general limits, then how can the law hope to fill the role that both science and society expect?

## The models and forms of regulations

A preliminary remark must be made at the outset. Genetic experimentation has specific characteristics of its own as compared to other similar areas of scientific research. To mention only a few, firstly, it could lead to a change, on a permanent basis, of the structure of the human being through germinal cell experimentation. Secondly, although that possibility is indeed remote, it may create some new life forms which, if given the chance to spread outside the controlled setting of scientific laboratories, may have a long-lasting impact on the environment. Thirdly, the experimental analysis of the human genome raises important questions about confidentiality and the ethical character of genetic information disclosure to the subjects of the experimentation themselves, to their families or lineage or to third parties [6].

I would like to address briefly two different questions related to the limits that law can impose on genetic experimentation. The

---

[6] See *inter alia*: D. Wertz and J. Fletcher, *International Perspectives on Voluntary Versus Mandatory Screening and Third Party Access to Test Results,* in: B. Knoppers and C. Laberge, eds., *Genetic Screening from Newborns to DNA Printing.* Ed. Excerpta Medica, Amsterdam, 1990, pg. 243.

first, is whether a national or international format of regulation is the most appropriate. The second, concerns the types of control through the legal process that could best achieve a harmonious balance between the demands of the scientific community and the concerns of society.

There is little doubt in my mind that ultimately we will have to achieve some form of international regulation of genetic experimentation. This branch of science is not limited by any national, political or geographical boundaries. The international characteristics of the Hugo Project are a clear reflection of the worldwide effort in that area. In genetics, one cannot seriously accept that certain types of experimentation which would be prohibited in a given country could readily be performed in another, especially where the dangerous character of the experiment is well-known or where there exists a general consensus on the social and ethical relevance of the prohibition [7]. One must realize, however, that international treaties or declarations are usually set in terms of vague and very general principles which consequently, may not be of considerable help when it comes to determining whether a particular type of experimentation should be allowed or not. On the other hand, we are yet far from forming a universal society in terms of ethics, social concerns and views on genetic experimentation.

Each of our countries has its own idiosyncrasies, with different cultural and historical backgrounds. Whereby, what is perceived to be proper and ethical in country X, may not be at all in country Y. Thus, even if a comprehensive international regulation was achieved, one would still want to allow a good measure of flexibility to accommodate local and national traits. However, what is encouraging and remarkable in that respect is the self-imposed, general peer control regulations process of the scientific community itself, of which the Asilomar Conference of 1972 is a good example.

Some forms of minimal universal regulation could however, be attained in two ways: one, by a general agreement on the basic conditions precedent to certain forms of genetic experimentation; and two, by developing within large political entities such as Europe or North America, some agreement on the type of experimentation, that as of now and until further notice, should definitely be prohibited. It is my fear however, that a meaningful, enforceable and sophisticated international regulation of genetic research is still a long way to come. Until then, and for the time

---

[7] See: J. Dausset, Les droits de l'homme face aux progrès des connaissances: proposition d'une addition à la Déclaration Universelle des droits de l'homme, 2nd International Journal of Bioethics 23, 1991.

being, national regulatory processes reflecting the consensus and expertise of the medical community are probably still the best way to achieve these goals and may indeed, through comparative experiences, pave the way to a more global and international future strategy.

What then ought to be the way for national law to set the limits of genetic experimentation? Time does not permit me to go into much detail and I will thus only attempt to give you briefly, my personal point of view. I will not attempt here to explore the legal limits of scientific experimentation in general, for they are well known. Therefore, I will only address the specifics of genetic experimentation.

First of all, the criminal law regulatory process should be used sparingly and only to prohibit those research activities on which a broad general social consensus to total unacceptability has developed. Several countries have already done this, mostly in the areas of the cross-fertilization of animal and human gametes, cloning, the replacement of the whole nucleus of the human embryo cell, etc. [8]. There is, I think, in that very small and limited area a certain role for criminal law to reflect deep-rooted social concerns of humanly unacceptable procedures. Probably, there is also a place for criminal law in the areas of genetic experimentations that present a high risk for the environment. One must note, however, that criminal prohibitions are not eternal and, with the advancement of science and social changes, some form of experimentation that may appear totally unacceptable today may very well be felt to be perfectly legitimate in a given number of years. Before using the somewhat heavy tool of criminal law rules, which nevertheless does have a certain degree of permanence, one should really be convinced of the importance and relative permanence of the proposed prohibition.

The second level of control over genetic experimentation concerns the researchers themselves and the laboratories in which research is conducted. There simply (and I will not insist on this point because it is well-known) has to be some form of public control over the practice of genetic experimentation through the licensing of laboratories and the control over the qualifications of their personnel. Millions of dollars are involved in the results of genetic research and no one can accept the premise that projected pecuniary benefits from the genetic experimentation are to be the sole goals and concerns which can

---

[8] For instance, Germany prohibits cloning and the creation of hybrids; Great Britain makes it a criminal offense to replace the nucleus of a human embryo cell (Human Fertilization and Ambryology Act, 1990); Denmark prohibits cloning, etc.

legitimate research. This type of control and regulation, mostly through administrative and civil law, is not specific to genetics and is well-known of other scientific disciplines. However, it has to be tailored to the specific particularities of this branch of medicine. It also involves of course, the rules concerning the safety of the scientific laboratories[9].

The third level deals with the very process of experimentation itself. Here I believe, the best form of control is not a strictly legal one but rather a bioethical, self-regulated and peer control one: control of how the experiment is carried out; control of how the consent is obtained; and control over the risk-ratio benefit, are best left to an enlarged scientific community decision process through research ethics boards or committees. Here again, at least in North America, we have the experience of the ethical research boards which must approve research projects and protocols and measure them to certain ethical standards[10]. One would hope however, for a greater public involvement in the process itself and for a larger measure of continuous and permanent control, rather than simply a preliminary and *ex post facto* one.

To briefly conclude this short and summary presentation, I would like to make three general remarks. First, everyone should be concerned with the development of genetics. Conferences like the present one are very important. For beyond the interdisciplinary meeting of specialists, they do have an important public educational value and impact. Second, it is only through general public education and the demystification of genetics, that one can hope to achieve a clear and harmonious framework setting the legal limits to human genetic experimentation.

Third, the geneticists should not regard the legal process, or indeed the intervention of law, as a bar to scientific progress but rather accept it as a symbol of the very high ethical and social responsibility that they carry because of the fact that they are dealing with human life and human dignity, and certainly with the future of mankind[11]. Such responsibility necessarily carries with it a legitimate concern of the legal process.

---

[9] See for instance: «BNA Sprcial Report: US Biotechnology: a Legislative and Regulatory Roadmap», Washington, 1989; «Genetic Manipulation», Law Reform Commission of Victoria, Report no. 26, 1992; «An International Approach to Biotechnology Safety», UNO Vienna, 1990; «Medical Research Council of Canada», Laboratory Biosafety Guidelines, Ottawa, 1990.
[10] See for instance: «Guidelines for Research on Somatic Cell Gene Therapy in Humans», Canadain Medical Research Council, Ottawa, 1990.
[11] See: «Human Dignity and Genetic Heritage», by B. Knoopers, Law Reform Commission of Canada, Study Paper, Ottawa, 1991.

# LEGAL LIMITS ON GENETIC EXPERIMENTATION

## Carlos M. Romeo Casabona *

Professor of Criminal Law and Dean of the Faculty of Law,
Universidad de La Laguna. Tenerife. Spain.

## Introduction

It has often been repeated and is well known that advances in biomedicine, that is, medicine and biotechnology, are making huge contributions to the wellbeing of individuals and humanity as a whole. At the same time, however, as the inevitable other side of the coin, the undesired effects of these advances are awakening concern over the potential hazards they represent to the individual and society [1]. Issues relating to organ transplantation, assisted reproduction and genetic manipulation are seen as particularly problematic [2], as is human experimentation in the quest for attaining biomedical progress.

As regards human genetics, it should be remembered that Spain has hosted an ongoing debate on the Human Genome Project for some years. Two important international workshops on «International Cooperation for the Human Genome Project» were

---

\* Keynote address.

[1] Romeo Casabona, Carlos M.: *La persona entre la Biotecnología, la Bioética y el Derecho* [*The person between biotechnology, bioethics and the law*], «Folia Humanística», no. 276, 1984, pg. 4.

[2] Association Internationale de Droit Pénal, *Droit Pénal et techniques modernes (Resolutions)*, «Revue Internationale de Droit Pénal», v. 59, 1988, pg. 1327.

held in Valencia in 1988 and 1990, and serve as valuable precedents for the present meeting [3]. Scientific study of the human genome is providing vast information about human biological nature and individual biological hereditary traits, including the identification of risk factors (predispositions) for the health of persons whose genome has been analysed. Consequently, the first major contribution of the Human Genome Project (the purpose of which let us not forget consists, succinctly, in mapping and sequencing human DNA) will be to furnish enormous amounts of highly valuable information and thus broaden humankind's self-knowledge. At the same time, however, such research —going beyond the scope of the said Project— will not be confined to exploring the genome only, to being a spectator to our genetic interior, but will open the doors to further initiatives, to intervening in the genome by means of recombinant DNA, to its manipulation and modification, perhaps irreversibly, with the honourable aim of curing defective, or even perfecting healthy, genes. Hence the blurring of the dividing line between therapy, in the strict sense, and eugenics (especially positive eugenics), opening the doors to the «eugenics temptation». The need to consider humankind as the agent and beneficiary of these discoveries is again brought into question, at the risk of reducing human beings to the subject matter of experimentation and manipulations.

In this way, investigation into human genetics offers the most recent (but not only) example of the lively ethical, philosophical, sociological and legal debates awakened or rekindled by modern science as to the *limits of genetic manipulation in human beings,* debates which are far from settled. Within the legal field the discussion primarily turns on whether the new situations call for adaptation of existing legal provisions or for the promulgation of new statutory controls on these activities. It is therefore essential from the legal standpoint to resolve a preliminary question: how should the law intervene, to what effect and on which aspects? As can be seen, this is initially a methodological problem which once resolved will contribute to developing appropriate responses for each particular case. This approach, by analysing the legal principles and values involved will, first, permit us to determine what must be supported, guaranteed and protected; second, delimit what needs to be regulated and limited; lastly, indicate what must be prohibited or punished, how severely and by means of which public instruments.

Although only partially and for certain spheres of activity, Spanish law already provides regulations directly or indirectly applicable

---

[3] See *Human Genome Project: Ethics,* published by Fundación BBV, Madrid, 1991.

to genetic innovations and human genome study [4]. However, Spanish criminal law, with its characteristic function of invoking penalties to protect certain legal values from serious or intolerable aggression, does not yet address these activities. Whether or not the criminal code should have such provisions is the fundamental question I shall address in this paper. The Criminal Code Bill of 1992, however, does envisage legal limits on different forms of human genome intervention or experimentation, and for such purpose lays down various criminal categories. Whatever the merits of the proposed regulations from a technical legal and criminal justice standpoint, and irrespective of whether or not the proposed Code is eventually approved, these new provisions are clear signs that the legislator has felt the need to intervene.

From another perspective, the right to scientific research also appears as an interest obviously worthy of protection but at times contraposed to other individual or societal values. The right to engage in scientific research is regarded as a projection of the right to scientific creation and as such primarily responds to the interests of the scientist or researcher, but also to the collective interest in promoting scientific progress and its general benefits for society. There thus arises another aspect which must be likewise guaranteed and protected: the dissemination and circulation of scientific knowledge and information. Articles 20.1.*b)* and 20.1.*c)* of the Spanish Constitution recognize and protect the right to scientific production and creation and to academic freedom, but establishes as a limit thereupon the respect for the rights recognized in Title I, by the legal provisions implementing it, and especially by the right to honour, privacy, to personal reputation, and to the protection of youth and childhood (article 20.4). Consequently, although the legitimacy of scientific research is recognized, this freedom –like all freedoms– is not unlimited. This once again reminds us of the need to determine those limits and to locate them among the collective as well as individual interests. In keeping with this dual vision article 44.2 of the Constitution, under the chapter on the principles governing economic and social policy, imposes on government authorities responsibility for promoting science and scientific and technical research in the general interest. It has been pointed out that the unbreakable limit is found in the human being, his development and immediate setting [5]. Along those lines, Eser has stated that the

---

[4] These and other human genetics investigation and experimentation are dealt with in more depth in the report I prepared together with Professor Juan Felipe Higuera Guimerá for the Spanish Ministry of Health and Consumer Affairs, entitled *El Derecho ante los Avances y Conocimientos de Ingeniería Genética* [*The Law and Genetic Engineering Advances and Knowledge*], 1992.

[5] Barbero Santos, Marino, *Fecundación asistida e ingeniería genética. Consideraciones jurídico-penales* [*Assisted fertilization and genetic engineering. Criminal law considerations*], «Ingeniería genética y reproducción asistida», Madrid, 1989, pg. 329.

limits to freedom of research must in any case be found where a medical or scientific procedure gives rise to violations of the civil or criminal code, clashing with the protection of a constitutionally or statutorily guaranteed interest [6].

Thus, there seems to be a common feeling that scientific activity should be pursued in such way that ethical and moral considerations not be ignored. Sensitive to this belief, professor Jean Dausset has proposed that the Universal Declaration of Human Rights include the following article: «Scientific knowledge should only be used in the service of man's dignity, integrity and future, but nobody can impede its acquisition» [7]. Briefly put, the proposal suggests that while no limitation can be placed on scientific knowledge per se or on its acquisition, its applications and derivations can be limited as required by individual and collective interests. In any event, while we must certainly agree that scientific research cannot be curbed as long as it serves only to increase human knowledge, this objective also comes up against limits (which must be set in the understanding that they are not uniform or applicable to how that human knowledge is applied) when its achievement involves using other persons or, even, other human biological realities, which poses another question in this discussion.

## Criteria for the intervention of law

As Eser [8] has already pointed out, within this ambit we can imagine different systems of step-by-step regulatory control of widely variable intensity and scope. The different steps range from an initial level of deontological self-regulation by the research community, to administrative law provisions, to the introduction of civil code protective statutes —or the strengthening of such instruments, we might add— and even, where necessary, to criminal prohibitions. Indeed, other areas of human activity are subject to this multi-faceted regulation with scaled levels of intensity, and I do not think such a regimen is any less apropos for biotechnology and the biomedical sciences in general as a means of providing the greatest possible room for the pursuit of research freedom

---

[6] Eser, Albin, *La moderna medicina de reproducción e ingeniería genética. Aspectos legales y sociopoliticos desde el punto de vista alemán* [Modern reproduction medicine and genetic engineering. Legal aspects from the German viewpoint], «Ingeniería genética y reproducción asistida», op. cit., pgs. 274 and ff.

[7] Dausset, Jean, *Les Droits de l'Homme face aux progrès des connaissances*, «Journal International de Bioéthique», vol. 2, no. 1, 1991, pg. 25.

[8] Eser, Albin, *Genética humana desde la perspectiva del Derecho alemán* [Human genetics from the perspective of German law], translated into the Spanish by C. M. Romeo Casabona, «Anuario de Derecho Penal y Ciencias Penales», 1985, pgs. 363 and ff.

while at the same time effectively curbing any socially undesirable consequences.

## 1. Ethical or deontological self-regulation: an exclusively complementary function

Appeals to ethics normally lead us to consider the area of professional ethics. It is not uncommon to finds attempts to invoke the latter as the exclusive vehicle for resolving potential problems, thereby keeping their control within the profession and away from the larger community. On the other hand, the situation is much graver when professional ethics are codified and imposed on professionals from outside. I say this imposition is external to the extent that the codes arise from professional organizations or associations in which membership is a prerequisite for practising the profession in question. Such situations imply the not necessarily voluntary acceptance of such deontological rules. This is particularly true when the professional ethics are not legally codified, as is the case with the Spanish Code of Medical Deontology and Ethics approved by the Spanish General Council of Medical Associations in 1990, substituting the previous Code of 1979 [9]. Nevertheless, irrespective of the question of the legal nature of deontological norms or the ethical principles regulating the most conflictive aspects of a profession, it is arguably unacceptable that regulation of professional issues directly affecting the society at large be left to the decision of the professional, either individually (personal ethics) or through the professional group to which he or she belongs (deontological norms). Government must therefore not abdicate its legitimate oversight functions in this terrain, and adopt regulatory controls if necessary, as it does in connection with other activities affecting society.

The foregoing is not inconsistent with a belief, as a first step, in self-regulation by researchers and the scientific community to which they belong in the pursuit of their research work. In this sense, we must recognize the important role of bioethics in its attempt to construct appropriate guidelines for resolving ethical conflicts on the basis of three fundamental principles: autonomy, beneficence and justice. Nor is there any contradiction in advocating the coexistence of legal regulation with professional ethical principles that reinforce interests and values deemed worthy of protection, such principles being conceived as guidelines or prescriptions for professional conduct or even as the highest ideals which ennoble the profession, more than the deontological code. Over the years we have had international examples of such an

---

[9] See Iglesias, Tomás, *El discutible valor jurídico de las normas deontológicas* [The debatable legal value of deontological norms], «Jueces para la Democracia», no. 12, 199, pgs. 53 and ff.

outlook in the form of formal declarations on specific subjects [10]. And there are examples at the national level, such as the guidelines or recommendations of the scientific societies of physicians, as is frequent in the United States and the Federal Republic of Germany. These initiatives has thus far yielded good results, in that they have been usually accepted as obligatory ethical references. Along the same lines, biomedical ethics committees can fulfil an important and helpful function in the decision-making process with respect to specific conflicts, similar to the role of clinical testing committees in the investigation of pharmaceutical and similar products. While these committees have a long tradition in some countries (particularly in the Anglo-Saxon world, perhaps favoured by the common law system and the importance it attaches to judicial case-law and precedents, as opposed to the continental European system, primarily based on normative provisions), in Spain their creation is just now under consideration in some hospitals. Lastly, the so-called National Bioethics Committees [11] are most appropriate for spotting new problems deriving from the most important biomedical advances and their application in human beings. They also work to offer guidelines and advice, which, though not binding, do carry special moral weight for the professional groups concerned and the general population, and call on government authorities to assume their responsibilities and take the appropriate institutional initiatives.

Spain's National Commission on Assisted Reproduction, though limited in scope and sector, could be patterned on this model. The Commission, whose creation was provided for by Act 35 of November 22nd 1988 on Assisted Reproduction Techniques, will be charged with advisory functions as well as other competencies of an administrative nature. The Act indicates that the Commission shall be «aimed at providing guidance on the use of these techniques, at collaborating with the government as to compiling and updating scientific and technical knowledge, and at formulating operating criteria for the Centres or Services where assisted reproduction techniques are performed, in order to facilitate their improved use» (section 21.1). Reinforcing the impression that the National Commission is modelled on the National Bioethics Committees is the Act's provision that committee members represent *inter alia* a «broad social spectrum» (section 21.3), thus

---

[10] See for example the Helsinki Declaration on human experimentation at the 18th World Medical Assembly (1964), revised by the Tokyo (1975) and Rome (1983) Assemblies.
[11] Numerous such committees have been formed in different countries, varying in function, structure, makeup and lines of dependence. The first was created in France by the President of the Republic: the *Comité Consultant National d'Ethique pour les Sciences de la Vie et de la Santé*. At the Madrid International Conference on National Bioethics Committees (March 1992) a proposal was put forward for the creation of an international committee.

indicating that the Commission is not to have a strictly technical character [12].

## 2.　Health administration control as a preventive measure

Government intervention in public health matters is fully accepted in advanced societies. We are witness to an increasing control by public authorities of health-care activity understood in the broadest sense of the term. This applies not just to the executive branch of government, which I shall take up ahead, but also to the legislative and judicial powers. This process is due to various concurrent factors, notably: 1) the health of the citizenry represents one of the prime policy goals of the present-day social or welfare state, which allocates sizable human, economic and material resources to such purpose; 2) the preservation of the individual's health must embrace the quality of public health care and diminish the risks involved, above all, from biotechnological development and the availability of new, complex, and potentially more harmful treatments; 3) this intervention is even more justified and even imperative in relation to health-care practices that possibly affect fundamental individual rights, such as life and personal integrity, liberty, privacy, the family, etc.

The public sector's role in medicine has consequently expanded, either as direct provider of health-care services or indirectly, in the form of collaboration with private sector medicine (by means of outsourcing contracts and agreements) or by financing private health care and research. In any event, whatever health-care system is adopted new administrative regulatory channels have been instituted for authorizing certain health-care services. These include personnel and material certification in health centres, professional certification for implementing or pursuing certain practices, follow-up of new treatments or of those still in the research and experimental stages, the stipulation of protocols, etc. These are more or less indirect procedures that allow the establishment of preventive measures whereby assurances can be provided in connection with some of the more delicate and potentially conflictive activities, conditions which may be particularly appropriate for human genome manipulations, as have been established in connection with certain microorganisms to avert the effects of their uncontrolled release into the environment. On the other

---

[12] For its part Spanish legislative Act 42 of December 28th 1988 on the donation and use of human embryos and fetuses or their cells, tissues or organs, provided for the creation of a National Commission to oversee the donation and use of human embryos and fetuses [in its first additional provision, sub-paragraph *f*)]. As in the case of the National Commission on Assisted Reproduction, the government has not yet approved the Royal Decree constituting the Commission even though both laws provided for such purpose a period of 6 months reckoned from the date of their respective enactment.

hand, when health-care professionals are directly employed by the government the authorities have a highly effective regulatory tool: the possibility of disciplinary action, with the application of sanctions and other corrective measures for the more serious infractions.

In Spain, this process has been gradually incorporated into the country's health-care system. The European Community recognizes the right to the protection of one's health, with such protection being incumbent upon the public authorities (section 43). This right was further implemented by the General Health Act (Act 14 of April 25th 1986) as to health-care delivery and creation of the National Health Care System. In addition, there are sectorial laws which regulate specific medical treatments and practices, such as organ extraction and transplantation, clinical autopsies, assisted reproduction techniques, clinical trials, etc. The regulations implementing these laws have conferred upon Spanish government health authorities an ever more significant and effective capacity to intervene in these matters. Taken as a whole they display the above-cited monitoring and intervention features: regulation of the lawful scope of activity, oversight to assure the quality of professional practice, and decisions aimed at safeguarding the relevant individual rights and legally protected interests.

In conclusion, if this growing protagonism has taken root in numerous complex biomedical activities, nothing should impede its extension to activities and investigation relating to human, animal or plant genetics. Such intervention must be understood to be fundamentally justified as a means of forestalling the potential hazards entailed in these and other biomedical science activities and not as a lever for government-run science or as a constraint on the freedom of investigation. The latter reservation does not argue against the government's legitimate function of encouraging and promoting those scientific branches most deserving support in the pursuit of general interests deemed opportune, or of restricting or eliminating financial support for research running counter to regulatory control and assurance mechanisms or having undesirable aims.

Two laws with a direct bearing on regulation of activities in human genetics have to be considered within this framework: legislative Act 42 of December 28th 1988 on the *donation and use of human embryos and fetuses or their cells, tissues or organs,* and Act 35 of November 22nd 1988 on *Assisted Reproduction Techniques.* The first is concerned with the donation and use of human embryos and fetuses or their cells, tissues or organs for diagnostic, therapeutic, research or experimental purposes (section 1) and specifically with genetic technology (section 8). The second regulates diverse aspects relating to assisted reproduction techniques, such as diagnosis, therapy, research and experimentation with gametes and pre-embryos or preimplantation embryos [13]. They attribute important oversight competencies to the government in connection with these activities, particularly to the commissions envisaged for such purpose. However, in some cases the commissions are given excessive discretion as to authorization for the pursuit of certain insufficiently delimited activities [e.g. sections 16.1.*k)* and 20.2.B.*n)* and *r)* of Act 35/1988]. The cases and circumstances in which authorization is discretional with the authorities or commissions should be expressly mentioned and defined by the Act, otherwise the scope of what is actually permitted or prohibited by the law is overly diluted.

As an ultimate reference both laws contain a catalogue of prohibited practices (serious and very serious offences), including some which are directly tied to genetic manipulation, and which are subject to administrative sanctions, that is, non-penal sanctions (section 20 of Act 35/1988 and section 9 of Act 42/1988). The different violations may be classified into several groups: *a)* those involving noncompliance with health administration rules; *b)* infringement of the rights or interests of persons involved in assisted reproduction techniques (users and donors); *c)* those involving protection of human biological «material» (gametes and pre-embryos); *d)* application of assisted reproduction techniques for purposes other than those envisaged under the Act; and *e)* prohibited genetic manipulation or experimentation.

As can be seen Spanish lawmakers have for now (without prejudice to their first attempt with the Criminal Code Bill of 1992) decided not to establish new criminal categories in these Acts under which to impose criminal sanctions on violators of its regulatory provisions. With respect to some of the serious offences contained in the Act on Assisted Reproduction Techniques, doubts are raised, not as to their prohibition (something that appears obvious) but as to which legal instrument should be used (penal or administrative). This uncertainty specifically arises in connection with the following conducts: the creation of human beings by cloning or other procedures aimed at racial selection [section 20.2.B.*k)*]; creation of identical human beings by means of any type of cloning or other procedure able to originate several identical human beings [section 20.2.B.*l)*]; parthenogenesis, or stimulating development of an ovule by thermal, chemical or physical means without its fertilization by a spermatozoon, which would give rise to only female offspring [section 20.2.B.*m)*]; sex

---

[13] Both acts were challenged as unconstitutional before the Spanish Constitutional Court in 1989 (no judgement has yet been handed down) by the Popular Party Group in the Congress of Deputies, which argued that the laws did not sufficiently protect certain fundamental rights.

selection or genetic manipulation for non-therapeutic or unauthorized therapeutic purposes [section 20.2.B.*n*)]; creation of pre-embryos of persons of the same sex for reproductive or other purposes [section 20.2.B.*o*)]; fusion of pre-embryos or any other procedure aimed at producing chimeras [section 20.2.B.*p*)]; human genetic exchange, or recombination with other species, for the production of hybrids [section 20.2.B.*q*)]; unauthorized transfer of human gametes or pre-embryos to the uterus of another animal species, or the inverse operation [20.2.B.*r*)]; ectogenesis, or the creation of an individual human being in a laboratory [section 20.2.B.*s*)]; creation of pre-embryos with sperm from different individuals for transfer to a uterus [section 20.2.B.*t*)]; simultaneous transfer to a uterus of pre-embryos originating from ova of different women [section 20.2.B.*u*)]; use of genetic engineering and other procedures for military or other purposes to produce biological arms or human exterminating weapons of any type whatsoever [section 20.2.B.*v*)]. The Act on donation and use of human embryos and fetuses or their cells, tissues or organs also raises doubts as to the criminal nature of some of the prohibitions it sets down, such as on all acts aimed at altering non-pathological human genetic inheritance [section 9.2.B.*a*)].

There thus inevitably arises the question of whether these legal instruments are sufficient or, on the contrary, others (such as criminal statutes) are needed in order to achieve adequate legal protection of the interests and values at stake. The creation of criminal categories in respect of the conducts prohibited by these laws (administrative offences) does not imply violation of the principle of *ne bis ni idem*, for only one type or the other would be applicable (the criminal or administrative sanction). Where such conflict arises under Spanish law it is clearly resolved in favour of preference for the criminal sanction.

### 3. Liability for harmful or hazardous acts

The legally available means for redressing these situations is the reparation of the damages occasioned, which pertains to the realm of civil law, and repression for that damage, fundamentally attributed to criminal law. This is not to say that the repressive function is exclusive to the latter or to minimize the important deterrent function that can be fulfilled both by civil and criminal law.

#### 3.1. Civil liability
As regards reparation of damages under civil law (there is now discussion of incorporating reparation of damages as a concrete penal instrument in criminal law), that is, of a finding of civil liability, three essential prerequisites must be met: 1) the occasioning of real, economically measurable damages; 2) culpability;

and 3) a causal link between the first two prerequisites. Legal doctrine and practice in North America –and more recently in Germany and France as well– holds that there exists an economically compensable damage in cases of children born with hereditary malformations in families with some known risk in their medical history but whose parents were nonetheless not offered the medically indicated prenatal genetic screening and corresponding genetic counselling; or where such tests or counselling were deficient (wrongful life) [14]. Judicial questions of this type have not yet been raised in Spain, although a similar complaint was recently reported (apparently a criminal complaint, which would not be likely to succeed), and is awaiting decision.

## 3.2. *The intervention of criminal law*

The role of criminal law in relation to a field as new as the one we are studying here should be guided by its traditional governing principles, but as those principles are currently understood [15], that is, consistent with the function of criminal law and the principles of minimum intervention and *ultima ratio* [16]. It was recalled above that criminal law has as its exclusive responsibility the protection of legal «goods», that is, of the fundamental principles, values and interests of the individual and community, from conducts that harm or endanger them whenever such conducts involve serious offence to the society's prevailing socio-ethical norms. Nevertheless, resort to criminal law should be reserved for situations of intolerable attack on the most important legal values and only when made strictly necessary by the insufficiency of other, non-penal legal instruments (administrative law, civil law, etc.). These criteria should also be applied in relation to the law's attitude toward human genetics, such that the place of criminal law in regard to that area should usually be accessory or non-existent, especially when other branches of law can fully satisfy the need to protect values and interests and limit undesirable activities. On the other hand, recourse to criminal law will be inevitable –but always exceptional– when dealing with particularly grave conducts in relation with interests or values worthy of heightened protection. Consequently, as indicated further above, the first limiting and sanctioning filter should be obtained from the laws regulating, curbing and sanctioning procedures for assisted reproduction (and not assisted reproduction per se), genetic engineering, and the use of human gametes and embryos for

---

[14] Crammer, Stephan V., *Pränatale Diagnostik und Fetaltherape*, in «Medizinrecht», 1991, pgs. 14 and ff, and Knoppers, Bartha M., *Human Dignity and Genetic Heritage*, Law Reform Commission of Canada, Ottawa, 1991, pgs. 54 and ff.

[15] For more on what follows see Cerezo Mir, José, *Curso de Derecho Penal. I Parte General*, 3rd edition, Tecnos, Madrid, 1985, pgs. 11 and ff.

[16] See Lahti, Raimo, *Criminal Law and Modern Bio-Medical Techniques. General Report*, «Revue Internationale de Droit Pénal», v. 59, 1988, pg. 611.

research purposes; in Spain, in the aforementioned Acts on Assisted Reproduction Techniques and on the Donation and use of human embryos and fetuses or their cells, tissues or organs. The same filtering function corresponds to civil reparation of the damages occasioned.

Although these criteria are clear, they are in practice difficult to specify. As mentioned earlier, they should reflect the community's dominant socio-ethical conceptions in relation to the different consequences of human genetics discoveries and activities, and at the moment it is not easy to find widely accepted points of agreement. In addition, varying perspectives on the role of criminal law –though generally accepting the core criteria set out above– can delay or accelerate its application. Thus under a conception of criminal law accentuating its preventive function, an ends-based rationale (the utilitarian conception) could lead to criminal sanction of conducts that endanger the principles of law whose protection is sought, even when such danger is merely potential, without the need for a specific case to have arisen (crimes of abstract danger); whereas a values-based rationale will emphasize the rights of the individual and the ideals of humanity and justice [17], thus tending to limit the application of criminal categories. Other sectors appeal to criminal law's symbolic function of reinforcing moral criteria in the face of deviant conducts, that is, demonstrating the moral error of the conduct, and emphasize its declaratory function in asserting the society's limits of tolerance [18]. Finally, others place more importance on the regulatory rather than the punitive function of criminal law (the latter itself would fulfil that regulatory function). In this approach certain conducts are not directly outlawed, but instead made conditional on compliance with determined conditions and procedures, whose infringement could give rise to criminal sanctions (similar to what occurs in economic criminal law) [19].

The foregoing undoubtedly confirms the complexity and difficulty of finding appropriate criminal justice criteria, and at the same time underscores the risk of expanding criminal law away from its essential function and principles of intervention, from which it should not stray, without forgetting the aspiration to the above-mentioned ideals of justice and humanity. Hence, having established this basic framework, further advance requires detecting and delimiting the legal principles or values or interests that could be affected by applications in the field of human genetics. Only after having identified those values will

---

[17] *Ibid*, pg. 611.
[18] *Ibid*, pg. 612.
[19] *Ibid*.

it be possible to analyse the conducts which could represent a threat thereto, assess their gravity, and tailor criminal policy accordingly. In any event, we cannot yet aim for definitive solutions: the possible consequences of human genome knowledge and its applications —some of which are still not practicable— are still not sufficiently known and, second, certain consequences which today may be deemed as undesirable or deviant could perhaps be viewed differently in the future, particularly if the undesirable effects can be prevented. In addition, it should be borne in mind that much of the genetic experimentation described in scientific literature is regarded as theoretically possible but not yet technically practicable, which raises the question as to whether criminal law's preventive function (where sanctions are deserved and needed) should be pursued even before such possibilities are realized.

## Legal values or goods meriting protection or heightened protection

Human genetics investigation and its potential applications may affect legal principles, or individual or collective interests or values. The task is to identify these, the protection they enjoy under our laws, and the gaps in that protection and to decide which legal instruments should be employed to guarantee adequate protection, according to their importance and the types of aggression to which they are exposed, without the recourse to criminal law being always necessary.

### 1. Individual goods or interests

Humanist and neo-personalist currents of recent decades have accentuated the recognition of human dignity and the free development of one's personality as individual values of the first order. These values often appear at the centre of many aspects of the debate concerning human genetics. The Spanish Constitution of 1978 expressly lays down in article 10.1 that «Human dignity, man's inviolable and inherent rights, the free development of his personality, respect for the law and for the rights of others are essential to political order and social peace». Frequent, indiscriminate and sometimes abusive appeal to these values and inattention to study of their overall place and precise function in the Constitution should not lead us to lose sight of their intrinsic importance. What I wish to stress here is the projection of these inherent rights onto the other fundamental rights and public liberties enshrined in the Spanish Constitution (similar to that of other similarly structured Constitutions), in the sense that the former give the latter greater constructive sense and cohesion, more than their conception as autonomous fundamental rights [20]. The principle of equality before the law, and, above all, its consequent ban on discrimination by reason of birth, race, gender, religion, opinion or any other personal or social condition or circumstance (article 14 of the Spanish Constitution), are also brought to the forefront by the discriminatory potential of certain human genome applications.

Most of the individual rights which could be affected by human genetics applications are specifically recognized in modern-day constitutions and international human rights declarations and conventions, and they have traditionally been conferred a special protection by criminal law. This is the case with human life, integrity (physical and mental), freedom of decision and self-determination, all of which are legal values directly protected in criminal law with respect to almost all forms of aggression. This, however, is not always the case, as I will attempt to demonstrate further below. There has been some flux in the protection afforded other legal interests, but the trend in recent years with respect to human rights is that they merit heightened protection in the face of new forms of aggression that were previously unthinkable or regarded as unimportant, such as with the life and bodily and mental (future) integrity of the fetus.

*1.1.    Life and integrity after birth. Genetic integrity*
1.    Just as occurs with some medical activities (diagnostic, therapeutic) that are new, still in the experimental stage or not yet consolidated –particularly the more aggressive ones or those affecting especially vital parts of the person– some aspects of the application of genetic techniques pose grave potential danger to the life, health or integrity of persons, including their genetic integrity. In general, criminal categories sanctioning homicide and bodily harm can satisfy the need for protection with respect to these conducts, including in very exceptional case those involving wilful misconduct (second degree or even first degree). In any case, we must ascertain whether or not criminal categories regarding injuries afford adequate protection from certain genetic actions on human beings after birth, whether performed for therapeutic or for scientific research or experimental purposes.

---

[20] In this sense see Valle Muñiz, José M. and González González, Marisé, *Utilización abusiva de técnicas genéticas y Derecho Penal* [*Abusive use of genetic techniques and criminal law*], in «Poder Judicial», no. 26, 1992, pgs. 126 and ff. Also, Mateo Pardo, Regino, *La «dignidad de la persona humana» y su significación en la Constitución española de 1978 a través de la jurisprudencia del Tribunal Constitucional* [*Human dignity and its significance in the Spanish Constitution of 1978 in the case-law of the Constitutional Court*] in «Escritos Jurídicos en Memoria de Luis Mateo Rodríguez», Universidad de Cantabria, 1992, 341 and ff (348 and ff).

2.  As is commonly known –and I will not delve into this here–
    genetic engineering is giving rise to a variety of manipulations
    of human genetic components. Most noteworthy among the-
    se is the potential offered by gene therapy [21] for curing se-
    rious genetically caused diseases or defects by means of the
    addition, modification, replacement or removal of genes. Dis-
    tinct types of genetic defects are involved: hereditary, when
    transmitted by the parents' genes; non-hereditary, when ano-
    malies are produced by unforeseen errors in the formation of
    sex cells; and congenital, when they occur during fetal develop-
    ment. For the moment these techniques are aimed at correcting
    defects of a monogenic origin, given the extreme difficulties
    posed in this sense by chromosomal aberrations (supernume-
    rary or absent chromosomes) and by plurigenic, multifactorial
    aberrations, with respect to which efforts are concentrated on
    preventing the environmental factors (in the broad sense) which
    may act as triggers. There are constant discoveries linking hu-
    man genes to often serious or deadly disorders (haemophilia,
    Huntington's chorea, thalassaemia, Duchenne myopathy, drepa-
    nocytosis, pigmentary retinitis, polycystic kidney disease, and
    such a connection is even suspected for cancer and certain
    acquired mental disorders) and to possible treatments for some
    acquired diseases, such as Aids. A distinction should also be
    made between manipulation of somatic and of germ-line cells,
    and between the different genetic diagnostic tests, including an-
    tenatal diagnosis (preconceptive and prenatal). The latter tests,
    in the context of possible subsequent therapy (or of abortion
    for eugenic reasons, where permitted under the country's laws),
    should be considered as lawful, provided they respond to the
    needs arising from the *lex artis* in each specific case, as I will
    further expound ahead.

    Genetic manipulation of somatic cells entails specific actions
    on those cells that do not affect the person's genetic pattern,
    because such cells do not transmit the alterations made to
    them to the person's offspring, given that they are neither
    responsible for carrying out reproduction nor affect the cells
    which actually do, the gametes. However, the effects of this
    type of intervention are not yet well known, and the possi-
    bility has not been ruled out that they can produce unpre-
    dictable spontaneous genetic mutations which could influence
    germ cells. The truth is that such manipulations seek to treat
    generally serious diseases in persons after birth (or in the
    unborn child once implanted inside the mother's uterus), as-
    suming, as the specific case may have it, the lack of more

---

[21] See Davis, Bernard D., *Limits to genetic intervention in humans: somatic and germline*, «Human Genetic Information: Science, Law and Ethics», Ciba Foundation Symposium 149, Wiley, Chichester, 1990, pgs. 81 and ff.

reliable therapeutic alternatives. A legal assessment of somatic cell gene therapy must take as its starting point that somatic cells and their components (including DNA) form part of the individual's personal integrity (bodily integrity and physical or mental health, according to the Spanish Criminal Code), within a subcategory we could term as «genetic integrity», and are consequently entitled to the protection afforded said legal interest under criminal law.

The following conclusions can therefore be established:

1)   Criminal law should regard somatic cell gene therapy as it does any other treatment (without prejudice to the relevant special considerations in respect of new or experimental treatments) that is, it is what is known as therapeutic experimentation, which implies submissions to the general guidelines and limitations commonly accepted for this therapeutic category (namely the weighing of risks and benefits, and the patient's informed consent without any external coercion whatsoever, e.g. for eugenic purposes) [22]; bear in mind that somatic cell gene therapy may be the only alternative to a grave or deadly disease, which situation would justify the risks (e.g. an unforeseen genetic mutation) faced by the patient; nevertheless, in connection with this for now still experimental therapy, consideration could be given to some form of flexible and swift pre-treatment external control (e.g. a multidisciplinary committee of specialists, but not only scientists, guided by a revisable list of diseases).

2)   Somatic cell gene therapy when in conformity with the lex artis is therefore lawful, and, moreover, does not even come under the bodily injuries criminal category;

3)   Any other, non-therapeutic action entailing alteration of the genetic components of a person's somatic cells does qualify as a bodily injuries criminal offence to the extent that it impairs the person's physical integrity or physical or mental health (section 420 of the Spanish Criminal Code), and the exact offence will depend on the medical care required, where such care is possible (sections 420, 421 and 582 of the Spanish Criminal Code), or on how these offences are configured in the applicable criminal code.

---

[22] Mayor, Federico, Genetic manipulation and human rights, «Modificazoni genetiche e diritti dell'uomo» (editor Guido Gerin), Istituto Internazionale di Studi sui Diritti dell'Uomo, Cedam, Padova, 1987, pgs. 141 and ff.

4) Nevertheless, these actions will be lawful if they are based on the informed consent of the interested party (the holder of the legally protected interest) and the laws of the country in question recognize the efficacy of such consent in relation to physical integrity and health issues (in Spanish law this is often indirect, through section 8.11 of the Criminal Code, concerning the legitimate exercise of a right or profession, provided there is other statutory support in this respect).

With respect to germ-line manipulations (germinal cells: gametes and totipotent embryos), the same criteria as those proposed for somatic cell manipulation should, in principle, be applicable. Bear in mind that the question we are dealing with here is not that of protecting gametes and zygote (although the effects of such therapy would certainly directly impact them, or better said, the human beings born after application of the germ-line gene therapy), but the prior question of the reproductive capacity of individuals presenting abnormalities in their reproductive cells or which manifest themselves immediately after their union, that is, that they can choose to have children without the risk of transmitting to them a genetic disease (hence the mention of this issue in this section). Germ-line gene therapy, however, raises other, more serious ethical and legal problems. Although it will surely contribute in the future to eradicating defects from the manipulated lineage (and lest us not forget that this is still only a future possibility), it will also bring about permanent genetic modifications that are transmitted to later generations and whose possible impact on the human species is not yet precisely understood [23], thus making it difficult to control the potential negative effects. The misgivings awakened by such as yet unknown effects have led some specialists to propose an outright ban on germ-line cell therapy and others to seek a moratorium until a fuller understanding is achieved. Lastly, there are those who hold that this therapy should not be rejected, because it will not be possible to see any actual risks to the human species as such until several generations have passed and the alterations are reproduced in other human beings.

The foregoing begs the resolution of several questions. First, to determine in these cases what should be understood by therapy in the strict sense and its possible differentiation

---

[23] For more on this discussion see Davis, *Limits to genetic intervention in humans: somatic and germline*, op. cit., 85, who believes the gene introduced would not normally displace the defective gene.

from manipulations aimed at genotypic or phenotypic improvements and not at correcting a clearly pathological condition. Second, given that other non-therapeutic germ-line manipulations will be genetically transmitted to offspring, to
determine if these cases involve some other legal interest
which transcends the collective meriting protection and, if so,
to identify that interest. I will explore this second aspect
further below. And lastly, in light of the second consideration,
to determine whether the law should allow germ-cell gene
manipulations of any kind, particularly if for non-therapeutic
purposes, or, if it does not so permit, should the prohibition
regard such conducts as criminal offences? This question will
also be explored further ahead (although I can now tell you
that the answer is affirmative). In view of the current situation, the most judicious course would seem to be support
for a moratorium insofar as concerns use (and an as yet still
future use and this would thus be a preventive measure) of
germ-line gene therapy only [24]. For the time being criminalization of such therapies does not seem called for. Their
curtailment should be a matter of administrative law and
serve as a criteria for the granting or denial of public funds
for related research or applications, without prejudice to the
possibility of allowing use for therapeutic purposes, according
to the merits of each specific case and a weighing of the
safeguards against undesirable mutations or aberrations, all as
evaluated by a committee of experts [25]. This proposal would
be greatly aided by the drawing up of a list of truly serious
hereditary diseases, which would serve as a frame of reference for possible authorizations. This would require that
such lists (which, of course, could be revised as often as
necessary) be the result of as broad a consensus as possible,
from the social as well as scientific standpoint, in order to
avoid exclusively scientific oversight and eugenic risks.

An overall evaluation of germ-line gene therapy must have
regard, moreover, to the already mentioned fact of its connection with human reproduction. Consequently, while certainly true that genetic engineering in the future will most
likely facilitate parenthood for persons who today run the

---

[24] In this regard see Resolution 6.8, Section II of the International Criminal
Law Association' *XIV International Congress on Criminal Law*, in «Kongressak-
ten», Vienna, 1989, pgs. 285 and ff, which envisages in support of such a
moratorium the establishment of, as minima, deontological guidelines and/or
a restrictive authorization policy.

[25] Along these lines, Lenoir, Noëlle, *Aux frontières de la vie: une éthique biomédicale à la française*, T.I., La Documentation Française, Paris, 1991, pg. 81,
who believes it should be pluridisciplinary and, at the present state of science,
is opposed to any germinal therapy experimentation as totally lacking in scientific and medical value.

risk of transmitting to their offspring genetic or hereditary diseases, the problem posed today –or, rather, when such genetic engineering becomes possible– is to consider whether or not to satisfy the desire of those persons to have healthy children by means of germ-line therapy before science is sufficiently prepared to avert the unknown negative effects; or to preclude that risk and have the affected persons confine themselves (that is, as with somatic cell gene therapy, without any kind of external compulsion for eugenic purposes) to using assisted reproduction techniques and pre-implantation diagnosis to assure the child will not inherit the feared diseases; or, finally, decide not to have children.

In addition to the above reflections, we should also consider that if measures are already being taken to control and limit, where appropriate, biotechnological laboratory applications so as to prevent uncontrolled release into the environment of microorganisms which could represent a hazard to the environment or to human beings [26], it would appear logical and even more justified to also allow some limitations on human genome interventions. Nevertheless, for now we should provide the appropriate frameworks for socially and legally favouring research aimed at a better understanding of the potential and benefits of this type of therapy, its consequences and unknown potentially harmful effects, and to find procedures and techniques to control and avoid such ill effects, except where what is actually questioned is the very use of the human «model», which would lead us to an ethical discussion of a different nature (to which I shall return further ahead).

In Spanish law the Act on Assisted Reproduction Techniques allows gene therapy and diagnosis (section 1.3), specifically for preimplantation embryos (pre-embryos *in vitro* or in the uterus), embryos and fetuses in the uterus on certain conditions: the national government must have issued a royal decree setting down a list of diseases for which therapy is possible with strictly scientific criteria (First Final Provision, d), the therapy must not influence non-pathological hereditary characteristics, and the aim is not race or individual selection (section 13.3, c and d, respectively). This broadly worded last condition suggests that Spanish law does not, in principle, exclude, germ-line gene therapy, without prejudice to the restrictions that could be introduced in this respect when the aforementioned list of diseases is published. Considered as relating to gene related are sex selection for therapeutic purposes, that is, as a means of impeding the transmis-

---

[26] See April 23rd 1990 Directive of the EEC Council on the environmental release of genetically modified organisms (90/220/CE).

sion of hereditary diseases linked to the sex chromosomes, and the surgical creation of beneficial genetic mosaics by grafting cells, tissues or organs of embryos or fetuses to patients in which they are biologically or genetically dead or missing (section 8 of Act 42/1988).

### 1.2.   Life and integrity pre-birth. Protection of the preimplantation embryo

1.   Abortion advocates have gained steady support and legislative backing for their positions, resulting in possible inattention to the legal protection of the unborn from their earliest stages of development. On occasion this disregard is deliberate and «consistent» with the limits sought on the protection of the unborn in connection with abortion. I will not enter into this controversy or the ideological and sociological issues that fuel it. What is certain is that biotechnology forces a reconsideration of the protection of the unborn in other aspects unrelated to voluntary abortion [27]. In any event, human life after conception and prior to birth, the life of the unborn, has always merited special penal protection from abortion with *mens rea* by a third party (again, I repeat, without here considering abortions performed with the consent or at the request of the mother and the circumstances in which voluntary abortion is decriminalized), but the same cannot be said with respect to negligent abortion. Genetic manipulations (and medical manipulation in general) can originate an increased number of the latter type of abortions, which should be prevented. In fact, negligent abortion performed by a third party should be punished, provided the presence of reckless negligence, regardless of the means used, or whether the result was foreseen [28]. Although legal professionals are not always aware of its importance, reducing the number of embryos within a multiple pregnancy also has criminal justice implications. By multiple pregnancy I am referring to when the woman is impregnated with various embryos by means of assisted reproduction techniques, whether by *in vitro* formation and transfer to the woman of more embryos than necessary or by hormone-induced ovular hyperstimulation of the woman. A multiple pregnancy achieved by these

---

[27] On Constitutional and penal law protection of the beginnings of human life see Romeo Casabona, Carlos M., *Human Life as a Value protected by Penal Law,* in «Le Droit face aux dilemmes moraux concernant la vie et le mort», Proceedings of the XXth Colloquy of European Law, Glasgow, 10-12 September 1990, Council of Europe, Strasbourg, 1993, pgs. 135 and ff.

[28] This proposal seeks to underscore the scarce punitive margin allowed by the current regulatory provisions of the Spanish Criminal Code, specifically section 412 as it now stands, if they are construed as only covering the negligent case and section 565 (and the fault set down in section 586 bis) is considered as not applicable in these cases.

means can actually endanger its eventual coming to term, due to the increased mortality of each of the embryos and to the risks such pregnancies represent for the health and even life of the pregnant woman. Several legal problems are involved which will not be considered in this paper, as they do not involve interventions in the fetal genome.

2. A comparison of various criminal justice systems (and the current Spanish Criminal Code) shows there are also gaps in the legal protection of the health and physical integrity (and later mental integrity) of the unborn, who are much more vulnerable as a consequence of the development of biomedical sciences (without prejudice to the necessary reminder that these sciences are also providing a greater understanding and better techniques to nurture the unborn child's development). The ensuing question is therefore whether or not the integrity of the embryo or fetus merits protection under criminal law. In my opinion it does[29], both as a consequence of the intrinsic importance of the legal interests involved and because, at least at present, most of the effects and handicaps of these injuries are difficult to treat and correct and will therefore persist throughout the life of the future child. In support of this view, I can cite the famous April 11th 1985 judgement number 53 of the Spanish Constitutional Court on the constitutional challenge to the law which decriminalized abortion in certain situations and medical indications. The high court held that the life of the *nasciturus* embodies a value that is constitutionally protected under article 15 of the Constitution («All have the right to life and to physical and moral integrity...»). I think this criterion can be properly construed as extending to the integrity of the unborn as well.

3. Today's broadened understanding of the different stages of embryonic and fetal development and the fact that modern assisted reproduction techniques allow embryos to be produced in laboratories and outside the uterus (pre-implantation embryos), together with the knowledge that they can be manipulated and are not necessarily destined to be implanted and develop in a woman, has led to two contradicting situations. First, there is a tendency to not consider as criminal

---

[29] As I outlined in 1981 in *El Médico y el Derecho Penal. La actividad curativa*, Bosch, Barcelona, 1981, pgs. 279 and ff, and developed in later studies such as *La protección jurídica del concebido. El feto como paciente* [*Legal protection of the unborn. The fetus as patient*], in «Revista Jurídica de Castilla-La Mancha», no. 7, 1989, 445 and 448. See also Cuerda Riezu, Antonio, *Límites jurídico-penales de las nuevas técnicas genéticas* [*Criminal law limits of the new genetic techniques*] in «Anuario de Derecho Penal y Ciencias Penales», 1988, pg. 442 (although from a different standpoint); Valle Muñiz and González González, *Utilización abusiva de técnicas genéticas y Derecho Penal*, op. cit., pg. 144 (argued on grounds similar to those presented in this text).

abortion the destruction of «excess» embryos (pre-implantation embryos or pre-embryos) produced by means of *in vitro*
fertilization and used as research material. For such an offence to exist the destroyed embryo must have been previously
implanted in the mother's womb or expelled (naturally or
artificially) therefrom after implantation, unless one wishes to
incur in an application of law by analogy, which in Spanish
criminal law is generally considered to violate the «principle
of legality» –there is no crime without a law, no punishment
without a law– and therefore not allowed. This issue is directly connected to the question of at what moment legal
protection of the embryo has effect. The present trend is to
consider the moment of implantation in the uterus for such
purpose [30]. The solution is certainly not easy when someone
destroys embryos or gametes that were obtained from a
couple for later use and are irreplaceable (i.e. when no more
gametes are available), in order to prevent the couple from
bearing offspring, or in order to prevent a researcher in possession of the gametes to continue his or her work. The latter
case could constitute a crime against property but this would
imply recognizing a reification of the human reproductive element or of the embryo itself. Such reification would surely be
inadmissible in relation to the first case; perhaps criminal coercion could be applied to that case, and if no criminal liability is
found, action for civil liability could be pursued.

Given the shortcomings pointed out above, some sectors
have called for the need to grant some form of legal protection, even penal protection in extreme cases, to the non-im-
planted embryo in order to prevent its manipulation (or some types of manipulations: those that are not aimed a
benefiting the embryo, i.e. diagnostic or therapeutic measures
aiming at its later implantation; see further above for the
remarks on somatic and germ-cell gene therapy). Advocates
of this position invoke different arguments, defining the scope
of sanctionable conducts more broadly or narrowly. Some
base their arguments on the view that the pre-implantation
embryo is inherently worthy of protection, others point to
the right to free development of the future person [31], and

---

[30] For more on the state of this question see Romeo Casabona, Carlos M.,
*La reforma del aborto: Límite mínimo, figuras delictivas y sistema de indicaciones*
[*Abortion reform: lower limit, criminal categories and medical-indication system*], in
«Propuestos para la Reforma Penal», Centro de Estudios Criminológicos,
Universidad de La Laguna, 192, pgs. 138 and ff, and in «Actualidad Penal»,
1991, pg. 137.

[31] Valle Muñiz and González González, in *Utilizacion abusiva...*, op. cit., pgs. 124
and ff (particularly pgs. 125 and ff and 132 and ff) maintain a restrictive
position. Conversely, Germany's Embryo Protection Act (*Gesetz zum Schutz
von Embryonen-Embryonenschutzgestez*) of December 13th 1990 has opted for
broad criminal coverage, as will be seen further ahead.

others appeal to the interests of humanity as a whole. In any event, proposals for criminal law protection of the preimplantation embryo do not necessarily contradict legal systems in which abortion has been decriminalized, above all if the legal value whose protection is actually sought is correctly profiled. Nevertheless, jurists seem to agree as to following: a) the prohibition of obtaining embryos *in vitro* for purposes other than procreation, such as for research or industrial use; b) the prohibition, backed by the threat of penal sanction, on implanting embryos which have been previously subject to any of these manipulations (that is, those whose purpose is not diagnostic or curative with respect to the embryo) [32]; and c) not allowing their development, *in vitro* or outside the body, beyond a specified period, usually fixed at 14 days.

This triple barrier constitutes a veritable retaining wall for a good number of undesirable genetic manipulations, with the last two having the specific purpose of impeding the birth of manipulated human beings. They place us within the framework of the so-called «embryo legal statute».

## 1.3. Genome analysis and individual freedom

1. The Human Genome Project and genome analysis will allow a person's genetic map to be completely known, making possible the prediction of future genetic diseases, even those with onset many years after the analysis is performed. As is known, this capability will allow a variety of preventive or curative measures to be taken before the disease manifests itself, particularly gene therapy measures, depending on the state of these techniques at each point in time. This knowledge, however, can suggest the adoption of certain measures which could gravely affect the individual's freedom or bring about discriminatory situations. Thus, for example, attempts could be made to justify, on collective health protection grounds, the mandatory imposition of genetic testing (genetic screening), of measures to avoid genetically defective offspring (contraception, sterilization, abortion), or to enhance the «genetic quality» of the affected persons by means of

---

[32] See Eser, *La moderna medicina de la reproducción...,* op. cit., pg. 288; Romeo Casabona, Carlos M., *La utilización de embriones y fetos humanos con fines de investigación genética u otros fines no terapéuticos* [*The use of human embryos and fetuses for genetic investigation or other non-therapeutic purposes*], in «Eguzkilore», Cuaderno del Instituto Vasco de Criminología, San Sebastián, no. 5, 1992, pgs. 151 and ff; Schreiber, Hans-Ludwig, *Der Schutz des Lebens durich das Recht an setnem Beginn und an setnem Ende,* «Festchrift fur Günter Schewe», Springer Verlag, Berlin, 1991, pg. 127; Valle Muñiz and González González, *Utilización abusiva...,* op. cit., pg. 134, although they hold that penal intervention is not justified.

gene therapy. The principle of individual autonomy continues to represent the indispensable reference that dispels and defeats all such initiatives.

2.  With respect to these possible therapeutic genetic manipulations, the patient's right to be informed enjoys the same legal recognition as has been granted for medicine in general since years ago, specifically embodied in various charters of patients rights and health legislations (in Spanish law, principally the General Health Act of April 25th 1986, section 10.5). The penal implications of omitting such information are very limited, however (and mainly turn on the fact that a properly informed patient is a prerequisite for the consent of the patient to have legal force in those offences for which such consent releases a third party from criminal liability), in some cases because there are no specific penal provisions addressing such omission and in others because it is seen as justifiable, without prejudice to any civil liability which could arise in connection therewith.

3.  Genetic diagnosis (preconception, preimplantation and prenatal) have very quickly become part of clinical practice as relatively accessible tests and demonstrates the extent to which advances in human genetics have already penetrated the daily life of the populace. They bear great influence on reproduction and family planning decisions and practices, with effects as yet difficult to properly assess.

Some aspects of prenatal testing are also of interest from a criminal law perspective [33]. Prenatal testing can be understood to refer to information on possible congenital defects of the fetus obtained by means of a set of procedures that biomedicine makes possible for such purpose. These screening techniques can detect the presence of disease or malformation in the fetus, and even predict the fetus' sex. Couples with a high risk of offsprings suffering abnormalities can also use it to confirm or rule out the presence of such abnormalities in the fetus. Thus, the fetus is the subject of prenatal diagnostic techniques, as opposed to preconceptive

---

[33] See the report of the Comité Consultatif National d'Ethique pour les Sciences de la Vie et de la Sante, *Rapport: le diagnostic prenatal et pertnatal. Le diagnostic d'une predisposition*, Paris, 1985, pgs. 4 and ff; Fraser, F. Clarke, *Diagnostic prenatal des désordres génétiques*, in «Cahiers de Bioéthique», no. 2, Quebec, 1980, pgs. 3 and ff; Powledge, Tabitha M. and Fletcher, John, *Recommandations concernant les problèmes moraux, sociaux et juridiques relatifs au diagostic prenatal*, also in «Cahiers de Bioéthique», no. 2, Quebec, 1980, pg. 92; Romeo Casabona, Carlos M., *El diagnóstico antenatal y sus implicaciones jurídicos-penales* [Antenatal diagnosis and its implications for criminal law], in «La Ley», no. 1751, 1987, pg. 6.

testing. Prenatal testing, like the latter, generally leads to some form of genetic counselling, in which two opposed conceptions are at work: the merely advisory and guiding role versus a more authoritative function, that is, one in which the medical specialist has the authority to, on the basis of the results obtained, impose certain measures (e.g. abortion) without the consent of the mother. Today there are a variety of medical techniques which provide early detection of fetal abnormalities. Amniocentesis is the one which currently allows diagnosis of the greatest number of congenital diseases. It entails certain risks, such as loss of the fetus, fetal injuries and infection, neonatal disorders, and complications for the mother (visceral perforation, premature detachment of the placenta, premature breaking of waters, infection, fainting and death of the mother, uterine contractions and premature labour, postpartum haemorrhaging). Nevertheless, the test has undergone continual improvement and its inherent dangers have been steadily reduced. Prenatal diagnosis per se does not affect gene integrity, but, like other genetic tests, can be employed as a prior step to genetic interventions

As opposed to those who view the role of prenatal diagnosis as an alternative to germ-line therapy that allows the same purpose to be achieved (to not have defective children) by means of selective abortion [34] as necessary, we should recall the wide range of diagnostic possibilities offered or which could soon be offered by prenatal diagnosis: *a)* reassure high-risk parents that the fetus does not present any disease or malformation; *b)* allow treatment (surgical, medicinal, genetic therapy) of the fetus in order to cure or alleviate determined anomalies, or fetal therapy; *c)* indicate the optimum delivery method in view of the malformations suffered by the fetus (e.g. a caesarean section); *d)* determine the post-delivery or later treatment to be followed with the newborn (preventive medicine); *e)* adopt a decision as to eugenic abortion where permitted by law (in Spain by section 417 bis number 1.3 of the Criminal Code, and in countries where abortion is allowed by medical indication and/or in the early stages of the pregnancy); *f)* accept the likely handicapped child or prepare the legal proceedings for his or her adoption by others or admission into a centre for abandoned children. The decision as to these options will depend on the personal convictions of the parents and the relevant legal regulations. In any event, it has been pointed out that this range of possibilities offered by prenatal screening, which after all will permit improve-

---

[34] Davis, *Limits to genetic intervention in humans: somatic and germline,* op. cit., pg. 86.

ments in obstetrical and neonatal care, should not imply an indiscriminate increase in abortions, thanks to the advances achieved in perinatology over recent years[35].

Prenatal testing may be classified as a therapeutic measure, as with any other diagnostic procedure, from the moment it aims as *treatment* of the fetus to the fullest possible extent[36]. It must be considered that such diagnosis does not constitute a bodily injuries criminal offence with respect to the mother or embryo insofar as it represents a potential benefit for both. This requires verifying the medical indication for screening, weighing the risks and advantages and acting in accordance with *lex artis*. This category is understood to include diagnostic techniques that still have a certain experimental component (therapeutic experimentation) and hence some risk (as occurs to a point with amniocentesis in light of the already described risks it entails). If screening is performed with a view to a eugenic abortion, the injuries produced by the diagnostic tests (in Spanish law generally equivalent to a bodily injuries misdemeanour and not criminal offence) are so minor as to be covered by the consent of the pregnant woman who suffers them in the first place.

In this context we must also recall preimplantation diagnosis as a prior step to subsequent *in vitro* genetic interventions on the embryo, and, moreover, as favouring the prevention of hereditary disease in the offspring by permitting a decision not to implant an embryo in which a serious abnormality has been detected. This possibility, given the necessary safeguards, should be viewed favourably. However, it can also lead to eugenic solutions: not only positive eugenics by means of such interventions, but also negative eugenics (e.g. the decision not to transfer the embryo to the woman even when the pathological conditions detected are not serious).

4.  Fetal therapy (or embryonic therapy, where such is the case) necessarily entails intervention in the mother's body in order to access the fetus (medications, transfusions, fetal surgery), even when the operation is performed *ex utero,* that is, extracting the fetus from the womb and later reintroducing it once the operation has been completed. The mother's consent is necessary for such therapeutic measures, but this raises the question of the legal implications of a mother's

---

[35] Carrera, *Diagnóstico prenatal: Un concepto en evolución* [*Prenatal diagnosis: An evolving concept*], in «Diagnóstico prenatal», (J. M. Carrera, editor), Salvat, Barcelona, 1987, pg. 8.

[36] See Eser, *Genética humana desde la perspectiva del derecho alemán,* op. cit., pg. 351.

refusal to allow such treatment (for religious reasons, for example). The answer must consider the legal nature of the conflict involved, weigh the competing interests (conceived more broadly than when weighing the legally protected values involved), and judge the risks incurred by the mother if the intervention is performed as opposed to those which arise for the fetus if not. The conflict could develop as one between the mother's freedom, and in some cases her right to health and integrity, and the life of fetus, in extreme cases, or at least its health and integrity in others. Criminal law has mechanisms for solving such conflicts (which can give rise to conflicting duties), when depending on the decision adopted a criminal offence is committed which affects the above-mentioned legally protected values: the defence of acting on necessity or in fulfilment of a duty. As is known, both defences are expressly recognized in the Spanish Criminal Code (section 8.7 and 8.11, respectively) [37].

5.  All these hypothetical, unjustified, compulsive interventions are an attack on individual liberty and merit penal sanction. Depending on the circumstances, they may constitute an offence of illegal detention, threat or coercion, with the last one being the most common. They do not always constitute a criminal offence, however; the compulsion required by the respective criminal category (in Spain, section 496 of the Criminal Code) may not always be present, for in these cases it is particularly easy for the intervention to be attributed to deception or error, thereby removing criminal liability, leaving only the possibility of civil or administrative liability. Second, it is very doubtful that these criminal categories can satisfactorily address the seriousness of the acts involved. Consequently, specific criminal categories should be provided for the more serious acts of disregard for the consent of the interested party in relation to the imposition of certain situations (e.g. an imposed pregnancy). The legal consequences of possible injuries to the fetus were already discussed earlier.

## 2.  Collective interests: the genetic integrity (and other similar values) of humanity

Although genetic manipulation and genetic engineering directly affect specific individuals, such actions on individual human genomes clearly have the transcendent capacity to affect the human species as a whole, its integrity, identity, individuality and inalterability, as well as the human legacy passed on to subsequent

---

[37] For more on this see Romeo Casabona, Carlos M., *La protección jurídica del concebido. El feto como paciente,* op. cit., pgs. 444 and ff.

generations. Hence the misgivings they awaken. Positive eugenics, genetic manipulation for racial or racist purposes, and those that in any way degrade the human species, say, by mixing it with animals, are widely rejected. There is concern with staving off any «modernized» resurgence of the eugenic trends which arose in the Anglo-Saxon world at the beginning of the century and the abuses committed under the German national-socialist regime. Even therapeutic genetic interventions, the legitimacy of which is generally accepted (with all the reservations mentioned above when affecting the germ-line) do not fail to stir concern and doubts as to their potential impact on altering the genome of the human species. That potential is openly discussed in relation to germ-line therapy. There is discussion of its possible use to fortify human resistance to certain diseases (e.g. cancer and other, viral diseases) or for negative eugenics, i.e. the elimination of pathological genetic material [38]. In keeping with the spirit of the above-mentioned moratorium until the consequences and effects of germ-line therapy are better known, it also seems advisable to refrain from definitive pronouncements on this eugenic proposal until we are in a better position to ascertain its possibilities and effects, and to control any undesirable effects if necessary. Judged in the hypothetical realm, however, the idea should be seen in a favourable light.

But the question which still stands is: are there new collective interests which merit legal protection and, if so, should the conducts that seriously endanger them be subject to penal sanction? We could cite (as yet only provisionally) certain interests which concern humanity as a whole [39], such as has been traditionally understood in connection with the right of peoples and the crime of genocide. This idea of the presence of a collective legal interest is what is to be highlighted here, without entering into consideration of whether it would at the same time entail individual legal interests and, above all, individual subjective rights (as we will now see is already being proposed), owing to the important and unforeseeable legal consequences to which they could give rise (e.g. as to the possessor of such rights, their scope and the persons thereby affected). These issues will nevertheless have to be contemplated in the immediate future. In any event, the way in which human genome interventions can affect and harm individual legal interests has been discussed earlier.

These generic values would serve to protect the inalterability of certain characteristics of the human species, its genetic variety

---

[38] For more on this see Eser, *La moderna medicina de la reproducción...*, op. cit., pg. 294.
[39] Lenoir, *Aux frontières de la vie: une éthique biomédicale à la françcaise*, T.I., op. cit., pg. 81, holds that «humankind is a value per se».

and plurality and, in the most extreme cases, the very survival of the human species, from the possible threats posed by eugenics or other biotechnological or genetic engineering propositions. At times the decision to provide protection may represent an instrument for at the same time protecting democratic values based on pluralism and equality, by preventing certain human beings from wielding dominion over others. It is well known that citizen indifference, homogeneity and docility have always been a temptation to the totalitarian state.

Although this line of argument needs to be explored more deeply, as a preliminary step I will outline some considerations which might be taken into account:

1.  The inalterability and intangibility of the human genetic heritage would give rise to the following prohibitions [40]: human genetic exchange (formation of hybrids); interspecies fertilization or interspecies transfer of embryos (from animals to human beings or vice versa) for any purpose or at any stage of development, except for certain time-limited diagnostic tests; the fusion of human pre-embryos or of interspecies pre-embryos (chimeras) for any purpose or at any stage of development; other actions aimed at altering human non-pathological genetic heritage. The last prohibition once again points to the need to distinguish between conditions which are pathological and those which are merely anomalous, different, rare or infrequent or slightly deviant [41]. These allusions to the normal and the pathological, which can only be mentioned here, are of pivotal importance to a reflection on future applications of genetic engineering. This reflection must not be confined to the sphere of biomedical analysis but taken up on the philosophical, sociological, ethical and legal terrain. The proposals put forward above with regard to germ-line gene therapy should also be taken into account in this connection, but I will here call special attention (as a clear illustration of the valuative and dialectical tensions which are potentially present and compel further reflection and discussion) to the fact that this emerging right to an unaltered genetic heritage could be opposed by a no less legitimate right to a healthy genetic heritage. Is this conflict real or apparent? The latter is most likely true; in reality both interests can be tended to, conciliated and even harmonized, but, as I have held throughout, only when future knowledge

---

[40] Valle Muñiz and González González, *Utilización abusiva de técnicas genéticas y Derecho Penal,* op. cit., pgs. 131 and ff.
[41] On this last aspect see Eser, *La moderna medicina de la reproducción e ingeniería genética. Aspectos legales y sociopolíticos desde el punto de vist Alemán,* op. cit., pg. 291; Knoppers, *Human Dignity and Genetic Heritage,* op. cit., pgs. 43 and ff.

has allowed us to more precisely understand the effects of intervention in the germinal line. In any event, this reflection only aims to stress that defence of an absolute right to an unaltered genetic heritage, if not nuanced, could bring to naught the benefits which will surely be obtained with gene therapy.

In connection with some of these questions, the Council of Europe's Recommendation of January 26th 1982 [42] asked that the catalogue of human rights include «the intangibility of genetic inheritance vis-a-vis artificial interventions» and that the necessary protection be provided by the adoption of the corresponding laws. The International Criminal Law Association, for its part, proposes that this right be protected by law, and that the transfer of human gametes for non-therapeutic purposes be prohibited. The association expressly advocates criminalization of experiments aimed at generating hybrids or chimeras through the fusion of human and animal cells [43]. These examples attest to the presence of interests affecting humanity, taken as a whole and as such worthy of maximum protection, which (as is suggested in the aforesaid Recommendation) could give rise to «new» rights of man, without prejudice to the fact that such a proposal requires profound debate and reconsideration of its actual significance and scope, in the absence of which, such a position, interpreted along different lines, could foster international conflicts and, even, the development of eugenic arguments contrary to the proposal's objectives [44].

2. The identity and uniqueness of human beings, as the right to individuality, to be oneself and different from others, accepting the complexity and variability of human nature: the creation of identical human beings by means of cloning [45] or other genetic procedures for any purpose (race selection, creation of «specialized» human beings or humanoids). Consider that genetic diversity can decisively contribute to preserving the human species in the face of infectious disease or other kinds of external agents to which a given genetic configuration might prove vulnerable.

---

[42] Council of Europe Recommendation number 934 of 1982.

[43] International Criminal Law Association, in Resolutions 6.1, 6.8 and 6.10, respectively, adopted at its *XIV International Congress on Criminal Law.*

[44] Knoppers, in *Human Dignity and Genetic Heritage,* op. cit., pgs. 29 and ff, warns of the risks which could arise from the assumption of that right, with highly interesting arguments which cannot be covered here.

[45] In this regard see the International Criminal Law Association, Resolution 6.9 of the *XIV International Congress on Criminal Law.*

3. Privation of the double genetic endowment, and thus of the male and female genetic line, to which could be added the potential risks to the health of the person so procreated: parthenogenesis, or the generation of a human being from only one gamete (egg); generation of embryos from gametes of persons of the same sex (xx, female: xx, xy, male); and from a different standpoint, ectogenesis, the development of an individual in a laboratory, although today this seems impossible.

4. Protection of the survival of the human species: the creation of biological or other weapons using genetic engineering; alterations of the environment by means of genetic engineering, particularly through the release of genetically modified microorganisms, so as to make it dangerous for or incompatible with human life.

Without preempting the further discussion and development warranted by these issues (including the identification of the legal interests involved), in principle, all these conducts are seriously detrimental to humanity and should be criminalized, provided we may assume a general consensus to exist in this respect. I will not take up here whether the corresponding criminal categories should be configured as injurious offences or, in some cases, as hazardous offences. Nor will I study whether the Criminal Code should include provisions in respect of all these conducts now or wait until they are scientifically feasible. At the same time these considerations serve as a reminder of the importance of reaching the broadest possible consensus in the international community in order to establish consistent guidelines accepted by all nations. This will prevent permissiveness or negligence by some states from giving rise to «genetic havens» and to achieve two objectives: to avert aberrant experiments and applications deemed unacceptable by the states and prevent the generation of inequalities in the scientific community with respect to research possibilities and resources.

## Outlook for the definition of new criminal offences concerning certain deviations arising from human genetic interventions

1. There are a number of countries whose legislation now includes offences directly related to assisted reproduction techniques. Far fewer address the activities typically related to genetic manipulation. The United Kingdom, for example,

enacted the Act on Human Fertilization and Embryology of November 1st 1990 [46], which includes a prolix catalogue of offences (section 41) and provides for sentence of up to 10 years imprisonment. The German legislature approved the Embryo Protection Act (*Gesetz zum Schutz von Embryonen-Embryonenschutzgestez*) of December 13th 1990 [47]. The latter is a rather singular penal law, for eight (sections 1 to 7 and 11) of its 13 sections lay down criminal categories and another includes an administrative violation. The penalties can reach a maximum of five years imprisonment in the most serious cases (artificial alteration of the genetic information in a human germinal cell, or its use for fertilization, section 5; creation of human clones and their implantation in a woman, section 6; the formation of hybrids and chimeras, as well as their implantation in a woman or animal, or the implantation of a human embryo in an animal, section 7). It also provides criminal sanctions for: sex selection for purposes unrelated to the prevention of Duchenne-type muscular dystrophy or comparable serious diseases in the future child, requiring in certain cases a report by the competent authority (section 3); the disposal of an embryo formed outside the body or extracted from the uterus before implantation is concluded; development of an embryo outside the body for purposes other than impregnation (section 2); and other practices, including diverse procedures which can give rise to extra embryos or supernumerary embryos, fertilization of an egg for purposes other than permitting a pregnancy in the woman who provides the egg, and surrogate maternity (section 1). In summary, the Act does not seek to regulate and guide the diverse practices it addresses, but instead describes and sanctions criminally prohibited actions, from which the sphere of what is permitted can be logically deduced. Along with this criticism of the method pursued, the other main criticism is that the principle of minimal criminal law intervention may have been violated. Some of the prohibited activities could have perhaps been better regulated under administrative law. Furthermore, the criteria adopted are more restrictive than those applied in other European countries, possibly placing German researchers at a disadvantage in this field [48]. In any case, even though the exclusively criminal penal content of this law strikes me as overly rigorous, it is much

---

[46] See Stellpflug, Marting H., *Embryonenschutz in England*, «Zeitschrift zür Rechtspolitik», 1992, pgs. 4 and ff.

[47] See Deutsch, Erwin, *Embryonenschutz in Deutschland*, «Neue Juristiche Wochenschrift», 1991, pgs. 721 and ff; Geilen, Gerd: *Zum Strafschutz an der Anfangsgrenze des Lebens*, «Zeitschrift für die gesamte Strafrechtswissenschaft», 1991, pgs. 289 and ff.

[48] Geilen, *Zum Strafschutz an der Anfangsgrenze des Lebens*, op. cit., 840 and ff.

clearer and more decisive in its handling of the conducts it prohibits –however questionably in some cases– than the comparable laws of Britain and Spain (the latter, as we know, do not include criminal offences), marked by a (probably calculated) ambiguity and uncertainty.

2.  In Spain the government submitted to Parliament a Criminal Code Bill (1992). Debate was postponed by the government's recent dissolution of parliament. In relation to the two human genetic offences contained in the two above-mentioned laws of 1988, the draft code seeks to penalize some particularly egregious practices: 1) the manipulation of human genes so as to alter a person's «vital constitution» for purposes other than the elimination or diminishment of serious disease or disability, whether by wilful misconduct or reckless negligence (section 167.1 and 167.3); 2) any other manipulation of human genes performed in violation of established legal provisions (section 167.2); 3) the application of genetic technology to determine a person's sex without the consent of the progenitors (section 168); 4) the donation, use or destruction of human embryos or fetuses, or their cells, tissues or organs, other than in the circumstances authorized by the law (section 169); 5) artificial insemination of a woman without her consent (section 170). In addition, the proposed code also defines injuries to the fetus as a criminal offence in the following terms: actions which, by any means or procedure, cause in a fetus injury or disease seriously impairing its normal development, or provokes therein a serious physical or mental disability, whether intentionally (section 165) or through reckless negligence (section 166), although the pregnant woman shall not be punished in the latter case. Most of these categories are intended to specify penal sanction for the prohibitions set out in the Acts of 1988. Not all the offences entail genetic manipulation, as some are specifically related to assisted reproduction techniques. The offence of negligence would potentially be applicable to manipulations of human genes for whatever purpose, including (since it is not specified) therapeutic, which seems sound.

Although it is beyond the purpose of this paper to enter into a critical appraisal of these proposed criminal code provisions, I will offer some partial reflections. First, the inclusion of these offences in the future Criminal Code should be viewed favourably (without here stating an opinion as to the most appropriate place for their inclusion, the Criminal Code proper or in a special criminal law), as an intent by the legislature to criminally sanction the most grievous practices relating to undesirable applications of biotechnology, but always subject to the principle of minimum intervention. Nevertheless, the translation of that intent into specific criminal categories has not been very fortunate. I will mention some examples. The reference to «vital constitutional type» introduces an indeterminate legal concept, generating legal uncertainty, as its meaning cannot be deduced from the law or from biomedical sciences. It is not a biological or genetic concept. It probably owes to reasons of legislative economy, but a more exhaustive treatment is inevitable and the demands of legal certainty require a more detailed taxonomy of specific criminal categories. This is in consonance with the «principle of legality» mentioned earlier («no crime without a law, no punishment without a law»). But even accepting the terminology of the draft code, it is even more difficult to distinguish between «vital constitutional type», «vital type» (expression employed in section 167.3 for reckless negligence) and «any other manipulation of human genes, performed in violation of the established legal provisions». Their systematic interpretation leads to the conclusion that there is no difference between the first two expressions, assuming that the word «constitutional» was inadvertently omitted in the second. And as we cannot ascertain the precise meaning of these expressions, neither can we reliably demarcate the scope of the third, which, moreover, obliges the courts to determine which of the established legal prohibitions (under Acts 35/1988 and 42/1988) entail manipulation of human genes and which do not. In this respect, the expression proposed during the parliamentary debate as an alternative to vital constitutional type («genotype») [49] is somewhat of an improvement but does not suffice to clear up the source of the ambiguity.

As for the crime of determining a person's sex without the consent of the progenitors, «determine» should presumably be understood to mean select not ascertain. In this case, since it is already generally prohibited by Act 35/1988, but permitted in some cases (to prevent diseases linked to the sex chromosome), the provision should be amended to include «except in those circumstances authorized by law». This leaves unresolved the doubt as to whether this criminal provision transgresses the principle of minimum intervention. If so, and if possible, it should not be classified as a crime of coercion, without prejudice to the fact that the latter criminal category needs to undergo a revision in order to better generally adapt and match it to the relevant genetic interventions in relation with certain atypical coercive conducts in the currently applicable Criminal Code [50].

---

[49] See *Official Gazette of the Spanish Parliament's,* Congress of Deputies, Series A, nos. 102-10, pgs. 536 and 623.
[50] Attempts have been made to improve the Bill's wording by means of amendments designed to differentiate the conducts authorized by the Act

In relation to the donation, use or destruction of human embryos and fetuses, etc., the general reference to the Act (apparently to Act 42/1988) could lead to criminalizing minor violations of no relevance to the intended protection. Moreover, that same general reference to the Act, without specifying which one, could give rise to overlap (conflict of laws) between the destruction of human embryos and fetuses as prohibited under section 169 and the crime of abortion. Nor should we rule out the possibility of conflicts arising between laws regarding genetic manipulation and those involving crimes of bodily injuries. The inclusion in this article of the offence of «those who fertilize human ova for any purpose other than human procreation», as proposed above, should be supported, but it is still not adequate, when considering the dubious classification under the currently operative legal provisions regulating these matters of the act of transferring to a woman lawfully manipulated zygotes and of maintaining an embryo *in vitro* beyond the 14th day of development, as well as of other actions, such as cloning, which strictly speaking do not involve genome alteration.

In summary, in addition to the specific foregoing criticisms, I think that the blanket criminal law method adopted in sections 167 and 169 should not be pursued in connection with such an important subject as genetic manipulation. Although undesirable, this method is at times inevitable, but I believe that its counterproductive aspects are intensified in this area. The prohibited practices need to be exactly identified and given a detailed description, even at the likely expense of an overly casuistic rendering. But above all, and as I have often stated, the legal interest (or legal interests) to be protected must be first well profiled, something which I believe has not yet been adequately achieved, as is suggested by the very heading given to the section on the offences here under consideration, which contraposes genetic manipulations to those involving embryos and fetuses.

---

from unauthorized practices, and by replacing the unfortunate term «to determine» (section 168: «Application of genetic technology or other techniques to select the sex of human offspring, in circumstances other than authorized by law, shall be punished... The more severe half of the sentence shall be imposed in cases where the progenitors did not give their consent. Sex selection performed in the circumstances authorized by law and without the consent of the progenitors shall be punished...». See *Official Gazette of the Congress of Deputies*, op. cit.). I continue to believe that this provision is counter to the principle of minimum intervention, it being sufficient to invoke the administrative sanctions provided for in Act 35/1988, including temporary closure of the centre (under the General Health Act, chapter VI), or the coercion offence, where applicable. Nor is it easy to understand the importance attributed to parental consent, given that the parents have no legally recognized authority in this respect and it has no effect (as opposed to what occurs with the abortion offence) on the fact of having a healthy child.

## Brief final considerations

The ideas, reflections, judgements, suggestions and conclusions presented throughout this paper must of necessity be considered as only provisional. The area before us is too complex for it to be otherwise. Despite the rapid advances and understanding attained, this field of exploration is still in its preliminary stages and hence our grasp of its potential and possibilities is likewise only beginning. Such precaution is further warranted by the fact that the future of humanity is more obviously affected by these developments than by those in any other area.

Hence the fundamental task before us is to remain alert to the ongoing investigations and their results, to persist in multidisciplinary debate, to provide legal instruments and agreements at the international level, to be cautious in legislative policy and open and willing to review and revise as necessary the criteria thus far adopted. If we are to assume that investigation of the human genome should not be curbed, we must also accept that it has to be controlled and that its possible applications and derivations must be analysed in each case. This should not necessarily stir any misgivings from the scientific community, for the future of humanity concerns us all. And, finally, while we can trust that the future may free humanity of serious hereditary disease, we should also adopt safeguards designed to prevent the resurgence of eugenics movements of the past which, if successful, this time around would now find available to them technical resources of irreparable effectiveness and precision.

# LEGAL LIMITS OF GENETIC EXPERIMENTATION

*Robert T. Stephan* [*]

Attorney General, State of Kansas, United States of America.

The development of genetics has brought hope to society in five areas.

1. Mankind can envisage control over its own destiny.

2. Predictability and control over genetic disorder.

3. Relief from gene therapy for catastrophic illnesses.

4. Improvement in the preservation and growth of plants, animals and food upon which the human race depends for its survival.

5. A more predictable and accurate use of curative medicine.

Increased concerns by professionals, both private and public, as well as the general population is increasing. The concerns center mainly on the protection of individual liberties and protection against permanent alteration of the human genome through germ-cell transfer therapy. Within the ambit of concerns is the reality of the situation that so-called «Genetic Therapy» is largely expe-

---

[*] Narrator.

rimental and research is, and can be, carried out on both an individual person or on human cells.

It was the Nazi atrocities in the name of scientific research that energized the realization of the need for rules and regulations. The Nuremburg Code and the Helsinki Declaration are examples of international rules. Legal rules in regard to experimentation on human beings generally require free and informed consent and a reasonably prudent ratio balancing risk and benefit. Society demands that scientific experimentation complies with legal and ethical concerns.

There is a delicate balance between the need for laws that protect individual liberty and the need for scientific research to be free from unnecessary restriction and the bureaucratic dictation of the principles of research and experimentation.

The use of criminal law to regulate genetic research should be used sparingly and with great caution. In the area of criminal law such enactments should only be utilized where the procedure acknowledged is reprehensible to society generally. It is preferable to control appropriate areas of genetic research through civil and administrative law. Responsible self-regulation is the best course of action to guide genetic research. If it is responsibly done, there will be less interest in governmental interference.

There seemed to be a general consensus that intervention into genetic research should be done cautiously and gradually. One theory advanced was that the first step in regulation should be ethical self-control. In this way there will be less limitation on scientific advancement. The second step would be to look to governmental power centered mainly in the health section. The health and welfare section of the government could exercise civil authority through the enactment of qualification standards, monitoring of activities and preventive limitations. This approach would allow public power to promote and unduly restrict scientific research.

If ethical self-regulation and/or administrative regulation fail, then the last recourse would be the enactment of a criminal code and this should be on a limited basis. Among others, some values to be protected are human dignity-equality and the integrity of the new-born.

There are numerous public views on the proper way to deal with genetic research. Some say that it should be prevented, others say there should be a moratorium and others say nothing should be done.

There was substantial discussion of Spanish law. Some statements were made that Spain had strong administrative laws that could penalize through the closing of a laboratory, a heavy fine or some other civil penalty and that a criminal law was not necessary. There was a contrary opinion given that administrative law was not enough and there should criminal sanctions. Naturally, abortion, when live beings and the quality of the foetus was mentioned by several of the speakers.

Several expressed concern about the difference in the laws of European countries. Because of the closeness of common borders, one of the speakers suggested that there should be a common European approach and attempts should be made to enact uniform laws among European Nations applying to genetic research.

Applications of regulations need more focus before decisions are made to prohibit genetic information from being disseminated. One speaker stated that a careful study should be conducted before legal enactments were endorsed. For example, he said advances in genetics made possible by the Human Genome Initiative will have a major impact on reproductive decision-making. At the most basic level, these choices involve the limits and scope of procreative liberty. Accordingly concerned people should:

1. Evaluate the extent to which ethical and legal concepts of procreative liberty entitle individuals/couples to use genetic knowledge to avoid offspring with genetic disease at premarital, preconception, preimplantation and prenatal stages of decision-making.

2. Evaluate the extent to which ethical and legal concepts of procreative liberty entitle individuals/couples to ignore genetic knowledge in decisions to procreate, and thus risk producing offspring with genetic diseases.

   The excellent presenters submitted information that would bring forward a spirited debate. Unfortunately as a result of time limitations, there was no group discussion of the issues raised.

**PAPERS**

# GENETIC MANIPULATION OFFENCES AND UNCONSENTED ARTIFICIAL INSEMINATION IN THE CRIMINAL CODE BILL OF 1992

## Antonio Cuerda Riezu

Professor of Criminal Law, University of León. Spain.

### Introduction

One of the most outstanding novelties of the Criminal Code Organic Bill of 1992 is the inclusion of several sections dealing with genetic manipulation and unconsented artificial insemination offences. These provisions were the first attempt in Spain to set down certain legal limits on what has been called genetic engineering, that is, to define specific crimes for the most dangerous conducts in this field. As is known, the early dissolution of the parliament resulted in the Bill being shelved before it could be approved, and its future is now uncertain. Nevertheless, it may be assumed that the next –and hopefully definitive– Criminal Code Bill will be based on the 1992 version analysed herein, so this analysis of the proposed criminal law provisions will not be completely fruitless.

The reflections which follow primarily focus on the draft regulations, but also touch on general aspects of genetic techniques. The proposed Bill will therefore serve as a platform from which I can raise questions and propose some specific solutions.

Now to understand –and criticize, where such is the case– the section of the proposed Code which deals with these matters, it

will be indispensable to first briefly review the historical evolution
of genetic techniques from the standpoint of criminal law. Once
this background has been given, I will turn my attention to the
proposed Bill itself.

## Historical background

The year 1988 was a watershed in the legal history of genetic
techniques, due to the enactment of two laws regulating the subject matter. It will therefore be useful to distinguish between the
situation prior to and subsequent to these Acts.

### a)   The pre-1988 stage

In the late 1960s the application of medical techniques designed
to overcome sterility in couples of childbearing age began to take
hold in Spain. These techniques are basically artificial insemination
and *in vitro* fertilization. The first Spanish semen bank was set up
in 1978. Somewhat later, in 1984, Spain witnessed its first birth
of a person born as the result of a pregnancy achieved by means
of *in vitro* fertilization and embryo transfer.

Logically enough, this development was in large part brought
about by the medical advances underlying the advent of these
techniques. But there also existed –and today still exists– a social
backdrop favourable to the spread of these methods. I am referring to a circumstance seen in most western countries, a certain
social pressure to have children. I would call this social pressure
«maternity and paternity compulsion», perhaps a response to
weak demographic growth in the occidental world. In any event,
raising children is associated with a measure of happiness, as if
having offspring necessarily implied good fortune for human
beings. Correlative to this pressure is the inverse phenomenon,
that is, a rejection or «penalization» of remaining single or of
childless couples; a conscious decision not to have children is not
well seen. In view of these sociological facts it is not surprising
that Spanish couples plagued by infertility should decide to put
themselves in a doctor's hands. Nor should it be forgotten that
the late 1970s witnessed the start of an economic upturn in our
country, a circumstance which likely influenced in the increased
use of these techniques, given their relatively high cost.

There was a legal vacuum in this area, that is, there was no legal
regulation of genetic techniques. But this does not mean that the
law did not take a stand on these techniques, declining to accept
or reject them. Quite the contrary. Our legal system recognized
the principle that «what is not prohibited is permitted». Since

these techniques were not illegalized under criminal or administrative law, their application per se was understood to be perfectly legal. Only in cases where their application resulted in an injury or danger to a legal right protected under criminal or administrative law was a sanction warranted. Thus, for example, if an artificial insemination procedure was improperly performed and the woman rendered definitively infertile as a result, the responsible party could be liable to sanction for a negligent injuries offence, but not for practising the insemination itself; and if the person who performed the insemination defectively was a public employee, he or she may have incurred an administrative offence and therefore be liable to administrative sanction.

This legal vacuum, however, sparked a genuine clamour for legal regulation of these techniques clearly delineating between lawful and wrongful activities. Doctors, members of parliament, and jurists called for legal provisions to mark the limits of these genetic methods and provide for their multiple consequences and implications, such as, for example, in paternity and other filiation disputes. In response to these calls for regulation, in 1984 the then member of Parliament Mr Rodríguez Sahagún moved that a Congressional Committee be formed to explore genetic techniques and their consequences. The motion was carried and the Committee, chaired by Congressman Marcelo Palacios, issued an in-depth multidisciplinary report –generally known as the «Palacios Report»– of a high scientific calibre. The Palacios Report was approved by a Plenary Session of the Congress of Deputies in 1986 [1], and served as the basis for two Bills drafted by the Socialist Party Parliamentary Group and enacted in 1988 [2]. These two new laws marked the beginning of a new legal period, which I will review below.

### b)   The post-1988 stage. The relevant legislation

The first of these statutes was Act 35 of November 22nd 1988 on Assisted Reproduction Techniques [3]. The second was Act 42 of December 28th 1988 on the donation and use of human embryos and fetuses or their cells, tissues or organs [4]. On February

---

[1] The report was entitled «Informe de la Comisión Especial de estudio de fecundación "in vitro" y la inseminación artificial humanas» [Report of the Special Committee for the study of human *in vitro* fertilization and artificial insemination], published by the Congress of Deputies, Madrid, 1987.

[2] I have dealt with these Bills in two other studies: Cuerda Riezu, «Límites jurídico-penales de las nuevas técnicas genéticas» [«Criminal law limits on the new genetic techniques»], *Anuario de Derecho penal y Ciencias penales (ADPCP)*, v. 41, 1988, pgs. 247-251; and «Otra vez sobre nuevas técnicas genéticas y Derecho penal» [«New genetic techniques and criminal law revisited»], *ADPCP*, v. 41, 1988, pgs. 413-429.

[3] Published in *BOE (Boletín Oficial del Estado* (Official State Gazette) no. 282, November 24th 1988; errors rectified in *BOE* no. 284, November 26th 1984.

[4] Published in *BOE* no. 314, December 31st 1988.

24th 1989 the Popular Party Parliamentary Group filed an appeal with the Constitutional Court challenging the constitutionality of the Assisted Reproduction Techniques Act, with respect to which the Court has not yet handed down an decision [5].

The two statutes have distinct scopes of application. The differences reside in the biological subject matter they address and the medical techniques they regulate. With respect to biological subject matter the distinction is as follows: the Assisted Reproduction Techniques Act refers to gametes and pre-embryos. Gametes are human sexual cells, that is, spermatozoa and ovules. The term pre-embryo designates the period from the ovum's fertilization to its attachment to the uterine wall, which usually takes place around the 14th day after fecundation. The Act on the donation and use of human embryos and fetuses covers the embryo and the fetus stages. The embryonic stage spans from uterine attachment through the third month of pregnancy; the fetal stage runs from the fourth month of pregnancy until the moment of birth.

The differences also hold with respect to the medical techniques regulated by the two Acts. The Assisted Reproduction Techniques Act refers to artificial insemination and *in vitro* fertilization, *in vitro* fertilization with embryo transfer, and to intratubaric transfer of gametes. For its part, the second of the aforementioned Acts regulates the donation and use of embryos, fetuses and their cells, tissues or organs.

The legal situation arising from the enactment of these two law may be said to be that genetic techniques are generally legal but subject to limits. I will now go on to explore both aspects.

It is my opinion that the generic legality of genetic techniques is perfectly correct. There are certain fundamental rights and liberties recognized under the Spanish Constitution and by other international human rights declarations that support and uphold the principle of generic legality. Human genetics investigation thus finds support in the right to scientific production [6]. The goal of alleviating or overcoming human infertility, which is the goal pursued by these techniques, is justified by the right to marry, the right to found a family, and the correlative obligation of the State to protect the family [7]. Moreover, since infertility is a disease, procedures aimed at its mitigation find support in the Constitu-

---

[5] See Palacios, *Reproducción Asistida. Discurso y Recurso*, 1990, passim.
[6] Article 20.1, *b)* of the Spanish Constitution.
[7] Articles 32 and 39.1 of the Spanish Constitution. Article 16.1 of the Universal Declaration of Human Rights. Article 23.2 of the International Agreement on Civil and Political Rights. Article 10.1 of the International Agreement on Economic, Social and Culture Rights.

tion's recognition of the right to protection of health [8]. In short, there exist legal norms of the highest order buttressing the general legality principle.

Nevertheless, that legality is not absolute, but subject to limits. And this is perfectly logical because the aforementioned fundamental rights and liberties are circumscribed by certain limitations. It should therefore come as no surprise that both Acts define offences and provide sanctions in connection with the cases where those limits are transgressed. Now, it has to be made perfectly clear that the offences and sanctions set down in both statutes are administrative and in no case criminal. This means that under current Spanish law there are no crimes, with their corresponding penal sanctions, for cases involving misuse of genetic manipulation. Or to put it more colloquially: nobody goes to jail for this. Of course, this holds so long as no other offence which is defined in the Criminal Code is committed, such as would be the case in the aforementioned example of the woman left infertile by a negligent artificial insemination.

In any event, one should not be misled into thinking that the administrative offences and sanctions provided for in the two statutes are lenient. Quite the contrary: they usually involve major offences, subject to fairly severe punishment. The fines range from half a million to one hundred million pesetas. The conducts which are administratively outlawed include, by way of example, the use of embryos, fetuses or their cells for the manufacture of cosmetic products; keeping fertilized ova alive *in vitro* beyond the 14th day period following fecundation; cloning, that is, the production of genetically identical individuals; the production of hybrid beings, half animal, half human, etc.

## The Criminal Code Bill of 1992

In the foregoing section [2.*b*)] I analysed the situation under current Spanish law. I will now refer to the 1992 Criminal Code Bill, which aimed to modify the status quo and introduce some criminal offences relating to genetic techniques. I will first take up the conducts which according to the Bill should be considered as criminal, and then offer a critical assessment of these regulations.

### a) *Criminal conducts in relation with genetic manipulation*

Leaving aside the abortion offence (sections 150 to 154), a striking feature of the Bill is its novel regulation of injuries to the

---

[8] Article 43.1 of the Spanish Constitution.

fetus (sections 165 and 166), categories not included in the currently applicable Criminal Code. They define the crime of impairing the physical or mental health of the fetus, with the latter term being understood in the broad non-technical sense, that is, as spanning all stages in the formation of a human being inside the mother's uterus. I proposed the creation of this offence some time ago, as the current abortion offence applies to actions involving the destruction of the product of conception, but not to conducts leading to the impairment of its health, impairment which may last beyond birth. This offence may be accompanied by mens rea or wilful intent or by gross negligence [9].

The Bill also includes the crime of genetic manipulation (section 167). The genetic manipulations receiving severest punishment are those which alter the vital constitutional type. Alteration of vital constitutional type may be committed with wilful misconduct or gross negligence. It is not clear whether this crime is applicable to actions involving pre-embryos, embryos or fetuses only, or if it can also be applied to actions carried out on persons after birth, as the latest medical advances seem to indicate is possible.

Another behaviour deemed criminal under the proposed Code is selection of the offspring's sex without the consent of the progenitors (section 168). This involves purposeful selection of the child's sex by a third party without the authorization of the future parents.

Section 169 of the Bill defines as a criminal offence the donation, use or destruction of human embryos or fetuses, or their cells, tissues or organs where such conduct is not authorized by the law. What this provision actually does is to convert into criminal offences –that is, into crimes– all the administrative offences set out in the aforementioned Act 42/1988.

And lastly, the Bill makes provisions for conducts involving artificial insemination of a woman without her consent (section 170).

### b) Assessment of the Bill within its scope

In view of the regulation which the proposed Criminal Code Bill of 1992 intends to introduce, certain questions come to mind.

---

[9] It is highly questionable whether the Bill permits punishment of fetal injuries produced by minor negligence. Although section 600.3 seemingly allows such a conclusion, that precept is included in Title I of Book III of the Bill, dedicated to «Offences against persons», and an embryo or fetus is obviously not a «person» in the legal sense.

*1. Is the criminalization of actions involving the new genetic techniques necessary?*

In order to answer this question we must first compare and relate the two 1988 Acts with the Bill's regulation. Such comparison reveals the following: each and every one of the conducts within the scope of the Bill already constitute administrative offences provided for in one of the two statutes already in force. Thus there could arise a double intervention by the State in the sanctioning of these conducts: there is administrative intervention, on the one hand, assessing heavy fines for the offences, and, on the other, there is penal intervention, providing prison sentences and other punishment for those same offences. Now, while it is true that pursuant to the constitutional principle *be bis in idem* a person cannot be subject to a criminal and administrative sanctions for the same offence, such double intervention can raise coordination problems between both sanctioning spheres, the penal and administrative.

This dual criminal and administrative law intervention appears in the Bill in a concealed, even disguised form. Section 168 punishes sex selection in offspring by means of genetic techniques «without the consent of the progenitors», seemingly implying that sex selection with the consent of the progenitors is permitted. But this impression turns out to be incorrect, because sex selection is prohibited under administrative law. In fact, the Assisted Reproduction Techniques Act provides administrative sanctions for sex selection in general; only permitting it where such selection is done for therapeutic purposes to avoid transmission of hereditary diseases [10].

In my opinion, administrative sanctions are sufficient for cases of application of genetic techniques which transgress the legally permitted limits.

Valle Muñiz and González González have expressed their opinion to the contrary. For those authors administrative sanctions are not sufficient in this area. They believe that the importance of the interests involved demands certain conducts be criminalized and punished the corresponding penal sanctions. They furthermore hold that administrative sanctions are not effective deterrents to the medical and pharmaceutical industries, whose economic power is such that administrative fines would not impede pursuit of the prohibited conducts [11].

---

[10] Sections 12.1, 20.2, B), n) and First Final Provision d) of the Act on Assisted Reproduction Techniques.

[11] See Valle Muñiz/González González, «Utilización abusiva de técnicas genéticas y Derecho penal» [«Misuse of genetic techniques and criminal law»], *Poder Judicial*, no. 26, June 1992, pg. 11, note 5, pgs. 117, 125 and ff, and 132.

I would answer the following to those objections. First, I do not deny the importance of the interests at stake in connection with the new genetic procedures. But I also believe very important interests are involved with respect to human beings after birth, and yet they are not offered as much protection. All the controls and precautions established for gametes, pre-embryos, embryos and fetuses do not apply with the same intensity for human beings after they are born. One draws the impression that the unborn are more fully protected than the born, which I believe is wrong. Second, the administrative sanctions provided for the offences defined in the 1988 statutes include not only heavy fines –from half a million to one hundred million pesetas– but also, for very serious offences, the closing of the establishment, facility or service where the prohibited conduct was carried out [12]. I think these sanctions do exercise a considerable deterrent effect for medical and pharmaceutical companies when they consider the possibility of contravening legal and regulatory provisions, especially when they run the risk of having their business premises closed down.

I therefore remain convinced that new criminal categories are not needed to impede improper genetic techniques, and that the current administrative provisions are sufficient.

2.  *Has the Bill made a reasonable selection of the conducts to be criminalized under the proposed Code?*
While I believe that new criminal categories are not necessary in this area, the question may be asked whether the proposed Code has made the most appropriate choice of conducts to illegalize. In this regard it should be recalled that a tenet of criminal jurisprudence is that criminal sanctions are in order only for those actions thought to represent a grievous threat to the most important societal interests. This is referred to as the principle of minimum intervention of criminal law.

Now, by the light of this principle the choice of criminalized conducts made by the Bill strikes me as highly questionable. There are very grievous actions which are not considered as criminal offences under the proposed Code. The creation of hybrids (half human, half animal), cloning human beings, or using genetic engineering for military purposes have been left out of the scope of the Criminal Code Bill. Furthermore, I have already indicated that the Bill considers unconsented artificial insemination to be a crime. But why then is unconsented *in vitro* fertilization and embryo transfer not likewise considered a criminal offence? A similar line of reasoning holds with respect to the criminalization of irregu-

---

[12] In accordance with section 36 of Act 14 of April 25th 1986, the General Health Act *(BOE* no. 102 of April 29th 1986).

larities in the donation, use or destruction of human embryos or fetuses and of their components. Strange then that no similar criminal sanction is contemplated for irregularities in the extraction and transplant of organs from human beings after birth [13].

*3. Is the duplication of provisions brought about by the proposed Code correct?*
Proper legislative technique demands that no more than one criminal law precept be applicable to the same conduct; otherwise there may arise problems of coordination in the enforcement of the redundant preceptas.

Yet the proposed Code incurs redundancies which raise difficult problems of construction. Section 169, for example, refers to the «destruction of human embryos and fetuses», a conduct which substantially coincides with the crime of abortion. The one possible way to differentiate the two offences would be to construe section 169 as referring to the destruction of human embryos and fetuses obtained *in vitro,* that is, in the laboratory, and abortion as consisting in the destruction of the product of conception originated in the maternal uterus. Another example of duplication: the same section 169 also refers to the «destruction of cells, tissues or organs of human embryos and fetuses»; but such acts are also covered by the offence of lesions to the fetus, set out elsewhere in the Bill, namely in section 165.

*4. Other questions*
In relation to the topic dealt with in the foregoing point, the following question arises: What criminal category applies to the conduct of a person who performs genetic manipulation of an embryo or fetus which is later born alive? The difficulty lies in the possibility of several different classifications: attempted abortion, injuries to the fetus, and genetic manipulation. The first step in choosing from among these possibilities would in principle appear to be application of a subjective criterion: if the intention is to terminate the pregnancy, it should preferably be classified as an attempted abortion. But if the intention is not to end the pregnancy but that the fetus be born with a physical or mental disability, then it would be a matter of choosing between an offence of genetic manipulation or one of injuries to the fetus. Here, two differentiation criteria are possible: 1) that the injuries to the fetus offence can only be committed when the fetus is in the mother's uterus, whereas genetic manipulation pertains to *in*

---

[13] In fact, Executive Act 30 of October 7th 1979 on the extraction and transplant of organs *(BOE* no. 266, November 6th 1979), which regulates this area with respect to human beings after birth does not set out any criminal categories or punishment, or any specific administrative sanctions. But violations of the provisions of the Act may be sanctioned administratively under section 35 of the General Health Act.

*vitro*, i.e. laboratory, manipulations; or, 2) to hold that the two offences are not differentiated by the type or site of intervention, and interpret all manipulation as a lesion, only more specific, and therefore of priority classification.

The complexity of this question once again shows that the Bill needs, at the least, a more precise rendering insofar as concerns offences stemming from the new genetic techniques. In my opinion the future Criminal Code should dispense with such criminal offences.

## References

**Albácar López, J. L.:** «Aspectos jurídicos de la manipulación genética: inseminación artificial» [«Legal aspects of genetic manipulation: artificial insemination»], *La Ley*, 1985, vol. 4, pg. 1051 and ff.

**Araújo Junior, J. M.:** «Técnicas biomédicas y Derecho penal» [«Biomedical techniques and criminal law»], *Revista Jurídica de Castilla-La Mancha*, no. 7, 1989, pg. 201-219, translated into Spanish by Rocío Cantarero Bandrés.

**Parliamentary Assembly of the Council of Europe:** «Recomendación relativa a la ingeniería genética» [«Recommendation regarding genetic engineering»], *Boletín del Ilustre Colegio de Abogados de Madrid*, 1986, no. 1, pg. 101 and ff, translated into Spanish by Martínez Val.

**Barbero Santos, M.:** «Fecundación asistida e ingeniería genética. Consideraciones jurídicos-penales» [«Assisted fertilization and genetic engineering. Criminal law considerations»], *Revista Jurídica de Castilla-La Mancha*, no. 7, 1989, pgs. 43-53. Also published in Marino Barbero Santos (editor), *Ingeniería genética y reproducción asistida*, Madrid, 1989, pgs. 305-320.

**Batlle, M.:** «La eutelegenesia y el Derecho» [«Eutelegenics and the law»], *Revista General de Legislación y Jurisprudencia*, vol. 17, 1949, pgs. 657 and ff.

**Bueno Arús, F.:** «El consentimiento del paciente» [«Patient consent»] in *Derecho Médico* (edited by Martínez Calcerrada), vol 1, Madrid, pgs. 273-296 (especially 292 and ff).

**Cuello Calon, E.:** *Tres temas penales (El aborto criminal. El problema penal de la eutanasia. El aspecto penal de la fedundación artifical)*, Barcelona, 1955.

**Cuello Calon, E.:** «En torno a la inseminación artificial en el campo penal» [«Artificial insemination and criminal law»], *Anuario de Derecho Penal y Ciencias Penales*, vol. 14, 1961, pgs. 195-206.

**Cuerda Riezu, A.**: «Límites juridicopenales a las nuevas técnicas genéticas» [«Criminal law limits on the new genetic techniques»], *Anuario de Derecho Penal y Ciencias Penales*, vol. 41, 1988, pgs. 247-251.

**Cuerda Riezu, A.**: «Otra vez sobre nuevas técnicas genéticas y Derecho penal» [«New genetic techniques and criminal law revisited»], *Anuario de Derecho Penal y Ciencias Penales*, vol. 41, 1988, pgs. 413-429.

**Eser, A.**: «Entre la "santidad" y la "calidad" de la vida. Sobre las transformaciones en la protección jurídico-penal de la vida» [«Between "healthy" and "quality" living. On transformations in the criminal law protection of life»], *Anuario de Derecho Penal y Ciencias Penales*, vol. 37, 1984, pgs. 747-781 (translated into Spanish by Patricia Laurenzo Copello).

**Eser, A.**: «Genética humana desde la perspectiva del Derecho alemán» [«Human genetics from the standpoint of German law»], *Anuario de Derecho Penal y Ciencias Penales*, vol. 38, 1985, pgs. 347-364 (translated into Spanish by Carlos M. Romeo Casabona).

**Eser, A.**: «¿Genética, "gen-ética", Derecho genético? Reflexiones político-jurídicas sobre la actuación en la herencia humana» [«Genetics, "gene-ethics", genetic law? Legal policy reflections on human inheritance actions»], *La Ley*, 1986, vol. 1, pgs. 1140-1147 (translated into Spanish by Carlos M. Romeo Casabona).

**Eser, A.**: «Problemas de justificación y exculpación en la actividad médica» [«Problems of justification and exculpation in medical activity»], *Problemas de la medicina y Derecho penal*, published by Santiago Mir Puig, Barcelona, 1988, pgs. 7-40 (especially pgs. 38 and ff), translated into the Spanish by Farré Trepat and revised by S. Mir Puig.

**Eser, A.**: «La moderna medicina de la reproducción e ingeniería genética. Aspectos legales y sociopolíticos desde el punto de visto alemán» [«Modern reproductive medicine and genetic engineering. Legal and sociopolitical aspects from the German standpoint»], in *Ingeniería genética y reproducción asistida*, by Marino Barbero Santos (editor), Madrid, 1989, pgs. 305-320.

**Fosar Benlloch, E.**: «La antropología y el derecho de la procreación humana. La procreación artificial y las manipulaciones genéticas en el mundo occidental. El informe de la Comisión especial de estudio de fecundación *in vitro* y de la inseminación artificial del Congreso de los Diputados-6 marzo de 1986» [«Anthropology and human procreation rights. Artificial procreation and genetic manipulation in the western world. Report of the special Congress of Deputies Committee for the study of *in vitro* fertilization and artificial insemination-March 6th 1986»], *Boletín del Ilustre Colegio de Abogados de Madrid*, 1986, no. 4, pgs. 63-81.

**Gallego Pérez, J. (moderator)**: «Debate: Aspectos Jurídicos» [«Debate: Legal aspects»], *Inovaciones científicas en la reproducción humana. Aspectos biológicos, psicosociales, antropológicos, éticos y jurídicos. I Congreso Nacional de Bioética*, Salamanca, 1987, pgs. 337-353.

**García Valdés, C.:** El Proyecto de nuevo Código Penal, Madrid, 1992 (especially pgs. 28 and 29).

**Herrero del Collado:** La inseminación artificial humana ante el Derecho penal, 1969.

Informe de la Comisión Especial de estudio de fecundación «in vitro» y la inseminación artificial humanas, Congress of Deputies, Madrid, 1987.

**Jiménez de Asúa, L.:** Libertad de amar y derecho a morir. Ensayos de un criminalista sobre Eugenesia y Eutanasia, 7th edition, Buenos Aires, 1984.

**Kaufmann, A.:** «Relativización de la protección jurídica de la vida?» [«Relativization of the legal protection of life?»], Problemas de la medicina y Derecho penal (Santiago Mir Puig, publisher), Barcelona, 1988 (translated into Spanish by J. M. Silva Sánchez), pgs. 41-57 (especially pgs. 46-48).

**Koch, H. G.:** «El control de la natalidad y el Derecho penal» [«Birth control and criminal law»], Eguzkilore, extraordinary no. 5, 1992, pgs. 123-131 (translated into Spanish by O. García Pérez).

**Lüttger, H.:** Medicina y Derecho penal, Madrid, 1984 (translated into Spanish by Enrique Bacigalupo).

**Lledo Yagüe, F.:** Fecundación artificial y Derecho, Madrid, 1988.

**Mantovani, F.:** «Problemas penales de la manipulación genética» [«Criminal law issues of genetic manipulation»], Doctrina Penal (Buenos Aires), no. 33/34, 1986, pgs. 9 and ff.

**Martínez Val, J. M.:** La eutelegenesia y su tratamiento penal, Madrid, 1954.

**Martínez Val, J. M.:** «La libertad de investigación en genética humana y sus límites» [«The freedom of research in human genetics and its limits»], Revista General de Derecho, no. 523, 1988, pgs. 2495 and ff.

**Palacios, M.:** Reproducción asistida. Discurso y recurso, Gijón, 1990.

**Peñalosa López-Pin, C.:** «Observaciones médicas y jurídicas acerca de la inseminación artificial humana» [«Medical and legal observations regarding human artificial insemination»], Boletín del Ilustre Colegio de Abogados de Madrid, 1986, no. 4, pgs. 17-31.

**Pérez Vitoria, O.:** Aspectos jurídicos de la inseminación artificial y de la fecundación «in vitro», Barcelona, 1985.

**Quintano Ripollés, A.:** «Biología genética y Criminología» [«Genetic biology and criminology»], Revista General de Legislación y Jurisprudencia, vol. 14, 1947, pgs. 597-608.

**Romeo Casabona, C. M.**: «Aspectos jurídicos de la experimentación humana» [«Legal aspects of human experimentation»], *Revista de la Facultad de Derecho de la Universidad Complutense*, monographic no. 11, 1986, pgs. 569 and ff.

**Romeo Casabona, C. M.**: «El diagnóstico antenatal y sus implicaciones jurídocpenales» [«Antenatal testing and its implications for criminal law»], *Problemas de la medicina y Derecho penal* (edited by Santiago Mir Puig), Barcelona, 1988, pgs. 81-124. Also published in *La Ley*, 1987, vol. 3, pgs. 798 and ff.

**Romeo Casabona, C. M.**: «Las respuestas del Derecho español ante los descubrimientos sobre genética y su aplicación al ser humano» [«The response of Spanish law to findings in genetics and their application to human beings»], *Eguzkilore*, extraordinary no. 5, 1992, pgs. 143-150.

**Romeo Casabona, C. M.**: «La utilización de embriones y fetos humanos con fines de investigación genética u otros fines no terapéuticos» [«The use of human embryos and fetuses in genetic investigation or for other non-therapeutic purposes»], *Eguzkilore*, extraordinary no. 5, 1992, pgs. 151-157.

**Romeo Casabona, C. M.**: «Algunas consecuencias vinculadas con la eugenesia y la reproducción humana: el diagnóstico preconceptivo y el diagnóstico prenatal» [«Some consequences related to eugenics and human reproduction: preconceptive and prenatal testing»], *Eguzkilore*, extraordinary no. 5, 1992, pgs. 159-166.

**Ruiz Vadillo, E.**: «Aspectos jurídicos de la inseminación artificial» [«Legal aspects of artificial insemination»], *I Simposium nacional sobre inseminación artificial heteróloga y bancos de conservación de semen*, Baracaldo, 1979.

**Ruiz Vadillo, E.**: «La investigación científica y el Derecho. Especial consideración de la ingeniería genética» [«Scientific investigation and the law. Special consideration of genetic engineering»], *Revista General de Derecho*, no. 504, 1986, pgs. 3645-3666.

**Ruiz Vadillo, E.**: «Investigación genética y Derecho penal» [«Genetic research and criminal law»], *Revista General de Derecho*, no. 528, 1988, pgs. 5791-5793.

**Serrano Rodríguez, M.**: «El aspecto penal de la fecundación artificial» [«The criminal law aspect of artificial fecundation»], in his book *Estudios penales Recopilación*, vol. 1, 2nd edition, Salamanca, 1967, pgs. 152-158.

**Serrano Rodríguez, M.**: «El aspecto penal de la fecundación artificial» [«Criminal law aspects of artificial fertilization»], in his book *Estudios penales Recopilación*, vol. 1, 2nd edition, Salamanca, 1967, pgs. 263-288.

**Soto Lamadrid, M. A.**: *Biogenética, filiación y delito. La fecundación artificial y la experimentación genética ante el Derecho*, Buenos Aires, 1990.

**Tamayo Salaberria, G.**: «Criminología y Bioética» [«Criminology and Bioethics»], *Eguzkilore*, extraordinary no. 5, 1992, pgs. 167-170.

**Valle Muñiz, J. M. and González González, M.**: «Utilización abusiva de técnicas genéticas y Derecho penal» [«Misuse of genetic techniques and criminal law»], *Poder Judicial*, no. 26, June 1992, pgs. 109-144.

**Zarraluqui Sánchez-Eznarriaga, L.**: «La naturaleza jurídica de los elementos genéticos» [«The legal nature of genetic elements»], *Revista General de Derecho*, no. 501, 1986, pgs. 2435-2468.

**Zarraluqui Sánchez-Eznarriaga, L.**: *Procreación asistida y derechos fundamentales*, Madrid, 1988.

# LEGAL PROBLEMS IN SOMATIC CELL AND GERM-LINE GENE THERAPY

## Juan-Felipe Higuera Guimerá

Professor of Criminal Law. University of Zaragoza. Spain.

The astounding genetic techniques currently under development (and those likely be developed in the future) already allow structural modification of the very components of human life. Given the vertiginous and rapid advent of these techniques and their personal and social consequences, it is not surprising, as Cerezo Mir has stated, that the related ethical and legal groundwork has not yet been firmly established.

Gene therapy is used to make changes in the composition of the cell. We thus have a direct «invasive» intervention on the genetic heritage of humanity, altering essential aspects of its structure and functions. Studies concerning human genetics have enormous potential benefit, which could be unnecessarily stifled if, as Vickers has said, an «uproar» is irresponsibly, and I would add «incompetently», organized. If said positive potential could not be controlled, we would be faced with a major problem. But, as I will try to demonstrate, I do not believe this to be the case.

The susceptibility of genetics to warped and even harmful applications has been obvious for some time now, as illustrated, for example, by the atrocious consequences seen in Nazi Germany. Recall the national-socialist regime's enactment of the sinister Hereditary Health Act of 1933. Under such a conception, new generations with hereditary diseases would have no place in society.

By means of gene therapy genes are transferred to or inserted in the cell, that is, a new version of the gene is introduced in the cell, a gene is modified, or an anomalous gene is eliminated and replaced with a normal one. The incredibly fast-paced advances being produced in this field often do not allow ethics and the law to adequately confront the implications of these dynamic innovations for all humanity.

I believe that the right to one's genetic identity forms part of the integrity and dignity of the human person and, as such, must be considered as an integral part of the fundamental rights the respect for which is guaranteed under the laws of each European Community member state and European Community law itself.

A distinction must be made between types of therapy sharply differentiated by their consequences and effects: *a)* somatic cell gene therapy and *b)* germ-line gene therapy.

### a)   Somatic cell gene therapy

Somatic cell gene therapy only affects the patient's corporal cells and, in principle, is, or should be, of no legal relevance whatsoever, given that, as Eser has said, it is one more curative medical therapy. Gene transfer in somatic cells does not pose any problem and should be governed by the same principles as apply to any organ transplantation. This type of therapy should therefore be subject to the same prerequisites as any operation or treatment: compliance with *lex artis,* subject to the adequately informed prior consent of the patient and a strict evaluation of the foreseeable risks and benefits.

Although this type of therapy is still in the experimental phase, it has been applied in isolated cases in some countries. Its application in humans is not widespread or systematic. Therefore, and in view of the possible dangers involved, the strictest constraints will have to be heightened and more rigorously applied when weighing the risks and benefits.

I think a distinction should be made between two types of experimentation, depending on whether the goals is to eliminate the patient's disease or simply to verify data and techniques. The former case is generally referred to as «therapeutic experimentation» or «experimental therapy». This consists in treatments whose effectiveness has not yet been fully established and which can therefore not yet be considered therapeutic remedies, all this assuming that the objective is to cure the patient.

The March 16th 1989 European Parliament Resolution on ethical and legal questions of genetic manipulation (Doc A 2-327/88, *Journal of the European Communities* no. C96/165) regards gene transfer in human somatic cells as a basically defendable form of treatment provided the affected person is informed and gives his or her consent. It rightly advocates reconsideration of the concepts of genetic disease and handicap in order to avert the danger that what are no more than simple deviations from genetic normalcy be medically classified as genetic diseases or handicaps.

### b) Germ-line gene therapy

Germ-line gene therapy is applied to cells in the germinal line (spermatozoa, ova and pre-embryos prior to 14 days after fertilization, phase in which the pre-embryos are totipotent), and its effects or results are therefore transmitted hereditarily, with the momentous and varied consequences this implies. The purpose of this type of therapy would be to impede the onset of hereditary diseases by replacing defective genes, that is, it aims to cure hereditary pathological conditions.

There is heated debate as to the possibility and propriety of this type of therapy, as to whether it should be permitted or absolutely prohibited, and, if the latter, whether such prohibition should be implemented via administrative law or be codified into offences and sanctions under criminal law.

The misgivings aroused by its possible effects have resulted in some specialists proposing outright prohibition, with others proposing a moratorium until more information is available. The problem surrounding germ-line therapy is the possibility of its use for eugenic purposes. Indeed, there hovers over this type of therapy the possibility, and hence danger, of it being employed to launch a «eugenic» programme, which in the case of a negative eugenic programme would entail arbitrary diminishment of handicapped life, and in a positive eugenic programme the end of normal life as a result of the strengthening of certain traits. In addition, this therapy harbours unpredictable risks to the individual and his or her offspring, as there is no guarantee that a mis-implanted gene will not have the secondary effect of destroying another gene and producing a different hereditary disorder.

Council of Europe Recommendation 1046 of 1986 prohibits interventions on embryos which affect «non-pathological» hereditary traits. The above-cited March 16th 1989 Resolution of the European Parliament insists that all attempts to «arbitrarily» recompose the genetic programme of human beings must be categorically prohibited and calls for criminalization of gene transfer to human germinal cells. In this spirit Rothley, for example, firmly opposes such therapy with different pragmatic and categoric arguments.

Lastly, the draft European convention on Bioethics (1992) provides in its article 10 that: «An intervention on the human genome shall not be carried out for other than therapeutic reasons and only if it does not affect the germinal line».

In my opinion, if germ-line therapy is authorized the relevant legal provisions should clearly and specifically set down, as is done in Spain for example, in the Palacios Report, that «gene therapy shall never influence non-pathological hereditary traits or be aimed at racial selection». Under Spanish law, «the performance of any act aimed at modifying non-pathological human genetic heritage» is considered as a very serious administrative offence [section 9.*b)*, *a)* of Act 42 of December 28th 1988]. In the new Spanish penal code such modification or alteration becomes a crime if carried out for any purpose other than the elimination or diminishment of serious diseases or handicaps. Germ-line gene therapy would be used exclusively to eradicate hereditary diseases once and for all, or put differently, «to eliminate the error forever», not just in the patient but in his or her offspring as well.

Eser, however, believes this neutralization of hereditary disease opens the door to possible manipulation of other properties and therefore considers it absolutely unacceptable. He goes so far as to call for criminal and not just administrative sanctions, citing the intervention's lack of selectivity and precision, the impossibility of controlling its consequence, and its lasting effects on future generations. He believes this therapy involves risks of such magnitude as to render it unacceptable, even for the natural sciences.

Suzuki and Knudston argue that while manipulation of somatic cells may be considered as pertaining to the realm of personal decision, manipulation in the germ line cannot. Any therapy affecting germinal cells should therefore be explicitly prohibited unless it has attained the consent of all members of society.

However, in my opinion, and in agreement with Professor Santiago Grisolía's thinking on these matters, germ-line gene therapy will not be used in a eugenic sense and will always respect the value of human dignity. We have to be optimistic and believe that the evolutionary aspects derived from genome study will be pursued by conscientious persons and not fall prey to outlandish eugenic ideas –including the so-called enhancement of the human genetic pool– and instead be concentrated on alleviating the genetic lesions which bring on disease.

But in order for germ-line gene therapy to be authorized, a set of very strict requirements and limitations, which I will describe below, would have to be met:

The patient would have to be properly informed and give his consent and, moreover, as this type of therapy clearly transcends the realm of personal decision, an international social consensus would also be necessary. It is up to society as a whole to expressly pronounce itself as to the what and how of such investigation, and as to its ultimate application. This type of therapy should be submitted to a series of *ex ante* and *ex post* preventive administrative social controls, and performed with maximum transparency pursuant to established protocols. It should always require the obligatory authorization of the relevant national and international Ethics Committees, before which the specific therapy should be previously presented. The consequences or effects which arise from germ-line gene therapy should be publicly disclosed.

Furthermore, in order to avoid abuses, a clear and exact catalogue of the hereditary disease to be eradicated should be drawn up, and the therapy should be applied in specialized centres with highly qualified personnel. This therapy should never be applied to minor deviations from genetic «normalcy» not qualifying as hereditary pathological conditions.

If germ-line gene therapy is to produce major potential benefits for all humanity, attention must be brought to bear on its well-planned control in order to limit and forestall dubious consequences, and it should perhaps not be insisted that the investigation continue.

Lastly, in closing, as Professor Marino Barbero Santos has said, «today the inviolable limit is called the human being, his development, his immediate contour and his dignity».

# LEGAL LIMITS ON GENETIC EXPERIMENTATION

## Andreas Klepsch

Directorate General for Science, Research and Development, Commission of the European Communities, Brussels. Belgium.

I would like to make briefly four points. I would like to state that there are principles and regulations and I would include in that legislative means which limit the freedom of research and all you basically need to do as a scientific administrator, and we do that, is to enforce that these limitations and regulations are enforced by the context of research. This was my first point. The second point is, that working for an organization like the EEC, this is not as simple as it looks, because of the level of the member states, there are different interpretations and there are gaps between the legislation and the rules and we may not allow these gaps to be abused. This is mainly a political question, but it can be regulated by legislative means, by contract means and by some collaboration. This was my second point. The third point is, when we do a work programme, we normally define what we are going to do and by that, we indirectly exclude many things. But in some cases, and I would say the Human Genome Programme is an example of that, we think it is necessary to state things we do not do. And what we do not do is any kind of manipulation of the germ line and we do not allow that. We have very specific announcements in our documents and, furthermore, we have applied some additional specific work safeguards to our work programme, to the contracts, meaning all research projects undergo an review before we finally commit the money and we finally attend to the contract. And there is an annex to our contracts stating our specific goals, like there should be no exclusive rights and exclusive exploitation in this respect to human DNA. This was my third point. The fourth and last point is that, of course, research also contributes to the development of legislation by just delivering data, materials, new knowledge, and this we call free normative research. Thank you.

# LEGAL LIMITS ON HUMAN GENETIC EXPERIMENTATION

## Lorenzo Morillas Cueva

Professor of Criminal Law. Principal of the University of Granada. Spain.

## Ignacio Benítez Ortúzar

Professor of Criminal Law. University of Granada. Spain.

I.  On the threshold of the 21st century jurists have no choice but to confront the realities of our age. At present, some of the traditional debates among criminal law jurists have lost their historic importance, while other fields of study have opened up and conducts which were until recently considered futuristic must now or soon be evaluated.

From this standpoint, and in exclusive reference to the human conducts of traditional relevance to criminal law by reason of their possible inclusion under Title VIII («Crimes against persons») of the currently applicable Spanish Criminal Code, which regulates criminal injury to persons per se (either protecting the life of the person: chapter I, «Of Homicide», with its aggravated categories of murder and parricide, also including punishable conducts related to suicide; chapter II, «Of Infanticide», as an autonomous category or an extenuated type of homicide; or protecting the physical and psychic integrity of the person: chapters IV and V, «Of injuries» and their «General Provision») and other conducts harmful to the development of human life not considered to be a person (chapter III, «Of abortion»), we see the disappearance in the present legislative arena of disputes over whether the death of a newborn caused, usually treacherously if one considers the victim's defencelessness, by its mother or maternal grandparents in order «to conceal the mother's dishonour» is less objectionable or less reproachable; or over whether the death of a descendant, ancestor or spouse is less objectionable or less reproachable than that of a third party. Such debates have given way to another type of legal discussion focusing on conducts carried out during the gestation of a new human being (no longer only in reference to the traditional abortion offence, but to other new offences such as «injuries to the fetus» or the so-called «genetic manipulation») or in conducts concerning the terminus of a human being (assisted suicide of terminal patients or euthanasia). With respect to both human gestation and human expiration, it is the task of students of criminal law to positively or negatively evaluate certain conducts practised by investigators in the natural sciences.

II.  This paper focuses on human genetic experimentation, mainly concentrating on experimentation prior to birth, the moment at which criminal law considers an independent human life to exist [1]. References to procedures which should not be considered as experimental [2] (because of their demonstrated effectiveness) or which do not involve human beings [3] will be kept to a minimum.

This will first require a conceptual delimitation of what is to be understood by human genetic experimentation, followed by a determination of which legal values are involved and need to be protected under criminal law. And last, we will explain what we view as limits of Spain's current criminal law,

---

[1] If the meaning of the term «genetic» is understood to be the same as «genic» it is possible to conduct genetic experiments (referring to genic) on living human beings. The problems posed in this case are the same as those accompanying any other type of experimentation in human beings, including issues of consent, the risk-benefit correlation, and the values and rights which may be involved (life, physical and psychic integrity, freedom and dignity).

[2] Such as assisted reproduction methods or prenatal testing per se, i.e. when not serving some other experimental purpose. For example: the attempt to *in vitro* fertilize a woman's ovum with simian spermatozoa, and later follow-up with prenatal testing.

[3] Taking man, his cells, tissues or organs as an experimental object. An example of non-human experimentation would be the creation of a transgenic sheep, by introducing goat DNA into a sheep embryo.

its gaps and the path which should be taken by the law currently in the making.

Experimentation consists in the purposeful observation of a fact or phenomenon in order to investigate its properties or causes. Human genetics is the science which studies human inheritance, its subject matter being that which is related to or concerns the reproduction, birth or origin of human beings [4], with genes being the biological unit of inheritance, the stellar figure of human genetics [5].

From these premises we may define human genetic experimentation as purposeful observation using new methods, techniques or substances applied to the fertilized human ovum prior to birth. But this definition does not cover the whole of prenatal human genetic experimentation; some genic alteration, modification or insertion could be made to an ovum or spermatozoon for use, for example, in an assisted fertilization procedure [6], which technique would then be applied to material that in no way can yet be considered a human being in the making, but which later on will give rise to a human being. Also qualifying as genetic experimentation would be the use of genetic material from a human being in formation in one that has already been formed, to an «owner of an independent human life». Thus the definition could be broadened to encompass purposeful observation by means of new techniques or substances applied to human germinal or reproductive cells which have already been fertilized as well as when this new technology is applied to unfertilized gametes for reproductive purposes [7].

---

[4] From the Spanish edition of the *Dorland Encyclopedic Dictionary of Medicine,* 26th edition, Interamericana. McGraw Hill.

[5] For this reason the terms «genetic» and «genic» have been used synonymously in many works, when in Spanish, strictly speaking «genetic» means relative or pertaining to inheritance, while «genic» means relative or pertaining to genes.

[6] Either *in vitro* or by means of artificial insemination.

[7] It should be made clear that experiments on unfertilized gametes for other than reproductive purposes do not constitute genetic experimentation. Spain's current legislation holds to this view. Section 14.1 of the law regulating assisted reproduction techniques (Act 35 of November 22nd 1988) sets forth that «gametes may be used independently for purposes of basic or experimental research» and section 14.3 provides that «gametes used in research or experimentation shall not be used to originate pre-embryos for procreative purposes». From the wording of the latter section it would appear that the possibility of creating pre-embryos for purposes other than procreation is envisaged under the Act, but section 3 of the same Act sets forth that «the fertilization of human ova for purposes other than human procreation is prohibited», and article 20.B)a. classifies «fertilizing ova for any purpose other than human procreation» as a very serious offence. The Act's statement of purpose asserts that the pre-embryo or pre-implantation embryo belongs to the pre-organogenesis stage, corresponding to the period from the ovum's

As with any other human experimentation, human genetic experimentation can be therapeutic or purely experimental [8]. Therapeutic genetic experimentation would consist in the application of new methods or techniques whose effectiveness in human beings has not yet been confirmed to gametes which are to be fertilized or to an already fertilized egg in order to avoid certain handicaps or diseases in the new human being. Pure or non-therapeutic experimentation would consist in assaying new methods or techniques on human reproductive material before or after fertilization but the direct aim of which is other than the elimination of genetic handicaps or defects; the aims could be various, including military (in the case of biological war), industrial (use of human genetic material in order to create cosmetic creams), surgical (using human genetic material to surgically treat a person suffering from Parkinson's disease) or pharmacological (use of this material as a medication). Also classifying as pure experimentation would be experiments seeking to cure a given disease or handicap in general and not in the specific embryo or individual subjected to the experiment. We will hereinafter refer solely to non-therapeutic experimentation.

Another distinction which is in order here is between experimentation involving somatic cells and that affecting the germ line. Human germ-line genetic experimentation is that experimentation conducted on gametes prior to fertilization, or immediately thereafter and before the nuclei of the ovum and spermatozoon combine, and affecting offspring of the embryo or individual on whom the experiment is carried out. Somatic genetic experimentation would be that experimentation performed on somatic cells, and as such of no influence on future offspring, specifically on non-reproductive cells of the already fertilized ovum, embryo, fetus or person.

One area of particular relevance to an evaluation of these practices is research involving pre-embryos, embryos or fetuses that are alive (or viable) or dead (or inviable).

---

fertilization through to its stable implantation in the uterus, a span of approximately 14 days.

From the foregoing it may be gathered that the law leaves the door open for the creation of pre-embryos by some method other than fertilization of the ovum. But article 20.B).o) also classifies as a very serious offence the «creation of pre-embryos of persons of the same sex for reproductive or other purposes».

[8] Helsinki Declaration of the XVIII World Medical Assembly (revised in Tokyo in 1975 and completed in Venice in 1983). Also, Romeo Casabona, «Aspectos Jurídicos de la Experimentación» [«Legal aspects of experimentation»], in the *Journal of the Madrid Universidad Complutense School of Law*, Monograph 11, in homage to professor Luis Jiménez de Asúa.

The foregoing shows that at present there is a range of experimental possibilities in the human gestation stage which criminal law must address and evaluate according to our society's fundamental values.

III. Once the conceptual limits of genetic experimentation have been defined, we must seek out the criminal law limits to the same, never losing sight of the ultimate purpose of criminal law –to protect the most fundamental legal rights from the most intolerable attacks– or the precision with which any such criminal limits must be set down, in keeping with the penal «legality principle» (no crime without a law, no punishment without a law). The moralistic and moralizing conceptions so typical of issues involving the origin and end of life should as far as possible be avoided [9]. Taking as a point of departure the generally held principle in Spanish legal doctrine that the development and application of genetic advances fall under the provisions of article 20.1.b) of the Spanish Constitution of 1978 [10], which enshrines scientific creation and production as a fundamental right, the possible limits must also be similarly grounded in fundamental interests or rights.

In order to find legal grounds for the possible criminal limits, the first requirement is a legal statute on human beings in formation. The traditional Spanish legal concept of human life in formation (or dependent human life) is insufficient, as most genetic experimentation does not affect life per se. There can be experimental practices which affect the health or physical or psychic integrity of that being in formation, with the attendant issues arising from the difficulty of confirming physical

---

[9] In this sense Cuerda Riezu has indicated that legal studies of the new human procreation genetic techniques first analyse whether these conducts are immoral or not, and then analyse whether they are legal or illegal, or whether they should be sanctioned by a law in the future; when the analysis should be carried out inversely, that is, to first see if the practices constitute a crime or misdemeanour under existing criminal law, and, if they do not match any of the existing offences, to then contemplate the possibility of their prohibition, applying legal criteria based on a social evaluation and not a specific moral attitude. «Límites juridicopenales de las nuevas técnicas genéticas» [«Criminal law limits on the new genetic techniques»], *Anuario de Derecho Penal y Ciencias Penales,* Volume XLI, Issue II, May-August, 1988, pg. 414.

[10] Along these lines, see: Ruiz Vadillo, «La investigación científica y el derecho. Especial consideración a la ingeniería genética» [«Scientific investigation and the law. Special consideration of genetic engineering»], *RGD,* no 504, 1986, pgs. 3652 and ff; Valle Muñiz-González, «Utilización abusiva de técnicas genéticas y Derecho penal» [«Misuse of genetic techniques and criminal law»], *PJ,* no. 26, pgs. 109 and ff; Cuerda Riezu, «Límites...», op. cit., pgs. 413 and ff; also Romeo Casabona, «Aspectos Jurídicos de la experimentación humana» [«Legal aspects of human experimentation»] on human experimentation in general (not just genetic), *RFDUC,* no. 11, monograph, pgs. 569 and ff.

or psychic alterations when the subject matter of the experiment (gametes before or after fertilization, or embryo or fetus) is different than the being in which the result is produced (the individual born after the experiment), or other practices affecting the dignity of a being who at the time of the experiment is not legally entitled to that dignity, nor able to pursue the free development of his personality as these rights have been traditionally construed.

Spanish law makes a unique distinction between three stages in the development of the conceived and unborn offspring: the pre-embryo, embryo and fetus. As set out in the statement of purpose of Act 35 of November 22nd 1988 on assisted reproduction techniques, the pre-embryo stage runs from fertilization of the ovum through to its stable implantation in the mother's uterus, 14 days later. The embryo stage, according to the statements of purpose of the aforesaid Act 35/1988 and of Act 42 of December 28th 1988 on the donation and use of human embryos and fetuses or their cells, tissues or organs, denotes the period from the stable implantation in the uterus until 2.5 months later. The fetal stage runs from 3 months after fertilization until the moment of birth.

A fourth stage could be pointed out here, actually a preliminary stage of relevance for human genetic experimentation, covering experimentation with gametes which are to be used in a fertilization procedure. It should not be forgotten, without entering into moral or ethical considerations, that these gamete alterations or modifications will later give rise to a human being, to a person. Imagine in this regard a healthy woman who has the AIDS virus injected into an ovum that she is going to use in an in vitro fertilization, disregarding her own bodily integrity, with the aim of giving birth to a child infected with that disease, or, somewhat less illogically, to obtain an embryo or fetus which could be used to investigate the therapeutic effects of vaccinations or medications previously tested in animals but not yet authorized for human use. Under the traditional concept this conduct would not be punishable, as no there is no applicable criminal offence. At most, she would be assessed an administrative sanction under paragraph *i)* of section 20.2.B) of Act 35/1988, or paragraph *x)* thereunder and its reference to section 14.3 of the same Act, which in turn refers to section 36 of the General Health Act insofar as concerns the applicable sanction. The penalty includes a fine ranging from 2,500,001 to 100,000,000 pesetas, plus a possible 5-year closing of the establishment on order of the national government's Council of Ministers or the regional government's governing council.

While this penalty may on first sight appear severe, it seems trivial if we consider the sums of money spent each year worldwide, and in Spain in particular [11], on the fight against AIDS.

Several consequences stem from the foregoing analysis: there arises the possibility of broadening criminal law protection beyond only dependent human life, as with the physical or psychic integrity of the unborn, or human dignity; current abortion laws therefore become insufficient insofar as concerns experimentation with the new genetic technology; criminal law protection must be graduated by and distinguish between pre-fertilization, pre-embryo, post-implantation embryo and fetal stages; full study, on the basis of present-day social values and circumstances, has to be given to defining the new legal values which need or do not need protection, bearing in mind that this protection will serve as a limit to the fundamental right to scientific production and creation laid down in article 20.1.*b)* of the Spanish Constitution. These premises point to the need for an overhaul of the legal protection of the unborn.

Graduation according to the different stages in which genetic experimentation is possible raises the question of who shall hold legal title to the interests we consider to be worthy of criminal law protection and, as such, constitute limits on a fundamental right. It appears obvious that the unborn cannot be the holder of these interests, nor, therefore, of the legal capacity for their protection [12].

In order to determine the legal interests which may be affected by genetic experimentation and need protection under criminal law we must begin with the Spanish Constitution of 1978 and the jurisprudence of Spain's Constitutional Court, which regards the protection of human life as a «process that begins with gestation, in the course of which a biological reality corporally and sensitively attains a human configuration, and which ends with death» [13]. The right to life, physical and psychic integrity, or health in the stages of human development prior to birth cannot be considered as fundamentally protected under the Spanish constitution, as these constitutional rights are set down as vested in the human person, and in these techniques no such person exists. We concur

---

[11] In Spain some ptas. 50 billion last year according to the daily newspaper «El País», April 3rd 1993.
[12] The Spanish legal world is divided as to the titleholder of dependent human life and the aggrieved party when the latter is attacked, but this is not the place to consider those issues.
[13] Constitutional Court Judgement 53/1985, in the fifth legal foundation.

with Valle Muñiz-González González's statement that the supreme values of the legal system (equality, liberty, justice and political pluralism) and the fundamental rights thereunder are intrinsic to human dignity [14]. The point is that, basing ourselves on a neo-personalist conception of dignity, genetic experimentation is beyond the constitutional scope of dignity, for a person does not yet exist when these experiments are conducted. We would therefore have to look for a conception of human dignity conceived as a collective jural interest, appertaining to the society as a whole. This does not sit well with article 10 of the Constitution of 1978, which refers in section 1 to the «dignity of the human person» and which in section 2 states that provisions relating to the fundamental constitutional rights and liberties shall be construed according to the Universal Declaration of Human Rights and other international treaties and related agreements ratified by Spain. In this sense, the first declaration of the Universal Declaration of Human Rights sets down that «all human beings are born free and equal in dignity and rights», also referring to the dignity of the individual human person, as it speaks of dignity from the moment of birth of the human being. Section 29 of Spain's Civil Code provides that «personality is determined by birth». Likewise the International Agreement on Civil and Political Rights, the European Convention for the Protection of Human Rights and Fundamental Liberties, the European Social Charter...

IV. In this section we attempt to briefly establish that according to the criminal legislation are as yet in force in Spain [15], all genetic experimentation not affecting the life of the conceived is, as things currently stand, of no relevance for Spanish criminal law.

Having seen in the preceding section that the currently operative concept of dignity is personalistic and individualized and at present allows for no interpretation of it as a collective interest, it becomes clear that the only legal interest or right enjoying protection under criminal law is the right to life, after Constitutional Court Judgement 53/85 which set forth that life commences with gestation. One possible solution would be to set down criminal categories for permanent offences, envisaging a unity of action from the moment the genetic experimentation begins through to birth, when the being does attain legal personality and which, by means of a

---

[14] Valle Muñiz-González González, «Utilización...», op. cit., pgs. 126-127.
[15] The situation in the Federal Republic of Germany is quite different after the enactment of the Embryo Protection Act (Embryonenschutzgesetz = EschG), in force as from January 1st 1991.

legal fiction, could be considered as the moment the offence is committed. This would consist to some extent in the introduction into Spanish criminal law science of what we may term an «obstruction offence», as it seems clear that intentional experimentation with human genetic material which does not affect life itself is currently permitted and not punishable, even in cases where, say, a mongoloid child is intentionally produced.

We will now consider the different points at which experimentation may take place.

a) In the pre-fertilization stage, various ova are extracted from a woman and their genetic code altered in order to adapt them for fertilization with simian spermatozoa. Several pre-embryos are created in this way and transferred, with her consent, to the woman's uterus, so as to assure implantation of at least one. Let us suppose that the experiment is successful, that is, the pregnancy is achieved and the woman gives birth to the offspring. This action would not be punishable because the experiment was conducted before the new being was even conceived and therefore before there was a human being «in formation».

Under current Spanish law this action would constitute an administrative offence, according to the provisions of section 20.2.B).*q)* or *r)* of Act 35/1988, comparable to cases where an ovum is stimulated by means of parthenogenesis or some other means of obtaining a female human being without the action of spermatozoa [section 20.2.B).*m)*] or human gamete genetic material is used for military purposes [section 20.2.B).*v)*].

No criminal sanctions can be applied to genetic experimentation carried out on gametes for reproductive purposes, as gametes are not yet human beings in formation and cannot therefore be said prior to fertilization to possess human life. But viewed from a different perspective, if the gametes are possessed not by the society, nor by the gametes themselves, but by their progenitors, then it would perhaps be possible to limit the right of the latter to alter the gametes. All the more so when the alteration will affect not only the product of the fertilization but all the descendants of the new being, that is, when the experimentation is genuinely germ-line experimentation. Then it would be possible to place limits on the progenitors' consent to such practices, based not only on the fundamental rights of persons enshrined in the Constitution but also on the governing principles of social and economic policy laid down in Chapter III of the Constitution. These principles have a markedly public and therefore collective character, particularly the ones included in article 43.1 on the protection of health, and 44.2, which expressly provides that «the authorities shall promote science and scientific and technical research in the general interest». But it would appear logical therefore that these limitations be framed within the limiting and sanctioning power of administrative law, as is done by the Act on assisted reproduction techniques.

The German Embryo Protection Act sanctions artificial alterations of human germ cells with penalties of up to 5 years imprisonment or fines [16].

*b)*   The period from the moment the ovum is fertilized until 14 days later, when it is implanted in the uterus and the so-called primitive line begins [17], with the appearance of the new genetic individuality, is markedly different than the previous stage. It too, however, is not regulated under Spanish criminal law statutes when this period occurs outside the mother's uterus, and perhaps inside the uterus as well [under section 20.B).*b)* of the assisted reproduction Act, obtaining human embryos by means of a uterine wash for any purpose is classified as a very serious offence; this practice could be considered as an abortion under chapter III in Title VIII of Book II of the currently applicable Criminal Code].

Experimentation in this pre-implantation stage raises diverse issues, depending on the value attributed to this first stage in the formation of a human being. Human individualization may be understood to begin with gestation or upon uterine implantation. Each leads to different conclusions.

If the formative stage of the human being is considered to commence the moment of fertilization, then the criminal law treatment of this stage is equivalent to that for

---

[16] ESchG, paragraph 5. In paragraph 8 it states that germ cells, within the meaning of the Act, are human ova and spermatozoa, and also the ovum penetrated by a spermatozoon, until fertilization is completed with the fusion of the two nuclei.

[17] This criteria is gaining ever increasing support; see *inter alia* Council of Europe Recommendation 1046 (CAHBI), the February 25th 1975 Judgement of the Constitutional Court of the Federal Republic of Germany, which indicates that human life begins 14 days after fertilization, the Warnock report, the Palacios report.

the embryonic and fetal stages. If, on the other hand, such commencement is considered to coincide with the appearance of the primitive line (this is the position adopted in Spanish legislation after Acts 35 and 42 of 1988) and, therefore, with its individualization, the situation is different. Experimentation that does not affect its viability is then solely and exclusively subject to administrative limitation, as with the pre-fertilization stage, and only the Act on assisted reproduction techniques is applicable thereto, even if fertilization has not been aided with any such techniques.

c) The embryonic and fetal stages of the unborn human being run from the 14th day post-fertilization [18] through to the moment of birth, and are differentiated approximately 2.5 months after implantation. Both stages are given the same protection under Spanish law. Cases where experimentation produces the fetus' destruction or its premature expulsion and consequent inviability are covered by section 411 of the Criminal Code, in relation to abortion, if the direct or indirect, but necessary object of the procedure is the destruction of the embryo or fetus. Section 412 of the Code would perhaps be applicable to cases where the fetus or embryo is destroyed because of the violent application of a procedure not otherwise so aiming, this would require a broad interpretation of the expression «violently occasioned abortion». Experimentation not affecting the viability of the embryo or fetus is not subject to criminal law provisions [19]. All this assuming the experimentation on the embryo or fetus occurs within the mother's uterus, otherwise, current criminal law has no applicable provisions, and it is the administrative sanctions set out in sections 32 to 37 of the General Health Act which are again invoked by section 9.1 of Act 42/1988 on the donation and use of human embryos and fetuses or their cells, tissues or organs.

Thus, consider the following example. Totipotent cells [20] are extracted from an embryo or fetus and transplanted to the brain of a person suffering from Parkinson's disease, without affecting the embryo or fetus' viability.

---

[18] According to Act 35/1988 the product of the gestation may not develop more time outside the maternal uterus, excepting, in effect, the days in which it has been cryoconserved.

[19] In this connection, see Cuerda Riezu, «Límites...», op. cit., pgs. 415 and ff.

[20] Cells in which function has not yet been differentiated and which, with their great adaptability and reproductive capacity, can therefore be transplanted to any other type of organism.

The child is born but with serious physical or mental handicaps. This action would not constitute a criminal offence, would only be subject to administrative sanction, and could even be authorized by public health or science authorities or by decision of the planned National Commission for the Follow-up and Control of the donation and use of human embryos and fetuses. Indeed, section 7.1 of Act 42/1988 provides that «basic investigations of human embryos or fetuses or their biological structures shall only be authorized when the requirements set out in this Act are fulfilled and on the basis of duly drafted project proposals to be studied, and approved or otherwise, by the public health or science authorities», without any reference as to whether such embryos or fetuses should be alive (or viable) or dead (or inviable), although such possible administrative authorization should be interpreted to only be applicable for cases where the embryo or fetus is dead or inviable, pursuant to section 2.e) of the same Act, which, under Chapter I, dedicated to general principles, provides that «the donated embryos or fetuses (or their biological structures) be clinically inviable or dead».

Within the meaning set out in the German Embryo Protection Act, the embryo is understood to be the human ovum from the moment the nuclei of the female egg cell and male sperm cell are combined through until birth. The embryo's totipotent cells receive equal treatment when they are capable of developing a human being [21]. The Act provides for sentence of up to 5 years imprisonment or fines for cloning [22] and for hybridization and formation of chimeras [23].

V.   The proposed Criminal Code of 1992 attempts to rectify the inadequacies described above. It introduces new criminal offences under titles IV (section 165 and 166) and V (sections 167 to 170) of its second book, applicable to practices which are completely unregulated under current criminal law provisions. Criminal law protection is thus provided from attacks on the physical or psychic integrity of the fetus, and from non-therapeutic genetic manipulation and destruction, donation or use of human embryos and fetuses, their cells, tissues or organs. Unconsented artificial insemination (which will not be discussed in this paper) is also prohibited, somewhat inconsistently with recent Spanish genetic manipulation and re-

---

[21]  ESchG, paragraph 8.
[22]  ESchG, paragraph 6.
[23]  ESchG, paragraph 7.

production legislation, namely Acts 35 and 42 of 1988, in an overuse of the much criticized blanket criminal law provision, occasioning many redundant sanctions. This is rather illogical when one considers the novel treatment of these techniques in Spanish legislation and that these pieces of legislation were drafted around the same time, notwithstanding that the Act 35/1988's statement of purpose already pointed to the existence of criminal law gaps in this area.

As regards to the four stages described above, we may make the following observations.

a) The stage prior to fertilization continues to have no criminal law relevance. Manipulation of human genes for purposes other than the elimination of serious handicaps or disease, and involving alteration of the vital constitutional type [24], is provided for in section 167.1 if done with wilful misconduct and in 167.3 if accompanied by reckless negligence. Where there is no alteration of vital constitutional type the conduct is regulated by section 167.2, whereunder only cases involving wilful misconduct are sanctioned. Now, in order for such an alteration of the «vital constitutional type» to occur the differentiated genotype must already exist. This may be understood to be the case as from the moment of fertilization or from implantation, but in no case when pre-fertilization gamete procedures are involved, as the said gametes only possess haploid chromosomes [25]. Hence, the constitutional type they encode is that of the individual from which they proceed and not that of the person they will contribute to forming after fertilization, which will depend on the union of the haploid chromosomes of the male spermatozoon with the haploid chromosomes of the female egg cell. Furthermore, the aforesaid section 167.2 is included under Title V, entitled «On genetic manipulation of human embryos and fetuses and on unconsented artificial insemination». Leaving aside the issue of unconsented artificial insemination, which is covered in section 170 and which could perhaps have been classified under a different category of offences [26], the title

---

[24] From a scientific standpoint, the expression «vital constitutional type» should be understood to mean genotype, that is, as the individual's entire genetic makeup.

[25] Human cells possess a set of 23 diploid chromosomes, that is, they form 23 pairs of homologous chains. Gametes, the human reproductive cells, are made up of 23 haploid chromosomes, that is, with only one chain.

[26] Obviously not as an offence against sexual freedom, as this is not the protected legal interest. This offence could arguably have been better classified under threats and coercion, since it seems there is clear transgression of the woman's freedom of choice as to whether or not to be inseminated. Criticism can also be brought to bear on the classification of *in vitro* fertilization as a form of artificial insemination. These two practices are clearly differentiated

refers to «genetic manipulation of human embryos and fetuses». Given the fact that Spain already has a legal definition of embryo and fetus, criminal sanction of genetic (genic) experimentation in gametes for reproductive purposes would thus require an interpretation by analogy *in malan partem,* a practice much frowned upon practice in Spanish jurisprudence. We may also question the name given to Title V, in the understanding that it encompasses three different concepts: genetic manipulation (sections 167 and 168, though the latter refers to the «determination of a person's sex», when it should state «selection of the sex of a pre-embryo or fetus»), the donation, use or destruction of human embryos and fetuses (section 169), and, lastly, unconsented artificial insemination (section 170). In this case, the title would only refer to section 167, which does not treat of genetic manipulation (understood as everything involving reproduction, birth or origin) but of the manipulation of genes. Presumably, the drafters of the proposed Code did not intend to sanction genotype alterations of the individual who carries the gametes, but alterations of the new being who would develop therefrom; especially when considering that the Bill makes no reference to the reproductive or non-reproductive use of these genically altered gametes (moreover, the Assisted Reproduction Techniques Act itself exempts from administrative sanction experimentation on gametes for other than procreative purposes).

Thus, even creating a hybrid, which prior to fertilization has no differentiated genotype, does not entail alteration of a constitutional type, as the latter would only come into existence upon fertilization (say, of a human ovum by simian sperm).

Hence, if the Criminal Code Bill of 1992 were in force, experimentation on gametes for reproductive purposes would be regulated under administrative law, that is, under Act 35/1988 on assisted reproduction techniques.

b) If the name given to Title V is construed to refer to three different concepts, genetic experimentation in the pre-embryo could be understood to be covered by the provisions of section 167, but only those experimental procedures involving manipulation of genes in the pre-embryo and which alter the vital

---

in Assisted Reproduction Techniques Act itself, although it seems clear that the intent of the Bill's drafter was to refer to both.

constitutional type, or which are done in violation of applicable legal provisions. Here, two problems arise:

1. Experimental procedures on the pre-embryo which do involve genic manipulation cannot be classified as the aggravated offence provided for in 167.1 (if done with wilful misconduct) or 167.3 (if involving negligence), even though they involve genetic experimentation, because the offence refers solely to genic alterations in the strict sense. This would exclude, for example, such conducts as the experimental creation of several identical beings by means of artificial multiplication of the fertilized ovum within the first 14 days after fertilization, because this does not entail direct manipulation of genes, but rather of cells, and the vital constitutional type is not modified. What this does create would be a certain number of genetically identical beings who, even if born, would never be able to demand their right to protection of a unique genetic identity that they quite simply do not have.

   Even the creation of chimeras by means of joining two human pre-embryos or a human pre-embryo with a pre-embryo of another species could not easily be included under section 167.1 (or 167.3), because the manipulation is carried out on the pre-implantation embryos' cells and not directly on their genes, although such practices do modify the vital constitutional type.

2. Paragraph two of section 167 provides for what we may call the «attenuated degree», or, the «residual offence». The paragraph is an abusive application of the much criticized «blanket» technique of criminal law provision, setting down that «any other manipulation of human genes performed in violation of established legal provisions...». We assume this is a reference to the already existing Acts 35 and 42 of 1988, but such vagueness violates the specificity and precision which should be observed by a new Criminal Code, and creates a tangle of overlapping and redundant sanctions.

   Close study of the aforesaid section 167.2 reveals major inconsistencies.

   *a)* It makes continuous reference to manipulation of human genes, raising serious problems given that Acts 35 and 42 of 1988 regulate the application of genetic techniques, understood in the broad sense of the term, that is, not only genic techniques. In fact, only the provisions contained in paragraph (n) and (v) of Act 35/1988's section 20.2B may be understood as referring to genic applications [27], and those paragraphs use the term genetic and not genic.

b) Assuming that the reference to manipulation techniques represents an error in drafting the intentions of the authors of the Bill, the spirit of which to address all procedures involving reproduction, birth or origin of human beings, as was made abundantly clear in the parliamentary discussion of the Bill, the real problem in invoking administrative law emerges. Act 35/1988 sets out no fewer than 23 cases constituting very serious violations of its section 20.2B, and paragraph (x) of said section is another generic clause comparable in that respect to section 167.2 of the proposed Code. Add to this the duplication of administrative and penal sanctions, as both Act 35 and 42 of 1988, as has already been stated, cite sections 32 to 37 of the General Health Act for the determination of sanctions. We believe that a new Criminal Code must not be born with such defects as glaring as those so often criticized in the still applicable Code, especially when considering that the practices it regulates were virtually unknown in the past but which may be rapidly upon us in the near future.

The foregoing reflections aside, it appears that whereas the proposed Code continues to classify the induced destruction or expulsion of the fertilized ovum during these first 14 days as abortion if the ovum is in the mother's uterus [28], if the pre-embryo was created by means of some assisted reproduction method, however, according to Act 35/1988 such destruction is not punishable. Without wishing to adopt moralist or moralizing positions, consider the inconsistency of the following examples. A young woman without a stable partner becomes pregnant and decides not to bear the child though it repre-

---

[27] Section 20.2.B).*n)*, «...sex selection or genetic manipulation for non-therapeutic purposes or for unauthorized therapeutic purposes».
Section 20.2.B).*v)*, «...the use of genetic engineering or other procedures, for military or other purposes, to produce biological or human extermination weapons of any kind».
[28] Title II of Book II of the Bill, «On Abortion», does not refer to this 14 day period, hence, it must be construed according to the traditional criteria, that is, the destruction or expulsion of the product of gestation any time from fertilization through, at least, the moment when the fetus is capable of autonomous life.

sents no serious risk to her physical or mental health. She undergoes a uterine wash to expel the fertilized ovum before its implantation. Now, take a married couple suffering problems of infertility who go to an *in vitro* fertilization centre and create the number of pre-embryos needed to assure impregnation. At the moment of implantation they have conjugal problems and decide to separate, also deciding to destroy the pre-embryos. In the first example, the woman could be convicted of an illegal abortion, whereas the couple in the second example would go unpunished. The subject matter is the same (the pre-embryo) and the conduct identical (its destruction); the first was created naturally but unintentionally and its destruction can be ruled illegal, the second was intentionally created for reproductive purposes, and its destruction is not punishable (by application of Act 35/1988 which permits revocation of consent for these procedures at any time within the first fourteen days of the pre-embryo's gestation).

c)  The stages we have called embryonic and fetal vary considerably with the Criminal Code Bill of 1992. Section 169 provides: «The donation, use or destruction of human embryos and fetuses, or their cells, tissues or organs, other than in the circumstances authorized by the law, shall be punishable by 1 to 5 years imprisonment and specific disqualification for employment, public office, profession or occupation for 1 to 4 years». This section is understood to complement section 167, the latter being applicable to gene manipulations that do not affect the viability of the unborn child, irrespective of whether they alter the vital constitutional type, with section 169 applying to all other genetic experimentation procedures with embryos or fetuses, whether viability is thereby impaired («destruction of embryos or fetuses») or not (all other cases).

With regard to these stages, section 169, too, makes use of the blanket criminal regulation technique, sanctioning all conducts performed «other than in the circumstances authorized by the law». The law referred to in this case is Act 42/1988, which bears a very similar name to that of the conducts provided for in section 169: «On the donation and use of human embryos and fetuses or their cells, tissues or organs». Redundant sanctions once again result, as

Act 42/1988 also refers to sections 32 to 37 of the General Health Act in connection with sanctions for acts classified as serious or very serious offences under Chapter IV.

What is more, other penal duplications are possible. Under correct enforcement of Act 35/1988 development of embryos and fetuses outside the maternal uterus is not permitted. The Act envisages the possibility of therapeutic experimentation or investigation until the 14th day, time at which the pre-embryo must be implanted or frozen for conservation, as can be gathered from the spirit of the Act, in section 11 (which treats of pre-embryos transferred to the uterus or frozen, and does not refer to embryos), section 15.1.*b)* (in reference to therapeutic experimentation within the first 14 days), or paragraph *s)* of section 20.2.B) (which classifies ectogenesis, or the laboratory creation of an individual human being, as a very serious offence). In this case the conducts provided for in section 169 of the Bill would be included in Title II of Book II of the proposed Code, concerning abortion, if they produce the death of the embryo or fetus, or Title IV of the same, which takes up injuries to the fetus, when the said conducts produce a major physical or mental disability in the fetus or a lesion or disease that seriously impairs its normal development. Since sections 165 and 166 (Title IV) only refer to lesions to the fetus and not the embryo, it is the provisions of the aforesaid section 169 that will apply to practices which, without affecting the life of the embryo, occasion disabilities, defects or diseases therein. This could be solved by providing penal sanctions for ectogenesis or development of the fertilized ovum beyond the first fourteen days post-fertilization, excluding those in which it was cryoconserved, and by including the term embryo in Title IV of the Bill.

Problems concerning the right to one's own genetic identity, the creation of chimeras, ectogenesis and ovarian stimulation that creates a new being without the need for fertilization by male gametes, and the rights, values and legal interests they involve, are not addressed by the Criminal Code Bill of 1992. It should be stressed that the approach to these issues must be rooted in the Constitution, perhaps in the construction of the dignity of the unborn child within the right to dignity laid down in article 10.1 of the Spanish Constitution of 1978 as a collective interest. Today, such an interpretation does not seem possible. As has always been the case historically, the law trails several steps behind society; in a few years we will see interpretations along these or similar lines.

# LEGAL LIMITS ON GENETIC EXPERIMENTS IN THE EUROPEAN CONTEXT

## Herman Nys

Professor of Medical Law. Editor of the *International Encyclopaedia of Medical Law*. Leuven University. Belgium.

### Introduction

I will limit my intervention to only one point: is criminal law the most appropriate instrument to put legal limitations on genetic experiments, supposed that such limitations are deemed necessary or at least desirable.

The programme of this session and especially the Spanish version of it seem to imply that this is indeed the case. I myself am not so convinced it is. And I may say that I feel supported in this by the two keynote speakers, Professors J.L. Baudouin and C.M. Romeo Casabona, after heaving heard their introductory papers.

### A consensus to legally prohibit germline cell therapy

Criminal law implies that a certain behaviour is prohibited. For example, germline cell therapy may be prohibited by law. Such a prohibition, it can be argued, would reflect the overall consensus that exists with regard to the application of germline cell therapy, at least in Europe. In particular, some continental European countries such as France, Germany and Switserland favour a prohibition of germline cell therapy, although it is fair to admit that only Germany has introduced criminal legislation to enforce the prohibition. For another more recent example where this consensus has been reflected I refer to the report of the English Committee on the Ethics of Gene Therapy, the socalled Clothier committee. But at closer look, the opinion of this committee does not simply coincide with the consensus. Indeed the Clothier committee recommended «that gene modification of the germline should *not yet* be attempted» [1].

The position of the Clothier committee is more in line with the conclusions of the Fifth International Summit Conference on Bioethics on the mapping of the human genome «that there were neither medical nor ethical justifications for the intentional genetic manipulation of human germline cells *at this time.*»

And the supposed existing consensus throughout Europe completely fades away if we take a more distant view. The Declaration of Inuyama has left the door for germline cell therapy widely open: «such therapy might be the only means of treating certain conditions, so continued discussion of both its technical and its ethical aspects is essential. Before germline therapy is undertaken, its safety must be very well established, for changes in germ cells would affect the descendants of patients» [2].

## Disadvantages of a legal prohibition

A legal prohibition of germline cell therapy, enforceable with criminal sanctions, will block this continued discussion of the technical and ethical aspects. Moreover, one can almost be sure that pressed by the scientific community certain exceptions to the prohibition will have to be accepted. This technique of exceptions to a general rule is, however, not without dangers.

First, there is a technical problem: formulating these exceptions will be very difficult because of the underlying technical complexities.

Second, once one accepts a few exceptions there is the danger that the legal prohibition itself will come under severe pressure. This can finally lead to a situation where the rule is not enfor-

---

[1] *Bulletin of Medical Ethics*, February 1992, 8-10.
[2] Council for International Organizations of Medical Sciences, XXIV-th Round Table Conference, *Genetics, Ethics and Human Values: Human Genome Mapping, Genetic Screening and Therapy*, 22-27 July 1990.

ceable or not enforced anymore. As we know this threatens the very concept of the «rule of law». And this is probably more endangering Western democracies than the hitherto unknown risks of germline cell therapy.

Finally, accepting exceptions to the legal prohibition of germline cell therapy could lead to a new eugenics, in which someone or some group will decide which diseases will be treated and which will not [3].

## Towards a common European approach

A legal prohibition of germline cell therapy in one or a few European states also will cause problems at a supranational or international level. One might say that this or these countries are exporting in a certain way their problems to countries that take a more reluctant attitude regarding the use of criminal law. We have seen this obviously in Europe with regard to abortion; we see it now regarding *in vitro* fertilization and experiments on human embryos.

A legal prohibition in one country puts the other countries before an accomplished fact. Especially in the context of the European Community this is not acceptable anymore. Wide variations among Member States with regard to bio-ethical regulations will finally create differences in the medical practices of the Member States and thus differences in the provision of health care. Such differences will create distortions in the free circulation of persons and services.

To avoid this, a common approach —in Europe at least at the level of the European Community— is urgently needed. I agree with what J. Elizalde has remarked in his keynote speach: it will be eventually up to the Member States to introduce enforceable legislation. But before doing so, the Member States should make every possible effort —much more efforts than up to now— to reach a common determinator. Meanwhile, they should not introduce in their own jurisdiction rules that, by their absolute nature, impede this common efforts.

---

[3] Capron, A. M., «Which Ills to Bear?: Reevaluating the "Treat" of Modern Genetics», *Emory Law Journal*, 1990 (39), 3, 858.

# GENETIC MANIPULATION PRACTICES DEEMED WORTHY OF PENAL SANCTION

## Jaime M. Peris Riera

Professor of Criminal Law, University of Valencia. Spain.

There are two features traditionally held to be intrinsic to criminal law. The first is its «fragmentariness», meaning that criminal law should not safeguard all legal interest or values but only those deemed worthy and needing protection, and that this protection should only be wielded against the most serious and intolerable transgressions. The other criminal law principle is its subsidiarity, to indicate that penal sanctions are appropriate only when the legal system can be guaranteed only through punishment; if there exists some other less costly measure, one which involves less sacrifice, than criminal law should not be employed.

We must therefore surmise that the intent of the drafters of the criminal categories set down under Title V in Book II of the Criminal Code Bill 1992 was to illegalize those practices relative «to the genetic manipulation of human embryos and fetuses and to unconsented artificial insemination» deemed to be grave and intolerable attacks on a «new» legal value and which only criminal sanction could avert. Otherwise, we would have to conclude that these two traditional features of criminal law have been overlooked in this first attempt at penal regulation of genetic manipulation excesses.

The succinctness necessarily required of a conference paper does not allow for a thorough treatment of the subject or of each of the new criminal offences which have arisen in connection with genetic manipulation. For such a fuller exploration we may refer to other detailed considerations which have already been published. In this paper I will concentrate on putting forth certain specific formulations with respect to *(a)* the legally protected value; *(b)* the categories of genetic manipulation in the strict sense; *(c)* what I have called qualified coercion categories; and *(d)* offences involving illegal genetic manipulation of human organic material.

## Legally protected value

Undoubtedly the task of describing a legal value harbours great difficulties. In a general sense, the term «legal value» is used to refer to all human values protected by law (this and nothing else is what is meant by legal value); it is a thoroughly new concept and seeks to span fields which are still unpredictable. The task becomes almost impossible if we do not itemize areas.

Thus, to begin with, in the definition of genetic manipulation categories there is a constant allusion to what the Code's drafters term «vital constitutional type». This expression is scientifically incorrect and can only offer a very rough approximation of the underlying legal value.

The same legal value cannot be recognized for the categories of unconsented artificial insemination and gender selection – perhaps that is why the former, in the preliminary draft of the Bill, was included as an offence against sexual liberty (?), which reference has been maintained albeit outdated in the Bill's introductory statement of purpose– and much less so for the strange category of illegal manipulation of human organic material.

In general, what seems to be safeguarded in these categories is the overall liberty of persons, rendered as a protection of the right of consent in the free pursuit of one's personal development. In such a specialized area as genetics, the Code's drafters should be expected to exercise more precision when drawing up the law's provisions. Clearly the expression «vital constitutional type», to which no expert can assign an unequivocal meaning, does not live up to this expectation. This defect is all the more serious when considering that the said expression is used –by contradistinction to the human genome as a whole– to distinguish the basic offence from the aggravated offence.

## Categories of genetic manipulation in the strict sense

The types of manipulation are set down in section 167 of the Bill. The first two subsections regulate the offences involving wilful misconduct and the third covers those involving negligence or simple fault.

### 1. Wilful misconduct offences

There is the basic offence (167.2) and an aggravated offence (167.1) based on alteration of what is termed as «vital constitutional type».

– The basic offence is defined residually, as a complement to the aggravated degree... «all other manipulations» that are «performed in violation of the provisions of the law». According to the only interpretation which, as will be seen ahead, can be attributed to the aggravated offence, this category seeks to encompass any intrusion into the genomic structure.

– Central to the construction of the aggravated offence is the result produced by the «alteration of the vital constitutional type».

From the tenor of the provision and its juxtaposition with the one that there follows, it might be imagined that the reference to vital constitutional type implies punishment of any alteration of the human genetic component. As will be seen ahead, this is the only possible interpretation.

Even if one reasons that what was actually intended here was to punish manipulations entailing a change in the genetic contents transmitted by inheritance (the distinction between somatic and sexual cells is pivotal, because only manipulations of the latter are transmitted to all offspring), if this is in fact what was meant, the Code's drafters have expressed themselves very poorly.

According to the way the proposed Code regulates the offences, it must be concluded –like it or not– that mere manipulation, with no result whatsoever, constitutes the basic offence and that manipulations which alter the human genetic component (irrespective of whether it is somatic cells or sexual cells which are affected) constitute the aggravated offence.

### 2. Negligent offence

The negligent offence (167.3) is solely reserved for cases where manipulation produces harm to what it terms the «vital type» (this paragraph of the draft Code does not include the word «constitutional») because of «serious» negligence.

## Qualified coercion offences

By this expression I refer to the offences provided for in sections 168 and 170.1, although technically these are not forms of coercion in the pure sense. Nonetheless, they feature the absence of consent by the holder of the legally protected interest.

### 1.  Unconsented gender selection

The legislature should rectify the grievous error committed by both the author of the draft bill and of the bill itself, for «selection» (which is what I imagine the provision seeks to punish) has been confused with «determination» (which is what it actually punishes).

As the provision currently reads, the reference to the absence of consent and not to its denial, makes punishable the action of someone who «fulfils» the desires of the progenitors «without» their consent.

### 2.  Unconsented artificial insemination

If the proposed Code is approved, this strange but imaginable offence could produce a serious sanctioning disparity between unconsented artificial insemination practices and other practices which, having insemination as their purpose, violate other legal values but do so «naturally».

Thus, for example, statutory rape of a minor compounded with deceit or misuse of authority, and in which the offender moreover seeks to impregnate and succeeds, would under the proposed Code receive a lighter sanction than artificial insemination. Does the legislature wish to reward natural insemination?

In the preliminary draft, these cases were not included in the list of sexual aggressions and, hence, a woman impregnated in this way would not be entitled to a legal abortion. This incongruity has at least been eliminated in the Criminal Code bill (by section 153.1.3).

## Offences involving illegal genetic manipulation of human organic material

Section 169 epitomizes the «fear» with which the proposed Code's drafters regard any practice directly or indirectly related to genetic manipulation.

It represses all conducts involving the donation, use(?) or destruction of «human embryos and fetuses or their cells, tissues or organs» except for the cases specifically authorized by law.

The wording of the section offers an image of indiscriminate protection of any and all human cells, disregarding the most minimal requirement of specificity and not respecting the principle of minimum intervention of criminal law.

In general, it is possible to view the criminal categories in a favourable light only insofar as their mere existence inevitably represents an advance.

If they are to be «saved» further effort will be needed to make the terms more scientifically precise and thus more specific. Many of the sanctions will have to be revised, in order to avoid serious transgression of the principle of minimum intervention, and their serious lack of harmonization, especially as concerns sanctioning proportionality, will have to be solved.

# THE USE OF GENETIC INFORMATION IN REPRODUCTIVE DECISIONS

## John A. Robertson

Professor, Law School, University of Texas.
United States of America.

## Thomas Watt Gregory

Professor, Law School, University of Texas at Austin.
United States of America.

The clinical use of genetic information offers potentially beneficial treatment or intervention for a wide variety of problems. Such beneficial clinical uses range from somatic or germline gene therapy to the use of genetic information for reproductive decision-making. At the same time, however, the clinical application of genetic knowledge poses many difficult ethical, legal and policy problems which now must be addressed.

To address these issues coherently and effectively, it is essential that several kinds of distinctions be made. One is between experimental and established use of genetic knowledge. Another is between the kinds of uses that will be permitted once the efficacy of particular genetic interventions are established.

In my view, the issues raised by experimentation with genetic interventions are no different conceptually, ethically and legally than the issues raised by any form of human experimentation. With the Nuremburg and Helsinki Codes for Human Experimentation as background, the United States and most countries of Western Europe have developed a workable, effective set of guidelines for regulating human experimentation, including genetic experimentation. In the early stages of genetic experimentation, supplemental review boards at the national level may be advisable, as now exist in the United States with the National Institutes of Health Recombinant DNA Advisory Committee (RAC). However, with time and experience, genetic experimentation should fold into the existing structure of local and national review of government funded research, and be assimilated to that set of regulatory controls.

Rather than address these issues in depth, I think it is more useful to think of the precise problems which use of genetic information will pose once experimental uses are established as safe and effective. To this end, I propose identifying and discussing some of the main ethical, legal and policy issues that will arise with reproductive applications of genetic knowledge. Although gene therapy is another important area of clinical application, reproductive uses of genetic informaiton pose a special set of problems which require careful attention. They are likely to be the most common and frequent site of application of new genetic knowledge, and therefore deserve attention in their own right. The following discussion will highlight the main issues in reproductive use of genetic knowledge as they are likely to arise and be perceived in the United States.

## The problem

Advances in genetics made possible by the Human Genome Iniative (HGI) will have a major impact on reproductive decisionmaking. Many couples will want to use genetic knowledge in making decisions to reproduce or to avoid reproduction. Others will want to avoid having to take genetic information into account. The extent to which they may or may not make reproductive decisions on the basis of genetic information, and the extent to which physicians or government may force or constrain such choices, are important policy issues growing out of the HGI. These issues will be faced at many levels of decisionmaking, and involve individuals, couples, physicians, genetic counsellors, legislators, judges and other policy makers.

At the most basic level, these choices involve the limits and scope of procreative liberty. By building on prior work on the meaning and scope of procreative liberty, it will be possible to: 1) evaluate the extent to which ethical and legal concepts of procreative liberty entitle individuals/couples to *use* genetic knowledge to avoid offspring with genetic disease at premarital, preconception, preimplantation and prenatal stages of decisionmaking; 2) evaluate the extent to which ethical and legal concepts of procreative liberty entitle individuals/couples to *ignore* genetic knowledge in decisions to procreate, and thus risk producing offspring with genetic disease.

## I. The reproductive importance of genetic knowledge

It is now a truism to note that new genetic knowledge produced by the HGI will have a great impact on all stages of reproductive decisionmaking. As more genes are identified and their functions noted, there will be a greater tendency to incorporate this know-ledge into all levels of reproductive decisionmaking, including pre-marital, preconception, preimplantation and prenatal stages. De-cisions to avoid or engage in reproduction will be increasingly made on the basis of genetic information. Individuals will desire such information so that they can minimize the risk of having offspring with severe genetic disease, while others will oppose this use because of its effect on fetuses, on women or existing persons with those conditions, or because they are opposed to intervening in this natural process. (Rothman, 1986). As genetic knowledge grows, many persons will want to take account of that increasing fund of knowledge. Others, who are opposed to or uninterested in the use of genetic information, may feel pressured by physicians or public health agencies to use this information. (Fost and Wilfond, 1990). Eventually, states may pass laws requi-ring that people learn or be informed of their genetic status and use that information in reproductive decisions.

*Types of genetic information.* At present genetic information, through carrier screening or prenatal testing, is usually sought to avoid offspring with serious genetic disease, such as Tay Sachs, sickle cell anemia and Down Syndrome (Holtzman, 1989). A clear trend also exists to undergo carrier or prenatal testing to obtain information about late onset conditions such as Huntington's di-sease, and diseases that have a widely variable expressivity, such as cystic fibrosis. Carrier and/or prenatal tests for neurofibroma-tosis, Duchenne muscular dystrophy, fragile X syndrome, hemo-globinopathies, colon cancer and other genetic diseases are also expected. (*New York Times,* 1991) As more genetic knowledge emerges, carrier and prenatal states will be identified in which there is a high risk that a fetus or offspring has a genetic trait that predisposes or makes offspring more susceptible to heart disease, cancer, diabetes, bipolar disease and the like (Nelkin and Tancredi, 1989).

*Stages of decisionmaking.* The different types of genetic informa-tion will be relevant to reproductive decisionmaking at several stages. Premarital screening of persons for their carrier status may influence mate slection. Persons already married may undergo preconception carrier screening to determine whether they are carriers of an undesirable gene. If preconception tests show that both partners are carriers, the couple that wishes to have biologically related offspring may then decide to reproduce with an identifiable risk of transmission of the genetic disease to offspring, or to conceive and then undergo prenatal tests to ascertain whether the fetus has the genetic trait in question. Some prenatal testing will be available at the embryo level prior to implantation, but most will occur after pregnancy begins through chorion villus sampling or amniocentesis. When fetal cells are effectively obtained from maternal serum, prenatal screening will occur on the basis of a maternal blood test early in pregnancy (Price and Elias, 1991). Depending on the results of the prenatal test, the woman may decide to terminate pregnancy on that basis or not implant embryos with the genes in question.

*Differing perceptions of relevance.*   An important aspect of these developments is that many couples, physicians, genetics counsellors and policymakers will have differing views of the importance of taking this information into account in reproductive decisions. Many persons will value the importance of prenatal means of avoiding offspring with genetic disease, and seek access to that information and then act on it. Persons agreeing with them may urge that all persons be made aware of their genetic status and use it in their reproductive decisions. Others will be less enamoured of the ability to shape the genetic characteristics of offspring. They may oppose carrier or prenatal testing because of its impact on prenatal life, its perceived disrespect for existing persons with genetic diability, its impact on women, or because of deeply-held values of not «manufacturing» or «commodifying» offspring or interfering with the natural process of reproduction. Reconciling these disparate views of the importance or desirability of using –or not using– genetic information in reproductive decisions is a major issue presented by the Human Genome Initiative.

## 2.   Access or avoidance: public policy and practice issues

The main public policy and practice issues that arise with the increasing growth of genetic knowledge and the resulting carrier and prenatal tests concern questions of *access to* or *avoidance* of this information in reproductive decisionmaking.

As noted, many couples desiring families will welcome access to genetic information because they view it as increasing their chances of having healthy offspring. In some instances, individuals, physicians or government may oppose this use of genetic knowledge because of the impact of prenatal screening on embryos and fetuses, on existing persons with genetic disabilities, and on women and offspring. If physician practice, public policy or law adopts this restrictive position, access to genetic information to avoid having offspring with genetic disease will be frustrated, thus raising a major issue of procreative liberty.

In other instances, individuals or couples may refuse to learn their carrier status or to undergo prenatal testing because they would not terminate pregnancy, or because they accept the outcome of the genetic lottery for their offspring or otherwise disagree with the goals of prenatal testing. Their wish to avoid using genetic information in reproductive decisions might conflict with the efforts of physicians, public health agencies or government to reduce the number of handicapped births. Such a goal might be driven by a desire to prevent the suffering which severe genetic disease can cause or by a desire to conserve on medical costs. These actors may encourage, pressure or even compel individuals to become aware of or to use genetic information in their reproductive decisionmaking. In the extreme case, they might favor prohibiting some couples from conceiving or carrying affected fetuses to term. Laws or practices that compel the use of genetic information in reproductive decisions would interfere with an individual's liberty to procreate as he or she chooses –without regard to the genetic outcome for offspring.

Given these disparate views, it is essential that families, physicians, genetic counsellors, public health agencies, legislators, judges and other policymakers be aware of the right to use or not use genetic information in reproductive decisions. In examining the ethical and legal arguments for and against rights to use or not use genetic information, and thus identifying the ethical and legal status of such rights, future work on this issue will assist the many persons facing such questions to come to terms with them in personal, professional and policymaking contexts.

It is essential, for example, that all actors be aware of the scope of any rights to have *access* to genetic information in order to avoid, either by premarital, preconception or prenatal actions, offspring with unwanted genetic traits or conditions. Scholarly investigation and analysis of rights to use genetics in reproductive decisionmaking will thus help to protect the interests of individuals/couples in making such decisions. It will also help physicians, ethicists, legislators, judges and policymakers who are trying to determine the limits of these rights to reach well-reasoned conclusions.

Similarly, scholarly investigation and analysis of the extent to which individuals/couples are free to *ignore* genetic information and risk having offspring with genetic disease whose birth could have been avoided will protect rights to procreate regardless of the genetic outcome. It will also help make physicians, counsellors, public health agencies and other policymakers aware of the limits of encouraging or requiring that genetic information be used against a person's will, and thus help prevent the creation of mandatory testing and use programs that override those rights.

Finally, analysis of the scope of rights to use or not use genetic information in reproductive decisions will lay the groundwork for investigating other ethical and legal issues arising from the HGI. For example, as gene therapy develops in safety and efficacy, the question of inserting genes into embryos and fetuses, with possible germline effects, will arise. In determining the acceptability of germline gene therapy, the procreative rights of parents to have healthy offspring must be addressed. When later ethical, legal and policy analysis addresses those issues, this project's analysis of the right to use or not use genetic information in reproductive decisions will provide a useful starting point for addressing those questions.

### 3.  Previous work on reproductive use of genetics

Because there is already a considerable literature on carrier and prenatal screening, scholarly attention to these issues need not replicate that work, but can build on it and extend it in several ways that have not previously occurred. For example, there is considerable legal scholarship on tort remedies for physicians and genetics counsellors who fail to inform or misdiagnose genetic risks, dating back to the 1970's (Waltz, 1973; Wright, 1978; Capron, 1979; Andrews, 1987, 1992; Annas and Elias, 1987). There have also been good studies of both voluntary and compulsory newborn and carrier screening programs (Reilly, 1977; National Research Council, 1975). However, no one has combined tort and policy analysis of these issues with the constitutional dimensions of procreative choice. Nor has the recent phenomena of American states granting physicians immunity for genetic torts, and the testing dilemmas presented by imperfect and socially premature carrier tests been tied together with tort and constitutional analysis. A synthesis of these several elements within an overarching framework of procreative liberty will make a unique and original contribution to the literature.

Similarly, there is a body of previous work on rights to ignore genetic information in reproduction that needs extension and revision in light of recent legal and genetic developments. Thus while there is an important body of literature on eugenic sterilization (Kevles, 1985; Lombardo, 1985; Reilly, 1991), no constitutional analysis of these issues based on an overarching theory of procreative liberty and recent judicial decisions exists. For example, there is not yet a definitive analysis of how the overwhelmingly strong opposition to forcible eugenic sterilization relates to current practices that permit some sterilization of the retarded or to the continued existence of *Buck v. Bell* (the Supreme Court case which upheld involuntary sterilization of mentally retarded persons) as a legal precedent. Nor has the ethical, legal or policy aspects of a temporary interference with procreation through mandatory contraception yet been analyzed. Finally, other than a 1974 article dealing with amniocentesis (Friedman, 1974), there have been few articles dealing with the legal and ethical aspects of state programs that strongly encourage or compel carrier or prenatal genetic testing in order to avoid handicapped births. Ethical and legal analysis is needed to provide an up-to date account of the extent to which ethical and legal accounts of procreative liberty includes the right to ignore genetic information in reproduction.

A more extensive account of the issues involved in using gentic information both to avoid and to engage in reproduction follows.

## The right to have and use genetic information in reproductive decisionmaking

Any such investigation must first apply the ethical and legal concepts of procreative liberty developed in earlier work (Robertson, 1983, 1986, 1992b) to various uses of genetic knowledge in decisions to avoid reproduction. It should look at freedom to use genetic knowledge at each stage of reproductive decisionmaking (premarital, preconceptual, preimplantation and prenatal), and then examine the extent, if any, to which the state or physicians may prevent, or must provide or facilitate, access to and use of genetic information by individuals/couples interested in avoiding offspring with genetic disease. This analysis will consider the extent to which competing considerations, such as respect for prenatal life, for persons with genetic disability or scientific uncertainty justify limiting access to or use of genetic knowledge in reproductive decisionmaking.

### 1. Private barriers

In addressing issues of access and use, the proposed research will distinguish between private and public barriers. In the section dealing with private barriers, it will address the extent to which physicians, genetic counsellors or other health care providers who are in a professional-client relationship are ethically or legally obligated to provide persons with genetic information, including carrier or prenatal genetic tests or offers or referrals for such tests. This section will relate the duties created by legal doctrines of informed consent and negligence as recognized in wrongful life and wrongful birth claims to questions of access and use of genetics in reproductive decisionmaking. It will consider failures to test or refer for testing due to ambiguities in the operative legal standard of care, as well as those based on technological or social prematurity of the test. The current debate over whether all married couples should be routinely screened for cystic fibrosis will be used as a model of other testing dilemmas (United States Congress, 1992). It will also evaluate the extent to which conscientious beliefs of the professional about abortion, existing persons with genetic disability or other factors may influence their obligation to provide genetic information or services. The role of insurance coverage in blocking or facilitating access to genetic testing will also be addressed.

Special attention in this part of the research should be given to statutes in 12 states that prohibit damages for wrongful birth due to physician negligence in diagnosing genetic or other conditions that would have led a woman to abort. These statutes need to be analyzed for their constitutionality and for their consistency with prevailing ethical and legal doctrines of the right to avoid reproduction, and their potential for decreasing the care with which physicians and laboratories provide or carry out genetic test.

## 2.   *Public barriers*

In additional to private barriers, the role of public barriers in obtaining or using genetic information must also be addressed. The emphasis here should be on state laws or policies that impede or prevent access to genetic tests desired by couples facing reproductive decisions, or that impede or prevent their acting on such information. This part of the study will examine the extent to which existing laws prohibit or impede access or use of genetic information, and the constitutionality of such bans. Since there are no direct limits now on carrier or prenatal testing per se, the main focus of this section will be on public policies that would restrict abortion on genetic grounds.

With *Casey v. Planned Parenthood of Southeastern Pennsylvania* (United States Supreme Court, 1992) upholding the basic right to terminate pregnancy until viability recognized in *Roe v. Wade* (United States Supreme Court, 1973) the power of the state to ban abortion for any genetic indication, including gender, susceptibility traits or reasons perceived as frivolous, is presently questionable. However, changes in the make-up of the Supreme Court could alter this situation and empower the state to ban abortion in many circumstances. If that occurs, the question of the extent to which particular states would or should recognize an exception to a general ban on abortion to permit abortion for genetic reasons would have to be addressed.

This section will analyze the justification for permitting or prohibiting abortion on genetic grounds, in terms of benefitting offspring, parents and society. It will also identify the extent to which proposed or existing anti-abortion laws (which are not currently operative due to *Roe v. Wade*) recognize an exception for genetic indications either before or after viability (Clayton, 1992). Variations in statutory language will be identified and analyzed, and their validity under constitutional doctrines of vagueness and fair notice assessed. The question of whether many of the conditions now sought to be avoided through prenatal diagnosis, such as Down syndrome and sickle cell disease, would qualify under that language will also be addressed. This inquiry is especially important, because those statutes use terms such as «fetal deformity» or «grave defect» (Utah Statutes, 1991) that have no readily ascertainable meaning.

This section will also consider ethical, legal and medical developments that affect access to preimplantation genetic diagnosis or embryo biopsy. The applicant will bring his previous work (Robertson, 1992a) on this topic up to date, and consider the relation between the ethical and legal status of abortion and embryo discard for genetic reasons. As the analysis will make clear, the legality of abortion does not necessarily control the disposition of embryos, and thus other concepts and doctrines must be used to evaluate the validity of public barriers to use of embryo biopsy as a way to prevent offspring with genetic disease.

## Right to ignore genetic information in reproductive decisionmaking

As previously noted, although many persons will wish to use genetic information to minimize the chance of offspring with genetic disease, other persons will refuse to be tested or to act on the results of such tests. Their refusal may be based on inadequate resources, ignorance of the inheritability of disease, or, more likely, on deeply held religious, moral or cultural views about prenatal life, the nature of reproduction and the worth of persons with genetic disability.

In refusing to make use of available genetic information, these couples will be knowingly risking the birth of offspring with serious genetic disease. Although many families cope well with genetic disease, some parents, siblings and affected children suffer greatly. Offspring with such disease may also require expensive medical and educational services, which may be inadequate in times of shrinking health care and social service budgets. Inevitably, some persons will question the right of persons knowingly to reproduce when there is a high risk of genetically disabled offspring for whom the parents will not provide parenting. Proposals for public policies to reduce such births can be expected, thus raising highly controversial and sensitive questions about the scope of the right to procreate.

Research analyzing these issues should address the question of when private health care actors and the state may inform, encourage or compel persons to use genetic information in reproductive decisions so that offspring with serious genetic disease will not be born. Drawing on earlier work on procreative liberty (Robertson, 1983, 1986, 1992b), it should first establish that a right to reproduce exists which would presumptively include the right knowingly to produce handicapped offspring. I will then examine competing interests that might limit that right, such as the interest in protecting offspring who will be handicapped and the interest in conserving medical and social resources for use by others. It should also consider the extent to which even apparently justifiable limitations on procreation would lessen respect for persons with disabilities generally or set an easily abusable precedent for state intrusion on procreative choice.

Proposals to encourage or compel the use of genetic information at various stages of reproductive decisonmaking should be assessed in light of this analysis of procreative liberty. Such analysis should proceed by first discussing the least intrusive interventions and progress to increasingly greater intrusions to discourage or prevent such births.

## I.   Subsidies and required notification

The least intrusive policies to discourage such births would be state subsidies for preconception and prenatal testing, so that access to the relevant information and the ability to act on it is provided, and laws that require health care providers to inform at risk persons of the availability of preconception and prenatal tests for specified genetic conditions. Of special interest in this regard are the California regulations that require physicians to inform pregnant women of the availability of maternal $\alpha$-fetoprotein screening to detect neural tube defects or Down Syndrome.

Although such policies can be defended as promoting reproductive autonomy, they carry the risk that they will be used by physicians, genetic counsellors and others in ways that effectively leave women with no realistic choice to say no to the preferred tests (Rothman, 1986; Lippman, 1992). In addition, to the extent that the state is promoting private actions to avert the birth of offspring with genetic disease, this action may be perceived as a denigration of the worth of disabled persons and the families that rear them (Asch, 1988). The analysis will evaluate these concerns in assessing the ethical, legal and policy benefits of state subsidies and required notification, and will identify guidelines in operating such programs that will effectively preserve the choice of women not to be tested.

## 2. Mandatory carrier and prenatal testing

It will also be necessary to assess and analyze the status of mandatory testing at both the preconception and prenatal stages of decisionmaking. Mandatory carrier testing would require that persons at risk for specified genetic traits be tested so that they will be aware of their genetic status and their risk of producing offspring with the specified condition. A key issue to be addressed is whether the intrusion on bodily integrity and personal privacy of mandatory preconception genetic testing has sufficient social benefits to meet applicable constitutional standards of validity –an inquiry that goes beyond most previous work on genetic screening laws (Reilly, 1977). This analysis will have to reconcile the relatively minor physical intrusion required for the test (blood test or mouth swab), the freedom the person tested retains to reproduce as he or she wills and the harm to privacy interests of having one's genetic status revealed even in a confidential setting. In addition to determining the constitutional status of mandatory preconception testing, this part of the study will also address the likely social costs and benefits of such a policy.

The constitutional status and policy benefits of mandatory prenatal testing should also be addressed. Manatory prenatal testing would assure that women are aware of the genetic status of their fetus, so that they could take that information into account in deciding whether to continue a pregnancy. However, prenatal testing by amniocentesis or chorion villus sampling is highly intrusive for the pregnant woman and risky for the fetus. The social benefits of informing women of fetal genetic status against their will would hardly seem sufficient to justify such a major bodily intrusion. An important issue, however, is whether mandatory prenatal testing would be acceptable if the test were done on maternal serum obtained from a blood sample (Elias and Simpson, 1992). If mandatory preconception testing by blood test is acceptable, would not a prenatal test by the same means also be acceptable? Would the prenatal timing of the mandatory test change this, because of the greater impact of unwanted knowledge when the person refusing testing is pregnant? This section of the research will confront these issues and relate them to HIV and other kinds of health testing that some have urged be made mandatory (Gostin, 1989).

### 3. Mandatory abortion, contraception and sterilization

It will also be essential to assess policies that prevent or prohibit persons at risk of producing offspring with genetic disease from having children. Although no such proposals are now seriously being considered, public officials periodically call for mandatory sterilization or contraception for welfare recipients. With an accelerating growth of genetic information from the HGI, calls for prohibitions on genetically at risk reproduction may also arise. Indeed, the development of the long-lasting contraceptive implant Norplant has already led to judically-imposed restrictions on reproduction by convicted child abusers and calls for legislation to pay welfare recipients for accepting Norplant (Arthur, 1992).

In assessing the constitutional and policy merits of such drastic reproductive interventions as mandatory contraception, sterilization or abortion, it is essential first to address the previous experience of mandatory eugenic sterilization in the United States (Kevles, 1985; Lombardo, 1985; Reilly, 1991). The current legal status of involuntary sterilization should also be described, and current cases that permit involuntary sterilization when benefit to the sterilized person is shown distinguished from that discredited tradition (New Jersey Supreme Court, 1981). Using these precedents, it will be possible to determine when, if ever at all, mandatory sterilization on genetic grounds is possible.

An important issue to be analyzed is the constitutional and policy validity of mandatory contraception through the use of Norplant or similar long-lasting implants for persons at risk of producing offspring with severe genetic disease. Since contraception, unlike sterilization, is temporary and reversible, it might appear to intrude less substantially on procreative choice, and thus be more acceptable as a policy for recalcitrant persons at risk of producing genetically affected offspring. This analysis will address the burdens and benefits of such proposals, and show that the argument for mandatory contraception, like the argument for mandatory sterilization, is not persuasive on either constitutional, ethical or policy grounds.

Finally, to round out the analysis the question of mandatory abortion in cases in which a prenatal test for a severe genetic disease is positive and the woman wishes to continue the pregnancy should be addressed. While such an intrusive policy would be hard to justify, the intrusion on reproductive choice might appear less than would arise with mandatory sterilization or contraception, because the ability to reproduce in other situations is still preserved. Ethical and legal analysis of the burdens and benefits of such a policy will complete the analysis of state efforts to prevent or prohibit persons at risk of having offspring with severe genetic disease from reproducing.

## Limitations of a rights-based approach

Although much of the research necessary to identify the limits of the right to use or avoid using genetic information in reproductive decisionmaking involves a traditional rights-based ethical and legal analysis, one must stay aware of the limitations of such an approach when applied to such a charged issue as genetics and reproductive choice (Glendon, 1991). Rights-based analysis has many virtues, but the personal and social social setting of reproductive decisionmaking is often as important as the formal structure of legal rights and duties. Wealth, gender, race, class and the structure of health care delivery systems all enter into whether and how effectively formal legal rights are exercised. As several commentators have shown in their accounts of the hidden values and coercive influences operating in prenatal diagnosis, a purely rights-based analysis that ignored these dimensions would be seriously deficient (Rothman, 1986; Rapp, 1987; Lippman, 1992). To avoid this incompleteness, any research into these issues should draw on feminist and critical literature as relevant to show the limitations of the rights-based approach that largely informs legal and ethical analysis. Such attention will help flesh out the full parameters and conflicts that arise with reproductive use of genetic information.

## Conclusion

This discussion of issues in reproductive use of genetic information that ethical, legal and policy analysis must grapple with shows the range of issues that must be faced as genetic research moves from the laboratory and clinical trial to established and accepted use. The ethical and legal issues that arise with experimental use of genetics are important and must be addressed before proceeding. But in the long run the major challenge from genetic innovation will be the uses that individuals, couples, physicians and society permit or discourage in everyday clinical settings and in human reproduction.

# Bibliography

**Andrews, L. (1987):** *Medical Genetics: A Legal Frontier.* ABA.

**Andrews, L. (1992):** *Torts and the Double Helix: Malpractice Liability for Failure to Warn of Genetic Risks,* «Houston Law Rev.» 29:149.

**Arthur, S. L. (1993):** *The Norplant Prescription: Birth Control, Women Control or Crime Control,* «UCLA Law Rev.» (forthcoming).

**Asch, A. (1988):** *Reproductive Technology and Disability* in «Reproductive Laws for the 1990's», Cohen and Taub, editors.

**Clayton, E. W. (1992):** *Reproductive Genetic Testing: Regulatory and Liability Issues, Fetal Diagnosis and Therapy* (in press).

**Capron, A. M. (1979):** *Tort Liability in Genetic Counselling,* «Columbia Law Rev.» 79:619.

**Elia, S. and Annas, G. J. (1987):** *Reproductive Genetics and the Law.* Yearbook Publishers.

**Elia, S. and Simpson, J. L. (1992) (eds.):** *Maternal Serum Screening for Fetal Genetic Disorders* (New York, Church Livingstone).

**Friedman, J. M. (1974):** *Legal Implications of Amniocentesis,* «UPA Law Rev.» 123:92.

**Glendon, M. A. (1991):** *Rights Talk: The Impoverishment of Political Discourse* (New York: Free Press).

**Gostin, L. (1989):** *The Politics of AIDS: Compulsory State Powers, Public Health and Civil Liberties,* «Ohio St. Law J.» 49:1017.

**Holtzman, N. A. (1989):** *Proceed With Caution: Predicting Genetic Risks in the Recombinant DNA* (Baltimore: Johns Hopkins University Press, 1989).

**Kevles, D. (1985):** *In the Name of Eugenics: Genetics and the Uses of Human Heredity.*

**Lippman, A. (1992):** *Mother Matters: A Fresh Look at Prenatal Genetic Testing,* «Issues in Reproductive and Genetic Engineering», 5(2):141-154.

**Lombardo, P. (1985):** *Three Generations, No Imbeciles: New Light on Buck v. Bell,* «NYU Law Rev.» 60:30 (1985).

**National Research Council (1975):** Committee for the Study of Inborn Errors of Metabolism, *Genetic Screening: Programs, Principles and Research.*

**Nelkin, D. and Tancredi, L.** (1989): *Dangerous Diagnostics: The Social Power of Biological Information* (New York: Basic Books).

**New Jersey Supreme Court (1981):** *In re Grady*, 85 N.J. 235, 426 A.2d 467.

**New York Times (1991):** *Doctors Link Gene to Colon Cancer*, Aug. 8, p. A9. (by Natalie Angier).

**Price, J. O.; Elia, S.; Wachtell, S. S. et al.** (1991): *Prenatal Diagnosis Using Fetal Cells Isolated from Maternal Blood by Multiparameter Flow Cytometry*, «Am J. Obstet Gynecol.» 165:1731-1737.

**Rapp, R.** (1987): *Moral Pioneers: Women, Men and Fetuses on a Frontier of Reproductive Technology*, «Women and Health» 13:101-116.

**Reilly, P. R.** (1977): *Genetics, Law and Society* (Cambridge: Harvard University Press).

**Reilly, P. R.** (1991): *The Surgical Solution: A History of Involuntary Sterilization in the United States* (Baltimore: Johns Hopkins University Press).

**Robertson, J. A.** (1982): *The Right to Procreate and In Utero Fetal Therapy*, «Journal of Legal Medicine» 3:333.

**Robertson, J. A.** (1983): *Procreative Liberty and the Control of Conception, Pregnancy and Childbirth*, «Virginia Law Rev.» 69(3):405.

**Robertson, J. A.** (1986): *Embryos, Families and Procreative Liberty: The Legal Structure of the New Reproduction*, «Southern California Law Rev.» 59(5):939-967.

**Robertson, J. A.** (1987): *Pregnancy and Prenatal Harm to Offspring: The Case of Mothers With PKU*, «Hastings Center Report», Aug. 1987, pg. 23 (with Joseph D. Shulman).

**Robertson, J. A.** (1988): *Rights, Symbolism, and Public Policy in Fetal Tissue Transplants*, «Hastings Center Report», Dec. 1988, pg. 5.

**Robertson, J. A.** (1989): *Resolving Disputes Over Frozen Embryos*, «Hastings Center Report», Nov./Dec. 1989, pg. 7.

**Robertson, J. A.** (1989): *Ethical and Legal Issues in Human Egg Donation*, «Fertility and Sterility» 52(3):353.

**Robertson, J. A.** (1990a): *Procreative Liberty and Human Genetics*, «Emory Law J.» 39(3):697.

**Robertson, J. A.** (1990b): *In the Beginning: the Legal Status of Early Embryos*, «Virginia Law Rev.» 76(3):437.

**Robertson, J. A.** (1992a): *Ethical and Legal Issues in Preimplantation Genetic Screening*, «Fertility and Sterility», 57(1):1.

**Robertson, J. A. (1994):** *Autonomy and Ambivalence: Reproductive Technology and the Limits of Procreative Liberty,* (forthcoming, Princeton University Press).

**Rothman, B. K. (1986):** *The Tentative Pregnancy* (New York, Viking).

**United States Congress (1992):** Office of Technology Assessment: *Cystic Fibrosis and DNA Tests: Implications of Carrier Screening.*

**United States Supreme Court:**
> *Buck v. Bell,* 274 US 200 (1927).
> *Roe v. Wade,* 410 US 113 (1973).
> *Casey v. Planned Parenthood of Southeastern Pennsylvania,* 112 S.Ct. 2791 (1992).

**Utah Statutes Annotated (1991):** *Criminal Code,* Sec. 76-7-302.

**Waltz, J. R. and Thigpen, C. R. (1973):** *Genetic Screening and Counselling: the Legal and Ethical Issues,* «Northwestern Law Rev.» 68:696.

**Wilfond, B. E. and Fost, N. C. (1990):** *The Cystic Fibrosis Gene: Medical and Social Implications for Heterzygote Detection,* «JAMA» 263:2777.

**Wright, E. E. (1978):** Note: *Father and Mother Know Best: Defining the Liability of Physicians for Inadequate Genetic Counselling* «Yale Law J.» 87:1488-1515.

# HUMAN GENE MANIPULATION AND THE LAW

## Jaime Vidal Martínez

Professor of Civil Law, University of Valencia. Spain.

### Introduction

Scientific progress has now made it possible to isolate genes or individual hereditary factors, determine their structure, and combine them, even surpassing the biological limits established by nature between distinct species of living organisms [1].

Studies and research carried on during this century, particularly in recent decades, have allowed genetics, in conjunction with other disciplines, to give birth to molecular biology, one of the most fruitful syntheses of modern science, with very promising and even already practicable applications in various fields. But this has also paved the way for certain activities that harbour considerable risks and thus demand legal regulation [2].

---

[1] Karl Sperling, «Ingeniería genética y Medicina genética» [«Genetic engineering and genetic medicine»], *Ingeniería genética y reproducción asistida,* published by Marino Barbero Santos, Madrid 1989, pg. 109.

[2] With respect to certain concrete questions such as prenatal diagnosis or the need to avoid discrimination in employment affairs, insurance, etc., there have been attempts at legal regulation and there even exists a certain body of legal literature.

Hence, it is not surprising from the scientific standpoint that, with molecular biological structure having been probed and its component nucleotides combined and reproduced, first in bacteria and later in higher animals, the idea should arise of undertaking the enormous task of sequencing the nucleotides of the human genome, and that the possibility be contemplated of one day remedying a large number of dysfunctions and diseases attributable more or less directly to human gene disorders or mutations [3].

Despite the fears voiced by scientists from various countries, which in some cases led to moratoriums on or suspension of funding for further research, the Human Genome Project is a reality on which diverse countries collaborate. This initiative is expected to provided doubtless benefits for the fields of preventive and predictive medicine, and obviously for the development of scientific and technical knowledge [4]. This, however, does not preclude scientific controversy, given the enormous costs of the Project and the grave shortage of medical care, including in basic aspects, suffered by broad sectors of the world population [5], irrespective of the grimmer possibilities which could be ushered in by human gene manipulation, bringing the very essence of humankind into play [6].

In my opinion, this grandiose research programme into the human genome should not be viewed as isolated from other scientific advances pointing to the possibility of humans intervening in their nature, which thus mark a turning point of unpredictable, and certainly unprecedented, consequences in the history of humanity [7].

Among the aforesaid scientific advances, the development of numerous techniques grouped under the common name of *in vitro* fertilization obviously accelerates the development of human genetics, as well as of other sciences and techniques which are enriched by the possibilities of new forms of human reproduction [8] and which are, in turn, polarized by the consideration of

---

[3] This question is dealt with, prior to the legal analysis, in the work *Dignité humaine et patrimoine génétique* working paper prepared for the legal reform commission of Canada by Bartha Maria Knoppers, Ottawa, Montreal, 1991, pgs. 5 and ff.

[4] Santiago Grisolía, *El Proyecto del Genoma Humano,* monographs published by the Consell Valencià de cultura, Valencia, 1990.

[5] Dr Jean Martín, «L'Homme dans la nature», *J Int Bioéth,* 1991, pgs. 34-45; «Bioéthique et economie: vers un temps de questions insopportables», *J Int,* 1992, pgs. 157-162.

[6] Javier Gafo, «El nuevo "homo habilis"» [«The new "homo habilis"»], *Ingeniería genética,* op. cit., pgs. 150-172.

[7] Jaime Vidal Martínez, «Derecho y Bioética» [«Law and Bioethics»], *Revista General de Derecho, Sección de Derecho y Bioética,* December 1992, pgs. 11959-11963.

[8] Carlos M.ª Romeo Casabona, «La persona entre la biotecnología, la bioética y el Derecho» [«The individual, between biotechnology, bioethics and law»],

the human embryo conceived *in vitro* [9]. In this context, and from the standpoint of talk of the «New Biology» or «Life Sciences», the Human Genome Project takes up scientific study of the ultimate citadel of human life, probing the possible interrelation in the purely biological arena with other forms of life of widely variegated complexity [10] and taking into account the radical distinction established in ethical and legal plans between human beings (persons) and other animal species inhabiting the Earth.

## Ethical aspects

The expected expansion of human genome knowledge should produce –is already producing– practical consequences of important bearing not only in the sphere of ethics, but for the world of law as well. These concerns include the violation of personal privacy rights made possible by familiarity with an individual's genetic map [11] and, even more troublesome, by the automated processing of such personal information. These possibilities are in any event the prelude to possible discriminations and a potential source of extremely serious ethical conflicts, all the more so when considering that advances in human genome knowledge are likely to outpace the attainment of solutions for the problems arising from said knowledge. What is more, that presumed genetic determinism is perhaps only part of the truth and further scientific knowledge will actually confirm the radical freedom of the human being, always exercised in a given context. To stress

---

Folia Humanística, January 1986; Jaime Vidal Martínez, «Las nuevas formas de reproducción humana: introducción y panorama general» [«The new forms of human reproduction: introduction and general overview»], *Revista General de Derecho*, September 1986.

[9] Jaime Vidal Martínez, «Algunos datos y observaciones para contribuir a la consideración jurídica del embrión humano concebido in vitro» [«Some data and remarks to contribute to the legal consideration of the human embryo conceived in vitro», in the book-homage to professor Lacruz Berdejo, vol. II, 1993: 2077-2015.

[10] Scientists have managed to endow microorganisms with the genetic capacity to produce nucleic acids and proteins, enzymes of medical or commercial utility which can be used directly or as means of producing substances such as hormones, antibiotics and suchlike (Ernesto di Mauro: *Il dio genetico*, Rome, 1991, pg. 74).

[11] The ethical and legal problems arising from individual genome knowledge and related discrimination are addressed in different papers included in the *Journal International de Bioéthique*, no. 3, vol. I, September 1990 and ff. The question of «El diagnóstico antenatal y sus implicaciones jurídicos penales» [Antenatal diagnosis and its criminal law implications] is examined by professor Romeo Casabona, *La Ley*, July 10th 1987. Recently, by the same author *El Derecho y la Bioética ante los límites de la vida humana*, Madrid, 1994, pgs. 373-386; «Aspectos jurídicos del consejo genético» [«Legal aspects of genetic counselling»], *Revista de Derecho y Genoma Humano/Law and the Human Genome Review*, no. 1 July-December 1994: 153-177.

genetics and disregard all environmental influences would therefore be senseless, and to attempt to modify human nature when we are barely beginning to decode the genetic code veritable madness.

It is precisely this possibility of modifying human genetic roots that poses the most troubling concerns, for, even where beneficial, such modifications could be uncontrollably subverted in other contexts, particularly in the case of germ cell alterations passed on to offspring. If to this we add the possibilities of testing combinations of genetic material without regard for therapeutic purposes, the prospects called forth by genetic manipulation become enormously worrisome, even when keeping a tight rein on our imaginations. Hence the term «manipulation», which per se carries a certain pejorative content.

That is why the Council of Europe, in its Recommendation 934 of 1982 on genetic engineering, asserted that the right to life and to human dignity entail a right to unaltered genetic traits [12].

It was soon after the decisive advances made in DNA recombination in the years 1973-1977 that there occurred the first birth of a human being conceived in vitro (1978), a technique which allows human embryos to be obtained, manipulated and subjected to experimentation. It is only logical that scientific advances of such magnitude and unforeseeable consequences have thenceforth occupied a preeminent position in the ethical reflection accompanying the new biology. These debates have given rise to bioethics, in which that which may be done and be obtained is contraposed against what should be done and the search for the common good, in some cases consisting in the preservation of our civilization's most essential values.

The ethics committees which have emerged in hospitals, and movements within the world of bioethics which have spread and even acquired national importance, are today also expected to address biomedical research and biotechnologies, be it for consultative purposes or with certain sanctioning powers. In any event, the interdisciplinary meetings on new forms of human reproduction demonstrate the growing concern with embryology, placing the possibilities brought about by human embryo manipulation at the focus of important recent regulations of these issues in European countries [13].

---

[12] Nevertheless, Knoppers has warned, this intended protective interpretation would lead to selection of individuals apt for procreation (op. cit., pg. 33). Recourse to the language of rights in the genetic arena favours conflicts (pg. 63).
[13] Paradigmatically in the legislation introduced in late 1990 in the United Kingdom and Germany.

Already at the international meeting on Cooperation for the Human Genome Project held in Valencia in October 1988, the need was raised for placing limits on the manipulation of human genetic material. Yet, many of the scientists interested in the Project believed that experimental procedures could only be regulated by the scientists themselves, acknowledging their responsibility to ensure that genetic information be used to enhance the dignity of the individual, requesting greater international cooperation and accessibility to such information for scientists from all countries [14].

In November 1990, addressing the ethical aspects of the Human Genome Project, the signatories to the so-called «Valencia Declaration» restated those principles, asserting that civilized society must respect human diversity, including genetic variations. The Declaration stated that the mapping and sequencing of the human genome will have great benefit for human health and wellbeing, concluding, *inter alia,* that somatic cell gene therapy may be admissible, but that germline gene therapy faces numerous obstacles, does not command general ethical consensus, and therefore requires broader debate as to its technical, medical and social implications [15].

The so-called Universal Scientific Responsibility Movement, in its 1989 Declaration, proposed that the following new article be added to the Universal Declaration of Human Rights: «Scientific knowledge must not be used except to serve the dignity, integrity and future of Man, but nobody can block its acquisition»; at the same time calling on the UN to pronounce itself on such issues as a prohibition on inheritable alterations of human genetic heritage in light of the current state of knowledge, which would not rule out treatment of genetic diseases by means of modifying non-reproduction cells.

The Human Genome Project has nevertheless stirred fears of a new eugenicist movement and of an ultimate long-term risk: the possibility of reprogramming the human genetic code for other than therapeutic purposes. Hence the position that the exercise of new powers should also entail new duties. Germ-line therapy, it is believed, could perhaps be acceptable in the future with the consent of the highest ethical and scientific authorities and after broad public debate based on full, complete and intelligible information [16].

---

[14] «Valencia Declaration on the Human Genome Project», October 24-26th 1988, in the work *Human Genome Project: Ethics,* op. cit., pg. 19.

[15] «2nd Workshop on International Cooperation for the Human Genome Project: Ethics, Valencia declaration on ethics and the human genome project», *J Int Bioéth,* 1991, pgs. 94-95. *Human Genome Project: Ethics,* various authors, Fundación BBV, Bilbao, 1993: 26-31.

[16] *Les Cahiers du MURS,* no. 26, 1991, contains several articles on these issues. See pg. 83.

The UNESCO organized International Workshop on Bioethics and the social consequences of biomedical research, held in Moscow in May 1991, stressed the need for guidelines and international coordination, displaying a nearly unanimous concern for the relations between bioethics and the law, while at the same time revealing how the fast pace of progress in biotechnologies makes it difficult to render societal morals into law. According to some of the opinions there expressed, the reasons for drafting specific regulations would have to be convincingly set forth, whereas others adopted the position that general legislation would be required given the novelty of certain issues such as gene therapy. Another proposal put forward was to follow the example of Ethics Committees such as the one set up in France, issuing consultative findings and recommending specific legislative provisions, in the express hope that certain main principles governed by the supreme value of human dignity would be enunciated at the international level [17].

However, the proliferation of Ethics Committees has in certain areas such as gene therapy led to rivalries and the birth of review or coordination bodies, while the steady advances in genetic engineering are demanding a continual updating of the applicable principles and conceptas [18]. The Human Genome Project, others assert, rests on unverified assumptions that the genes are a phototrace of the organism and that gene information will facilitate treatment and care [19]. However, the use of this knowledge in performing gene therapy still entails major uncertainties and also requires ethical study translated into a specific programme for evaluating the ethical, legal and social consequences of the Human Genome Project [20].

It may therefore be concluded that modification of human germ cells for therapeutic or preventive purposes presents much greater difficulties than modification of somatic cells and is not currently contemplated, given that any changes so effected could affect a patient's offspring. The safety of such procedures must therefore be fully assured, and researchers and therapists will

---

[17] Bioéthique et droits d l'Homme. Rapport final et recommandations de la reunion internationale sur la bioéthique et les conséquences sociales de la recherche biomedicale. Moscow May 13-15th 1991, UNESCO. The text contains some of the information and proposals from participants at the Moscow Workshop.
[18] Odetter Valabreg e-Wurzburguer, «Introduction chez l'homme de materiel genétique modifié. La thérapie genique», J Int Bioéth, 1990, 245-263, pg. 259.
[19] Council for responsible genetics, «What's Wrong with the Human Genome Initiative?», J Int Bioéth, 1990, 221-224, pg. 221.
[20] Without disregarding the religious aspects of the subject, Albert S. Moraczewski, «The Human Genome Project and the Catholic Church», J Int Bioéth, 1991, 229-234. G. R. Dunstan, «Gene Therapy, Human Nature and the Churches», J Int Bioéth, 1991, pgs. 235-240.

bear a great responsibility to see to it that their benefits reach developing countries as well [21].

Numerous practical questions are raised by the Human Genome Project, and the varied interests associated with so far reaching an initiative are such that all concrete manifestations of the Project, such as genetic manipulation, must be carefully examined. It must not be forgotten that a result of a failure by specialists to assuage the attendant fears and concerns could be growth in government controls and excessive regulation.

It appears that continued investigation of human genetics could lead to substantial improvements in the human condition by the elimination of disease and suffering. Assuming also the existence of risks, and perhaps dangers, continued public and legislative tolerance is vital. International Declarations coincide in affirming the value of this knowledge insofar as it is universally applied to human health [22].

In 1987 the Ethics Committee of the Australian Research Council issued genetic therapy regulations briefly setting out simple principles limited to genetic therapy in somatic cells: (1) to improve the health of persons suffering from serious hereditary diseases and ruling out, on the grounds of inadequate understanding, therapy in the germ line; (2) all attempts to introduce DNA in human cells should be considered experimental and as such subject to the relevant legal provisions; (3) the therapy should be limited to diseases in which the defect is attributable to a single gene pair and therefore not attempt to correct multiple errors in the presence of other medical guarantees; and (4) with the acceptance of the Institutional Ethics Committee, taking into account the depth of the knowledge, prior experiences and other considerations.

Given their origin, these principles are official rules not laws. They imply specific sanctions; for example, the threat of cutting off government funding and the official publication of the names of institutions or persons not abiding by the principles, all of which appears to be a reasonable regulation at the present time for this specific field of biotechnology [23].

[21] In this sense see Norio Fujiki, «Scientist's responsibility», *Les Cahiers du MURS*, op. cit., pg. 81.

[22] CIOMS, «Genetics, Ethics and Human Values. Human Genome Mapping, Genetic Screening and Gene Therapy; The Declaration of Inuyama», *J Int Bioéth*, 1991, pgs. 96-98.

[23] Scott Russel, «Regulation of Human Gene Therapy in Australia», *J Int of Bioéth*, 1991, pgs. 87-93.

## Issues of legal regulation

The study of artificial reproduction techniques, namely of IVF and its close relation with genetic manipulation, has uncovered a series of difficulties as to the legal regulation of these activities[24].

– The technology surrounding artificial procreation continues to develop. The same applies, I believe, to DNA sequencing techniques. Even though the basic underlying knowledge has not seen much change in the last decade, any statutory regulation nonetheless runs the risk of becoming obsolete as from the moment of its enactment.

– The specific events to which such statutes would be applicable are not readily amenable to precision definition, a question of enormous importance if criminal sanctions are to be established. Thus, for example, in connection with the issue before use here, cloning could lead to the division and development of totipotent cells, or future techniques allowing identical human cells to be obtained from any cell.

– No laws should be laid down in areas which interfere with the sphere of personal autonomy and are difficult to enforce. We might here include the freedom of the researcher or scientist, who would not be able to properly pursue his work while subject to suffocating regulations, not to mention, strict oversight of his activities.

– Unsuitability of criminal sanctions for biomedical law, save in those aspects which directly transgress society's values and arouse moral indignation. In my opinion, these could include genetic manipulation for non-therapeutic purposes, with respect to which sanctions could be applied to such manipulation in the germ line for purposes other than aiding a patient suffering from a serious hereditary disease for which no other cure exists. In any event, the scope of the sanction should be calibrated taking into account the drastic effects it could have on scientists and scientific development[25].

– The need to clarify the civil aspects of all such statutes of this type as may be established or proposed, in two senses: denying the existence of private rights over human beings or aspects of personality, human embryos, individual genetic heritage, or human genome composition; and that the concession of the relevant authorizations should not imply complete lifting of liability.

---

[24] Russell Scott, «Regulation of Artificial Procreation: Law, Ethics and Other Options», J Int Bioéth, 1990, pgs. 102-110.
[25] Op. cit., pg. 105.

## Certain legal texts regulating genetic manipulation

Although legislative regulation is certainly not the only option with respect to areas such as new forms of human reproduction, human embryo research and genetic manipulation, there has recently been seen a proliferation of legal texts which address more or less directly the regulation of these subject:

1. *Reference to Spanish Acts 35 and 42 of 1988 on assisted reproduction techniques and donation and use of human embryos and fetuses, or their cells, tissues and organs*

The aforesaid legal texts lay down a detailed regulation of areas such as human embryo research and experimentation (including the inadequately profiled category of human pre-embryo) and a large set of activities in the field of human genetics. This apparently does not preclude future genetic engineering legal regulation [26] and implementing rules, which have not yet been enacted, down, and the creation of determined bodies (National Commission on Assisted Reproduction and National Commission for the followup and control of the donation and use of human embryos and fetuses), whose absence creates what I believe is a grave situation of legal uncertainty as to all these important issues [27].

The preamble to Act 35/1988 asserts the need for science to be able to act unfettered within the limits, according to the priorities, and at the pace dictated by society, maintaining respect for the fundamental rights and liberties of man. The issues involved are of enormous responsibility and must not be left to the free decision of scientists. The regulation of research in and experiments on gametes and fertilized ova is justified by the need to prevent embryological material from being used in a voluntarist or uncontrolled fashion.

In this apparently indirect or secondary form (note the thrust of section 1-4 of Act 35/88), the aforesaid Act regulates research and experimentation on gametes and pre-embryos (sections 14 to 17). Research in viable living pre-embryos is only authorized

---

[26] As recognized by the Parliament member who proposed Spanish Acts nos. 35 and 42 of 1988 during the parliamentary commission discussion 333, pg. 11122.

[27] Contrast the principles which inform the Legislative Motions which gave rise to Acts 35 and 42 of 1988 with the constitutional and civil principles of the Spanish legal system, in my work «Nuevas formas de reproducción humana», Madrid, 1988.

It should also be borne in mind that in 1989 a challenge to Acts 35 and 42 of 1988 was brought before the Constitutional Court, which has not yet handed down its decision.

if the non-pathological genetic heritage is not altered [section 15.2.*b*)], and the fertilization of human ova for any purpose other than human procreation is prohibited (section 3). In what I consider excessive detail, section 16 of Act 35/88 refers to basic research into the origin of human life, cellular differentiation and organization, gene and chromosome structure...and any such other research as whose authorization is considered appropriate. A chapter is set down of infractions and penalties (section 20) in which, with similar detail, a series of very serious violations (see paragraph K et seq) are enumerated, referring to activities, such as cloning and ectogenesis, which involve genetic manipulation, which in paragraph *n*) is expressly mentioned together with sex selection and criminalized when performed for non-therapeutic and for unauthorized therapeutic purposes. With respect to the application of the sanctions set out, reference is made to the General Health Act (sections 32 to 37), which provides for fines (section 36) without prejudice to civil, criminal or other concurrent liabilities (section 32 of the General Health Act).

The preamble to Act 42/88 on the donation of embryos and fetuses makes express reference to scientific and research freedom, conditioning it to such constitutionally recognized values as the protection of the body and life, the capacity of the affected person to decide, and human dignity. That scientific activity should not be pursued oblivious to ethical and moral considerations is a conquest of the democratic and civilized world in which social and individual progress are based on respect for human dignity and freedom.

Taking into account the new therapeutic procedures that use transplants or implants of embryonic cells or organs and advanced genetic technology, and the existence of abuses in the use of embryological and fetal materials, chapter II of Act 42/88 addresses activities with embryos and fetuses. Chapter III deals with genetic research, experimentation and technology, emphasizing the functions of the National Commission for the followup and control of the donation and use of human embryos and fetuses (section 7). Section 8 contains a detailed, but not exhaustive, description of these activities with human or recombinant genetic material, alluding *inter alia* to the use of molecular gene cloning in order to manufacture substances having health-care or clinical utility, sex selection for therapeutic purposes in the case of chromosome linked diseases, the surgical creation of beneficial genetic mosaics, to the application of genetic technology for purposes of recombinant DNA research and study in the cells of human beings or simple organisms... In addition, section 9 of Act 42/88, referring, like Act 35/88, to sections 32 to 37 of the General Health Act sets out a list of serious and very serious violations [section 9.B.*a*)], «The performance of any action aimed at modifying non-pathological human genetic heritage».

Despite the extraordinary detail of the regulation contained in Acts 35 and 42 of 1988, the first judicial application of the Assisted Reproduction Act, in my opinion, served to demonstrate the inadequacy and internal contradictions of said legislation in a case which pivoted on an instance of sex selection classified as a very serious violation under section 20 of the said Act.

In commenting this court decision, I will express my opposition to the judgement eventually handed down by the court, which overruled the initial permission to use a sperm filtration technique for purposes of sex selection, equating it, along with other sex selection techniques, to genetic manipulation, within the meaning of section 20 of Act 35/88 and sections 8 and 9 of Act 42/88. This explains why the regional court of appeals of Barcelona referred to a genetic manipulation in the origin of the individual identity code of the human embryo [28].

In agreement with the opinion of the Court of first instance for the aforementioned case, I believe that said technique can hardly be considered a serious violation, especially when the expert witnesses detected reasons to permit a practice which is scarcely medical and much easier to justify in moral terms than many others which are consented and even favoured by Spanish legislation on assisted reproduction techniques. It would therefore be advisable for any eventual regulation to make a clear distinction between «sex election» techniques and those techniques involving «sex selection» by means of manipulating the embryo or genuine manipulation of human genes, and to establish a distinct treatment for each, particularly insofar as concerns the levying of sanctions, having regard also to the existence or absence of therapeutic purpose [29].

### 2. Reference to the Human Fertilisation and Embryology Act 1990 (United Kingdom)

The technological revolution brought about since 1978 by *in vitro* fertilization and the development of these techniques for extracorporeal fertilization of human ova necessarily influence the questions here under discussion. The Governmental Commission of Investigation created in the United Kingdom to address these questions gave rise in 1984 to the Warnock Report, which re-

---

[28] Jaime Vidal Martínez, «Choix de sexe: commentaire d'une decision judiciaire appliquant la loi espagnole sur les techniques de reproduction assistée», *J Int Bioéth*, 1992, vol. 3, no. 1, 5-12, note 26.
[29] The Court's decision could in my opinion be considered equitable given the circumstances of the case and its forced classification as an instance of genetic manipulation. I believe it would be preferable to assign different terms: sex election and sex selection, in the application of the differentiated legal treatments.

commended that investigation be allowed in human embryos during the first 14 days after fertilization, with the requisite permit from a statutory body, and that genetic manipulation, cloning and the creation of hybrids between human beings and animals be outlawed [30].

Years later, after heated parliamentary debate which extended outside the Parliamentary Houses, in my opinion notably influenced by the legal treatment of abortion issue in the United Kingdom, the Human Fertilisation and Embryology Act (HFEA) 1990 was approved, establishing provisions in connection with human embryos created outside the body and setting up the Human Fertilisation and Embryology (HFE) Authority, in addition to other related provisions [31].

For our purposes here, it should be emphasized that the Act's centre of gravity is the living human embryo whose fertilization has been completed and which has been obtained outside the human body, also including the ovum in the process of fertilization.

The HFEA lays down prohibitions in relation to human embryos which cannot be lifted by an administrative license, whereas other activities require a specific license from the HFE Authority. Noteworthy among these prohibitions is that «No one shall place in a woman embryos and other gametes other than living human ones» (section 3.2); and that no license shall authorize storing or using an embryo beyond the 14 day period following fertilization, placing a human embryo in an animal, replacing the nucleus of one of its cells with the nucleus of a cell taken from another person, or embryo, or subsequent development of the same.

Save for these restriction, licenses may be granted for purpose of research with human embryos (section 11). The Act itself (HFEA) is extremely casuistic and defines as criminal offences a series of activities. Hence sections 3.2 and 4.1's prohibition of mixing living human gametes with animal ones, punishable with imprisonment of up to 10 years, a fine or both.

### 3. Reference to the German Embryo Protection Act

On December 13th 1990 the German Federal Parliament approved an Embryo Protection Act, which provided for prison sen-

---

[30] The «Warnock Report» is dealt with in the study cited in note 9.

[31] Virginia Bolton, John Osborn, Denise Servante, «The Human Fertilisation and Embryology Act 1990. A British Case History for Legislation on Bioethical Issues», describes the political and chronological context of this legislation, *J Int Bioéth.* 1992, pgs. 95-101. References to the parliamentary debate of this Act are in the study cited in note 9.

tences of up to 5 year or monetary fines for persons performing certain actions aimed at artificial human fertilization, research with human embryo and genetic manipulation [32].

Paragraph 8 of the Act contains a definition of the concept of human embryo. The Act regards as human embryo the fertilized human ovum capable of development as from the moment the cells are fused, as well as all totipotent cells extracted from a human embryo which can divide and develop into an individual given the presence of the other requisite conditions. The human ovum is considered capable of evolution in the first 24 hours after cell fusion, and the Act defines germinal cells as those cells which give rise to a single cellular line in the fertilized ovum.

Under the German Act, artificial fertilization or conservation of an ovum artificially penetrated by a sperm cell may only be performed by a physician. Any other person so acting is liable to imprisonment of up to 1 year or a fine of up to 5,000 deutschemarks. Prison sentences of up to 3 years may be imposed on a person provoking extracorporeal development of an embryo for purposes other than producing a pregnancy. Fertilizing a human egg with semen selected so as to choose the sex of the offspring is punishable by up to 1 year in jail or a fine.

The harshest sentences –5 years in prison or a fine– are reserved for the events provided for in paragraph 5 –altering the hereditary information contained in human germ cells or their use for artificial fertilization– although certain exceptions are recognized for cases where alteration of the germ cell genetic information is not intended. Similar punishment is provided under paragraphs 6 and 7 of the Act for cloning, production of monsters (chimeras) and hybrids, descriptions of which are also included. Like punishment is established for implanting embryos so obtained or a human embryo in an animal.

In referring to the principles and antecedents of the German Embryo Protection Act, I alluded to different studies of the Act's Draft Bill which were presented in an German-Spanish workshop on Genetic Engineering and Reproductive Medicine held at the German Institute in Madrid in 1980 [33].

The general impression produced after the Act's publication is contradictory. It attempts to repress abuses arising in connection

---

[32] This Act is also referred to in my study «Algunos datos y observaciones...»; see note 9.
[33] *Ingeniería genética y reproducción asistida*, cited in note 1.

with the new reproduction techniques, but the development of those techniques will require the law to be frequently updated [34].

However, the human embryo conceived *in vitro* is quite clearly at the centre of gravity of the new legal provision, and the contrast with the overall thrust of contemporary foreign regulations such as the British Act of 1990 jars established legal doctrine. Taking into account the territorial application of criminal law and the non-applicability by analogy, moreover, doubts arise as to the future of said legislation.

Yet the starting point of said Act is the state's obligation, laid down in the German Constitution, to protect the dignity of man (article 2.2). These objective assessments of the Constitution restrict the individual right to self-determination (article 2.1) and scientific and research freedom (article 5.3).

## Some final thoughts

Throughout this paper I have stressed the extraordinary importance for science of the discovery of the DNA genetic message and the ambitious Human Genome Project. In addition, *in vitro* fertilization techniques which allow the observation and manipulation of human embryos usher in possibilities which are unprecedented in the history of humanity; humans may perhaps free themselves of terrible diseases and disorders, but they also run the immense risks entailed in modifying their essential nature.

The preceding pages have also underscored the commonly felt need to place ethical and even legal limits on the growing domain of areas of knowledge whose practical applications are only beginning to be glimpsed.

That is why I believe in some cases there has been a certain haste in setting down legal norms to regulate such complex questions, the ultimate consequences of which have only been very partially revealed and, moreover, which do not command a wide consensus in the ethical sphere. This is all the more true when we consider that the most noble aspect of genetic manipulation, the advance of biomedical sciences, allows for huge differences in the participation in those scientific advances by the different peoples inhabiting a world made ever smaller by that very scientific progress.

---

[34] E. Deutsch, *Fetus in Germany:* «The Fetus Protection Law of 12, 13», 1990, *J Int Bioéth,* 1992, vol. 3, no. 2, pgs. 85-93.

Science is in the process of ever more clearly accepting that human life begins the moment the ovum is fertilized by the spermatozoon. As such, the promulgation of a legal gestation calendar which does not provide protection for human beings in the embryonic or fetal development stages, but instead aims to make possible the manipulation or destruction of those lives, strikes me as a dehumanizing trend that could mark a major step backwards in our civilization.

At present, genetic manipulation already represents a very real threat to human liberty. In such circumstances it would appear obvious that it is the law in general, and civil law in particular, which must guarantee this essential principle of freedom for human society and specifically for persons, precluding discrimination of whatever kind.

That is why I have elsewhere [35] maintained the need to reconstruct these legal instruments in order to address these new problems, proposing an ethic of responsibilities more than an ethic of rights.

Within Constitutional Law there is a need for clarification of the ultimate connection between the principle of personality and the principle of community that exists in issues in which the future of human beings is in question. It is therefore not a matter of avoiding clashes between the researcher's activity and human rights, but rather of placing the human being at the centre of all law, as is done (paradigmatically so in my opinion) in article 10.1 of the Spanish Constitution.

In the field of Civil Law I believe the concept of person and determination of personality should be reconstructed so as to preclude manipulation of a human being from the moment of conception, given that such manipulation is now possible, and assuring that all manipulation of individual human genomes be done for purpose of benefitting the specific person undergoing said manipulation.

In the field of Administrative Law statutes of this type should confine themselves to setting down the controls needed for enforcing any liabilities which arise from genetic manipulation activities by scientists, in the firm understanding that said constraints should be kept to a minimum and that liability cannot completely disappear, in my opinion, when a human being is acted on, just as neither is it possible for restrictive laws to make freedom of scientific investigation ever completely disappear.

---

[35] Paper presented to the Second International Meeting of the Milazzo Group (Genetics) (July 1991) in *Revista General de Derecho,* March 1993, 1991-2.

In the field of Criminal Law, finally, according to the legal principle of minimum intervention, criminal sanctions should be reserved for those extreme cases which offend community morals, with the scope of statutes in other fields of law being clearly set out and a precise criminal law definition of the relevant offences.

## ADDENDUM

The current diversity in certain countries, even within the European Community, as to the legal treatment of genetic manipulation strikes me as improper. Such conditions make very difficult the necessity, proportionality and adaptation to the pursued purpose that are required by Criminal Law. Nor can the protected legal interest be precisely defined in such a setting, as the said interest must draw on principles of universal scope: human dignity, rooted in genetic privacy, and its premise and corollary, human liberty.

I add my voice to the school of thought that believes science will continue to advance in the understanding of the human genome, and that Law will for each case find the necessary instruments for ensuring said knowledge be used to benefit genuine human progress, given the immense, transcendent importance of the values at stake. I believe this will require us to overcome the raw laws of the market and purely utilitarian notions, and to further develop, both in the world of science and in the world of law, the principle of responsibility.

*(February 23rd 1995)*